Studio 2 VERT

Teacher's Guide

www.pearsonschools.co.uk

✓ Free online support
✓ Useful weblinks
✓ 24 hour online ordering

0845 630 33 33

Tracy Traynor

Heinemann
Part of Pearson

Heinemann is an imprint of Pearson Education Limited, Edinburgh Gate,
Harlow, Essex, CM20 2JE.

www.pearsonschoolsandfecolleges.co.uk

Heinemann is a registered trademark of Pearson Education Limited

Text © Pearson Education Limited 2011
Edited by Sara McKenna
Designed by Emily Hunter-Higgins
Typeset by Kamae Design, Oxford
Original illustrations © Pearson Education Limited 2011
Illustrated by Caron at KJA Artists
Cover design by Emily Hunter-Higgins
Cover photos © Corbis: Terra; Getty Images: Eloy Ricárdez Luna; Pearson Education Ltd: Sophie Bluy; Shutterstock.com: Gualtiero Boffi, M.M.G.

First published 2011

15 14 13 12 11
10 9 8 7 6 5 4 3 2 1

British Library Cataloguing in Publication Data
A catalogue record for this book is available from the British Library

ISBN 978 0 435 02999 9

Copyright notice
All rights reserved. No part of this publication may be reproduced in any way or by any means (including photocopying or storing it in any medium by electronic means and whether or not transiently or incidentally to some other use of this publication) without the written permission of the copyright owner, except in accordance with the provisions of the Copyright, Designs and Patents Act 1988 or under the terms of a licence issued by the Copyright Licensing Agency, Saffron House, 6–10 Kirby Street, London EC1N 8TS (www.cla.co.uk). Applications for the copyright owner's written permission should be addressed to the publisher.

The CD-ROM accompanying this book contains editable Word files. Pearson Education Limited cannot accept responsibility for the quality, accuracy or fitness for purpose of the materials contained in the Word files once edited. To revert to the original Word files, re-load from the CD-ROM.

Printed in the UK by Ashford Colour Press Ltd

Acknowledgements
Every effort has been made to contact copyright holders of material reproduced in this book. Any omissions will be rectified in subsequent printings if notice is given to the publishers.

Scheme of Work CD-ROM
Important notice
This product is suitable for use on a Windows® PC only. It will not run on Macintosh OS X.

System requirements:
- OS: Windows XP* sp3. RAM: 512MB (1GB for Vista) 1GHz processor (2GHz for Vista)
- Microsoft Office 2003*, Adobe Flash Player 9*, Adobe Reader 8*, Internet Explorer 7*/Firefox 3

*or later versions

Playing the product
If the disc is loaded into a CD/DVD drive on a PC it should autorun automatically. If it does not, please browse the disc and double-click **RB32.bat**.

Active content
Your browser security may initially try to block elements of this product.
If this problem occurs, please refer to the Troubleshooting document which can be found in the root of this CD-ROM.

Installation instructions
This product may be installed to your local hard drive or to the network.
Further instructions on how to do this are available from the central menu.

VLE Pack
The root of this disc contains the content from this product as a zipped SCORM 1.2 Content Pack to allow for convenient uploading to your VLE.
Please follow the usual instructions specific to your VLE system to upload this content.

Contents

Introduction   4

Module 1	**T'es branché(e)?**	17
Module 2	**Paris, je t'adore!**	47
Module 3	**Mon identité**	75
Module 4	**Chez moi, chez toi**	104
Module 5	**Quel talent?!**	133
Module 6	**Studio découverte**	163

Introduction

Course description

Studio is a fully differentiated 11–14 French course in three stages – *Studio 1* for Year 7, *Studio 2* for Year 8 and *Studio 3* for Year 9. The Year 7 resources also include a separate short book, *Accès Studio*, which enables flexibility in teaching the language according to pupils' prior experience of learning French at Key Stage 2. In *Studio 2 Vert* pupils can be assessed at National Curriculum levels 1 to 5.

Studio 1 and *Studio 2* are suitable for use on their own as a two-year Key Stage 3 course.

The course has been written to reflect the world pupils live in, using contexts familiar to them in their everyday lives and teaching them the vocabulary that they need to communicate with young French people of their own age on topics that interest and stimulate them. They are introduced to young French people and given insight into the everyday life and culture of France and other French-speaking countries, encouraging intercultural understanding.

At the same time, *Studio* ensures that pupils are taught the language learning skills and strategies that they need to become independent language learners. The four elements of the Key Stage 3 Programmes of Study (Key concepts, Key processes, Range and content and Curriculum opportunities) and the five strands of progression in the Key Stage 3 Framework for languages are fully integrated into the course. In addition, pupils have the chance to experience cross-curricular studies and are given regular opportunities to develop and practise the personal, learning and thinking skills required to operate as independent enquirers, creative thinkers, reflective learners, team workers, self-managers and effective participators.

The *ActiveTeach* DVD (see details on pp. 6–7) provides easy-to-use and exciting technology designed to add dynamism and fun to whole-class teaching, together with a wealth of interactive activities for pupils to enjoy and learn from both in class and independently.

Differentiation

Studio 2 Vert is written for those pupils who will progress at a moderate or slow pace through the National Curriculum levels in Year 8. Pupils who are able enough can reach Level 5 by the end of the book. Clearly pupils will work at different levels and at different paces, and every module caters for the given range of National Curriculum levels in the following ways:

- There are differentiated activities within the target range of NC levels in all four Attainment Targets throughout the Pupil Book.
- Ideas are given in the Teacher's Guide for simplifying and extending the Pupil Book activities.
- *En plus* units at the end of every module contain longer reading and listening passages to provide opportunities for extension work.
- The *À toi* section at the back of the Pupil Book provides extra reading and writing activities at reinforcement and extension levels.
- The *Studio 2 Vert* workbook provides further reading and writing activities at reinforcement and extension levels.

Studio 2 Vert

Pupil Book

- Full coverage of the Programmes of Study and updated Key Stage 3 Framework for languages
- Assessment right from the start
- Exciting video introducing pupils to the lives of young people in France
- Fully integrated grammar explanations and practice ensuring logical and rigorous progression
- Opportunities for cross-curricular topics and emphasis on language learning skills
- Fully integrated opportunities for PLTS

The Pupil Book consists of five core modules and a sixth optional module (see p. 5). Modules 1 to 5 are subdivided as follows:

- Five double-page core units – these contain the core material that must be taught to ensure that all the key language and grammar is covered in Year 8.
- *Bilan* – this is a checklist of 'I can' statements, allowing pupils to check their progress as part of Assessment for Learning.
- *Révisions* – optional revision activities that can be used as a 'mock' test preceding the end-of-module *Contrôle* in the Assessment Pack.
- *En plus* – an optional unit in which no new core language is introduced. The unit can therefore be missed out if you are short of time. However, these units contain lots of useful activities and tips for developing language learning skills,

including longer reading and listening passages and opportunities for oral presentations.
- *Studio Grammaire* – two pages where the key grammar points introduced in the module are explained fully and accompanied by practice activities.
- *Vocabulaire* – two pages of module word lists for vocabulary learning and revision, plus a *Stratégie* tip box to help pupils acquire the skills they need to learn vocabulary more effectively.

Module 6, *Studio découverte,* is an optional module with a more cross-curricular focus. The module consists of three units, each one dealing with a particular theme – world geography and French-speaking countries, science and the French Revolution. These units can be taught as regular units or developed as project work for more individual study. As Module 6 is the last in the book, it is ideal for less directed work in the final half-term of the school year. You can choose to work through all three units in the usual way, or to focus on one particular theme. Each of the units can be taught on its own earlier in the school year if you prefer.

At the back of the Pupil Book there are four further sections:
- *À toi* – self-access differentiated reading and writing activities. *À toi A* contains reinforcement activities for lower-ability pupils, and *À toi B* contains extension activities for higher-ability pupils. These are ideal for use as homework.
- Verb tables.
- *Stratégies* – one page reminding pupils of the language learning strategies they learned in *Studio 1*.
- *Mini-dictionnaire* – a comprehensive French-English glossary, organised alphabetically and containing all the vocabulary encountered in *Studio 2 Vert*. There is also a list of the French rubrics used in the Pupil Book.

Teacher's Guide
The Teacher's Guide contains all the support required to help teachers use *Studio 2 Vert* effectively in the classroom:
- Clear and concise teaching notes, including lesson starters, plenaries and PLTS references for every unit.
- Full cross-referencing to the National Curriculum Programmes of Study and the updated Key Stage 3 Framework for languages.
- Cross-referencing to the Foundation Certificate of Secondary Education in French.
- Overview grids for each module highlighting grammar content and skills coverage.
- Answers to all the activities.
- The complete audioscript for all the listening activities in the *Studio 2 Vert* Pupil Book.
- Guidance on using the course with the full ability range.

The accompanying CD-ROM contains a customisable scheme of work offering complete help with planning, and showing how the course covers the National Curriculum Programmes of Study and Key Stage 3 Framework for languages.

Audio CDs
The audio CDs contain all the recorded material for the listening activities in the Pupil Book. The different types of activities can be used for presentation of new language, comprehension and pronunciation practice. The material includes dialogues, interviews and songs recorded by native speakers.

This material is also contained on the *ActiveTeach* DVD. Therefore, if you buy *ActiveTeach* and can play audio using your computer, you can play all the listening activities from there.

Please note: the audio CDs and *ActiveTeach* do not contain the listening material for the end-of-module tests and end-of-year test. This material can be found in the Assessment Pack (see p. 6).

Workbook
The *Studio 2 Vert* workbook contains a page of activities for each double-page unit in the Pupil Book. It fulfils a number of functions:
- It provides self-access reading and writing activities designed to offer the pupils enjoyable ways of consolidating and practising the language they have learned in each unit.
- It gives extra practice in grammar and thinking skills, with integrated activities throughout.
- Revision pages at the end of each module (*Révisions*) help pupils revise what they have learned during the module.
- Module word lists (*Vocabulaire*) with English translations are invaluable for language learning homework.
- The *J'avance* pages at the end of each module allow pupils to record their National Curriculum level in each Attainment Target and set themselves improvement targets for the next module.
- NC level descriptors in pupil-friendly language at the back of the workbook allow pupils to see what they must do to progress through the NC levels in all four Attainment Targets.

Assessment Pack

The Assessment Pack is a CD-ROM containing all the assessment material required to assess pupils in Year 8 against the National Curriculum Attainment Targets, as well as self-assessment sheets.
- End-of-module tests in all four Attainment Targets – listening, speaking, reading and writing
- End-of-year test in all four Attainment Targets
- Covers National Curriculum Levels 1 to 5
- Target setting sheets

The audio CD contains the recordings of the listening tests. The CD-ROM contains all the sheets for the tests in PDF format and as Word files. The Word files can be customised to suit your individual needs.

ActiveTeach

ActiveTeach is a powerful and motivating resource combining the 'book on screen' and a wealth of supporting materials – providing you with the perfect tool for whole-class teaching and individual practice and revision on a PC.
- Use the on-screen Pupil Book with all the listening activities included.
- Zoom in on areas of text and activities to facilitate whole-class teaching.
- Build your own lessons and add in your own resources to help personalise learning.
- Use fun and motivating electronic flashcards to teach new vocabulary.
- Consolidate language using the whole-class interactive games.
- Use the video clips in Modules 1 to 5 to introduce your pupils to the lives of young French people.
- Teach and revise grammar using PowerPoint® presentations.
- Download and print off a variety of extra worksheets for consolidation of grammar, thinking skills and learning skills – ideal for follow-up work, cover lessons and homework.

Plus *Le Studio* pupil environment for:
- **Practice** using games and flashcards
- **Revision** of grammar and vocabulary
- **Self-assessment** of reading, listening and grammar skills

A Quick Tour in *ActiveTeach* provides you with an overview of the most common features. Fuller instructions can be accessed by clicking on the question mark icon in the top right-hand corner of the book on screen.

In addition to the interactive activities in *ActiveTeach*, there is a wide variety of extra worksheets that can be used to consolidate and extend pupils' learning as follows:

Module 1

Learning skills	Pronunciation of *–er* verbs
Grammar skills	Present tense of *avoir* and *être*
Thinking skills	Identifying sentences
Learning skills	Forming longer sentences
Grammar skills	Present tense of *aller* and *faire*
Thinking skills	Odd one out!
Assignment	Mon site Internet préféré (with NC assessment)

Module 2

Learning skills	Infinitives
Grammar skills	Expressions with infinitives
Thinking skills	Opinions
Thinking skills	Fact or opinion?
Grammar skills	Perfect tense and negatives
Learning skills	Mind mapping – learning vocabulary
Thinking skills	An ideal outing
Assignment	Une attraction touristique (with NC assessment)

Module 3

Grammar skills	Adjectival agreement
Thinking skills	Friendships
Thinking skills	Odd one out!
Learning skills	Proof reading
Grammar skills	Adjectives and the near future
Grammar skills	Using more than one tense
Assignment	Ta passion, c'est quoi? (with NC assessment)

Module 4

Learning skills	Looking up adjectives in a dictionary
Thinking skills	Making deductions
Thinking skills	Truth and probability
Grammar skills	The partitive article
Learning skills	Having fun with language!
Grammar skills	The near future
Assignment	Une petite pièce (with NC assessment)

Module 5

Thinking skills	Understanding precise meanings
Grammar skills	Modal verbs
Learning skills	Working things out
Learning skills	Quality of language
Grammar skills	Using more than one tense
Assignment	Ta classe a du talent? (with NC assessment)

Module 6

Learning skills	Predicting language
Thinking skills	La vie d'un scientifique
Thinking skills	Un cours d'histoire

Assignment (*Défi*)

The worksheets for Modules 1 to 5 include a collaborative assignment or challenge (*Défi*) to be carried out in pairs or groups.

The assignments consist of two worksheets, one containing the instructions for the task, the other providing preparation tasks and language to help the pupils.

The focus of the assignments is to help the pupils develop further their extended speaking and writing skills in cross-curricular contexts while fostering PLTS.

Incorporating ICT

Appropriate use of Information and Communication Technology (ICT) to support modern languages is a requirement of the National Curriculum. Suggestions of ICT activities (word-processing, using email, videoconferencing, researching on the internet, etc.) have been included in the Teacher's Guide and are identified by the symbol.

Grammar coverage

Grammar is fully integrated into the teaching sequence in *Studio* to ensure that pupils have the opportunity to learn thoroughly the underlying structures of the French language. All units have a grammar objective so that pupils can see clearly which grammar structures they are learning. The key grammar points are presented in the *Studio Grammaire* boxes on the Pupil Book pages, and fuller explanations and practice are provided in the *Studio Grammaire* pages at the end of each module. In addition, there are grammar PowerPoint® presentations in *ActiveTeach* for presenting new grammar concepts to classes, followed by interactive practice activities that can be used with whole classes or for individual practice. Worksheets focusing on the key grammar topics taught in *Studio 2 Vert* are also provided in *ActiveTeach* and can be printed off for individual pupil use.

Grammar points explained and practised in *Studio 2 Vert*:
- present tense of regular –*er*, –*ir* and –*re* verbs
- present tense of *avoir, être, faire, aller, venir, prendre*
- perfect tense of regular verbs
- perfect tense of irregular verbs
- perfect tense with *être*
- perfect tense: asking questions
- the near future (*aller* + infinitive)
- using a range of tenses (present, perfect, near future)
- reflexive verbs
- modal verbs (*vouloir, pouvoir, devoir*)
- infinitives
- the imperative
- negatives (*ne ... pas*)
- *c'était/j'ai trouvé ça* + adjective
- adjective agreement
- possessive adjectives
- prepositions
- the partitive article
- quantities with *de*
- *il faut* + infinitive
- masculine, feminine, singular and plural: nouns, subject pronouns, the definite article, the indefinite article, adjectives and possessive adjectives

Coverage of the Programmes of Study in *Studio 2 Vert*

In *Studio 2* the four elements of the Programmes of Study – 1 Key concepts, 2 Key processes, 3 Range and content and 4 Curriculum opportunities – are comprehensively covered, as follows:

---

1 Key concepts
Pupils need to understand the key concepts that underpin the study of languages in order to deepen and broaden their knowledge, skills and understanding. As these are implemented in all modules of *Studio 2*, they are not listed in the module grids but simply summarised here for reference.

1.1 Linguistic competence
a developing the skills of listening, speaking, reading and writing in a range of situations and contexts
b applying linguistic knowledge and skills to understand and communicate effectively

1.2 Knowledge about language
a understanding how a language works and how to manipulate it
b recognising that languages differ but may share common grammatical, syntactical or lexical features

1.3 Creativity
a using familiar language for new purposes and in new contexts
b using imagination to express thoughts, ideas, experiences and feelings

1.4 Intercultural understanding
a appreciating the richness and diversity of other cultures
b recognising that there are different ways of seeing the world, and developing an international outlook

Activities specifically designed to give pupils the opportunity to develop in the other Programmes of Study areas appear throughout *Studio 2*. The tables which follow show examples of these. Further details are given in the module grids throughout the Teacher's Guide.

2	**Key processes**	
2.1	**Developing language learning strategies** Pupils should be able to:	
a	identify patterns in the target language	M1 U1, M4 U2, M5 U2
b	develop techniques for memorising words, phrases and spellings	M2 *Stratégie*, M3 U3, M5 *Stratégie*
c	use their knowledge of English or another language when learning the target language	M2 *En plus*, M3 U5, M5 U1
d	use previous knowledge, context and other clues to work out the meaning of what they hear or read	M4 U4, M5 *En plus*, M6 U1
e	use reference materials such as dictionaries appropriately and effectively	M4 U1, M4 U5, M5 U3
2.2	**Developing language skills** Pupils should be able to:	
a	listen for gist or detail	All core units and *En plus* of every module
b	skim and scan written texts for the main points or details	M4 U3, M5 *En plus*, M6 U3
c	respond appropriately to spoken and written language	All core units and *En plus* of every module
d	use correct pronunciation and intonation	M1 *En plus*, M4 U1, M5 U2
e	ask and answer questions	M2 U3, M3 U1, M4 U1
f	initiate and sustain conversations	M3 U1, M5 U2, M5 U4
g	write clearly and coherently, including an appropriate level of detail	M1 *En plus*, M2 U2, M4 U1
h	redraft their writing to improve accuracy and quality	All core units and *En plus*
i	reuse language that they have heard or read in their own speaking and writing	M2 U1, M2 U4, M3 U1
j	adapt language they already know in new contexts for different purposes	M3 U1, M3 U3, M6 U2
k	deal with unfamiliar language, unexpected responses and unpredictable situations	All video episodes, M4 U5, M6 U1, M6 U2

3	**Range and content** The study of language should include:	
a	the spoken and written forms of the target language	All core units and *En plus*
b	the interrelationship between sounds and writing in the target language	M2 U5, M3 U5, M5 U2
c	the grammar of the target language and how to apply it	All core units and *Studio Grammaire* pages
d	a range of vocabulary and structures	All core units and *En plus* of every module
e	learning about different countries and cultures	All modules
f	comparing pupils' own experiences and perspectives with those of people in countries and communities where the target language is spoken	All modules

4	Curriculum opportunities	
	Pupils should have the opportunity to:	
a	hear, speak, read and write in the target language regularly and frequently within the classroom and beyond	All core units and *En plus* of every module
b	communicate in the target language individually, in pairs, in groups and with speakers of the target language, including native speakers, where possible, for a variety of purposes	All core units and *En plus* of every module
c	use an increasing range of more complex language	Units 4 and 5 and *En plus* of every module
d	make links with English at word, sentence and text level	All core units and *En plus* of every module
e	use a range of resources, including ICT, for accessing and communicating information in the target language	All core units and *En plus* of every module
f	listen to, read or view a range of materials, including authentic materials in the target language, both to support learning and for personal interest and enjoyment	All video episodes, all core units and *En plus*
g	use the target language in connection with topics and issues that are engaging and may be related to other areas of the curriculum	All core units and *En plus* of every module, especially Module 6

Coverage of the Revised Framework for languages (2009)

Studio ensures full coverage of the five strands of progression in the Key Stage 3 Framework for languages (2009):
1. Listening and speaking
2. Reading and writing
3. Intercultural understanding
4. Knowledge about language
5. Language learning strategies

To help you with your **long-term planning**, the framework overview grid on p. 10 gives examples of where each learning objective is met in the Pupil Book.

To help you with your **medium-term planning**, the overview grids at the start of each module in this Teacher's Guide indicate the particular objectives that are met in that module.

To help you with your **short-term (lesson) planning**, the overview boxes at the start of each unit indicate the particular objectives that are met in that unit.

Learning Objective	Module and unit
1.1/Y8 Listening – understanding on first hearing	M1 U2, M3 U3
1.2/Y8 Listening – new contexts	M2 U4, M3 U1
1.3/Y8 Listening – (a) understanding language for specific functions	M4 U4, M5 U2
1.3/Y8 Speaking – (b) using language for specific functions	M4 U4, M5 U2
1.4/Y8 Speaking – (a) classroom exchanges	M1 U1, M6 U2
1.4/Y8 Speaking – (b) unscripted conversations	M3 U3, M5 U4
1.5/Y8 Speaking – (a) unscripted talks	M1 U2, M5 U5
1.5/Y8 Speaking – (b) using simple idioms	M3 U1, M5 U4
2.1/Y8 Reading – authentic materials	M2 U3, M5 *En plus*
2.2/Y8 Reading – (a) longer, more complex texts	M4 *En plus*, M6 U1
2.2/Y8 Reading – (b) personal response to text	M6 U3
2.3/Y8 Reading – text features: emotive	M3 U2, M5 U4
2.4/Y8 Writing – (a) using text as stimulus	M2 U1, M3 U2
2.4/Y8 Writing – (b) organising paragraphs	M4 *En plus*, M6 U3
2.5/Y8 Writing – using researched language	M5 *En plus*, M6 U1
3.1/Y8 Culture – changes in everyday life	M6 U3
3.2/Y8 Culture – (a) young people: aspirations	M5 U1, M5 U3
3.2/Y8 Culture – (b) customs/traditions	M3 *En plus*, M4 *En plus*
4.1/Y8 Language – sounds/spelling exceptions	M3 U4
4.2/Y8 Language – increasing vocabulary	M3 U2, M5 U4
4.3/Y8 Language – gender and plurals	M1 U3, M3 U1
4.4/Y8 Language – developing sentences	M2 U2, M3 U1
4.5/Y8 Language – (a) range of verb tenses	M3 U4, M3 U5
4.5/Y8 Language – (b) range of modal verbs	M2 U1, M5 U2
4.6/Y8 Language – (a) range of questions	M2 U2, M3 U4
4.6/Y8 Language – (b) range of negatives	M1 U1, M2 U5
5.1 Strategies – patterns	M3 U4, M5 U2
5.2 Strategies – memorising	M2 *Stratégie*, M4 *Stratégie*
5.3 Strategies – English/other languages	M3 *Stratégie*, M6 U1
5.4 Strategies – working out meaning	M2 *En plus*, M4 U3
5.5 Strategies – reference materials	M4 U5, M5 U3
5.6 Strategies – reading aloud	M1 U5, M2 U5
5.7 Strategies – planning and preparing	M4 *En plus*, M5 *En plus*
5.8 Strategies – evaluating and improving	M1 *En plus*, M3 *En plus*

Coverage of Personal Learning and Thinking Skills in *Studio 2 Vert*

Activities supporting PLTS development are included throughout the course. Key examples are highlighted in the Teacher's Guide using the PLTS icon **PLTS**: one PLTS is identified in each unit, with Modules 1–5 all featuring the full range of PLTS. A selection of these is listed below, with details of how they meet the curriculum requirements.

Personal Learning and Thinking Skills	
I Independent enquirers	Pupil Book activities throughout the course (e.g. M1 U1 ex. 5, M4 U2 ex. 3); ICT-/other research-based activities (e.g. M6 U1 ex. 8)
C Creative thinkers	Regular activities developing skills strategies (how to improve listening/speaking, etc.) (e.g. M2 U3 ex. 5); activities requiring pupils to identify patterns and work out rules (e.g. M3 U1 Starter 1); activities requiring creative production of language (M5 *En plus* ex. 6)
R Reflective learners	Ongoing opportunities to assess work and identify areas for improvement (e.g. M2 U2 ex. 7, M4 *En plus* ex. 5), including all *Bilans* and Plenaries (e.g. M6 U3 Plenary)
T Team workers	Regular pair and teamwork activities (M6 U2 ex. 7), including many Starters; regular peer assessment (e.g. M1 U5 ex. 2); links with partner schools (e.g. M5 U4 extension suggestion after ex. 6)
S Self-managers	Ongoing advice on managing learning (e.g. M5 U5 ex. 6), including strategies to improve learning (e.g. M3 *Stratégie*)
E Effective participators	Opportunities throughout the course for pupils to contribute (e.g. M2 U5 extension suggestion after ex. 7), including discussions based on module openers, presentations (e.g. M3 U2 ex. 8) and all Plenaries (e.g. M5 U1 Plenary)

Pupils may find the following short forms useful as a reference in class:

I am a/an …	Today I …		
Independent enquirer	**PLTS**	**I**	worked on my own to find out something new
Creative thinker	**PLTS**	**C**	used what I know to work out or create something new
Reflective learner	**PLTS**	**R**	thought about what I've learned and how I can improve
Team worker	**PLTS**	**T**	worked well with other people
Self-manager	**PLTS**	**S**	took responsibility for improving my learning
Effective participator	**PLTS**	**E**	took part in the lesson in a positive way

Coverage of the Foundation Certificate of Secondary Education (FCSE) in French in *Studio 2 Vert*

Studio can be used to teach the Key Stage 3 FCSE qualification from AQA. The following table shows where each of the FCSE units and sub-topics can be taught using *Studio 2 Vert*. The FCSE units and sub-topics that do not appear in the *Studio 2 Rouge* or *Vert* grid are covered in *Studio 1* or *Studio 3 Rouge/Vert*. A separate leaflet is also available showing the FCSE coverage across all three stages of *Studio* (*Studio 1, Studio 2 Rouge/Vert, Studio 3 Rouge/Vert*).

Unit 1 – Meeting people

Sub-topics	Where in *Studio 2 Vert*
Personal information	Module 3, Unit 1 Module 3, Unit 5 Module 5, Unit 1
Family members	Module 3, Unit 5
Pets	
Physical/character descriptions	Module 3, Unit 1 Module 5, Unit 4 Module 5, *En plus*
Time	Module 2, Unit 3
Clothes and colours	Module 3, Unit 4
Places	Module 2, Unit 1 Module 2, Unit 2
Sports and hobbies	Module 1, Unit 1 Module 1, Unit 2 Module 1, Unit 3 Module 1, Unit 4 Module 1, Unit 5 Module 3, Unit 3 Module 3, Unit 5 Module 5, Unit 1 Module 5, Unit 5 Module 5, *En plus*
Jobs	

Unit 2 – Home life

Sub-topics	Where in *Studio 2 Vert*
Types of accommodation	Module 4, Unit 1
Rooms in a house	Module 4, Unit 2
Description of own room	Module 4, Unit 2
Daily routine	
Jobs around the house	
Household equipment	Module 4, Unit 2
Members of the family	
Family relationships	
Pocket money	

Unit 3 – Education and future plans

Sub-topics	Where in *Studio 2 Vert*
School subjects and opinions	
School items	
School report	
Classroom language	
Types of school and location	
School routine	
Aspects of school life	
Study plans	
Career plans	

Unit 4 – Holidays

Sub-topics	Where in *Studio 2 Vert*
Activities	Module 2, Unit 1 Module 2, Unit 2 Module 2, Unit 5
Aspects of holidays	Module 2, Unit 4
Weather	Module 1, Unit 5 Module 3, Unit 2
Places in a town	Module 2, Unit 1 Module 2, Unit 2
Holiday destinations	Module 2, Unit 1 Module 2, Unit 2 Module 2, Unit 3 Module 3, *En plus*
Literature about places to visit	Module 2, Unit 3 Module 2, *En plus* Module 3, *En plus*

Descriptions of holidays	Module 2, Unit 1
	Module 2, Unit 2
	Module 2, Unit 4
	Module 2, Unit 5
	Module 2, *En plus*

Unit 5 – Travel and accommodation

Sub-topics	Where in *Studio 2 Vert*
Transport and opinions	
Hotel bookings	
Accommodation	
Prices	
Holiday activities	Module 2, Unit 1
	Module 2, Unit 2
	Module 2, Unit 3
	Module 2, Unit 4
	Module 2, Unit 5
	Module 2, *En plus*
Traffic signs	
Accommodation descriptions	

Unit 6 – Leisure

Sub-topics	Where in *Studio 2 Vert*
Sports/hobbies	Module 1, Unit 1
	Module 1, Unit 2
	Module 1, Unit 3
	Module 1, Unit 4
	Module 1, Unit 5
	Module 1, *En plus*
	Module 2, *En plus*
	Module 3, Unit 3
	Module 3, Unit 5
	Module 5, Unit 1
	Module 5, Unit 5
	Module 5, *En plus*
Invitations – accepting and refusing	Module 5, Unit 2
Time	Module 2, Unit 3
Places	Module 2, Unit 1
	Module 2, Unit 2
Locations	Module 2, Unit 1
	Module 2, Unit 2
Clothes	Module 3, Unit 4

Unit 7 – Celebrations

Sub-topics	Where in *Studio 2 Vert*
Celebrations/festivals in target language country	Module 3, *En plus*
	Module 4, Unit 4
	Module 4, Unit 5
	Module 6, Unit 3
Organising a celebration	Module 4, Unit 5
Invitations – venue, time, transport	Module 4, Unit 4
Gifts	
Activities at a celebration	Module 4, Unit 5
Food and drink	Module 4, Unit 3
	Module 4, Unit 4
New Year resolutions	
Clothes	Module 3, Unit 4

Unit 8 – Health and fitness

Sub-topics	Where in *Studio 2 Vert*
Parts of the body	
Common ailments – at the doctor's/pharmacy	
Food and drink vocabulary/menus	Module 4, Unit 3
	Module 4, Unit 4
Healthy vs. unhealthy lifestyle	
Sports/forms of exercise/ways of keeping fit	
Giving/receiving advice on diet/exercise	

Unit 9 – Food and drink

Sub-topics	Where in *Studio 2 Vert*
Food and drink vocabulary	Module 4, Unit 3
	Module 4, Unit 4
Shopping for food	Module 4, Unit 4
Ordering in a restaurant	
Likes and dislikes	Module 4, Unit 4
Recipes	Module 4, Unit 4

Unit 10 – Region and environment

Sub-topics	Where in *Studio 2 Vert*
Description and location of home	Module 4, Unit 1 Module 4, Unit 2 Module 4, *En plus*
Opinions on different houses	Module 4, Unit 1 Module 4, *En plus*
Description and location of area	Module 3, *En plus* Module 4, *En plus* Module 6, Unit 1
Facilities and activities within an area	Module 3, *En plus* Module 4, *En plus* Module 6, Unit 1
Positive and negative aspects and opinions on a particular area	Module 4, *En plus*
Environment issues	
Opinions on environmental issues	

Unit 11 – Media

Sub-topics	Where in *Studio 2 Vert*
Free time activities	Module 1, Unit 1 Module 1, Unit 2 Module 1, Unit 3 Module 1, Unit 4 Module 1, Unit 5 Module 3, Unit 3 Module 3, Unit 5
Types of TV programme and films	Module 1, Unit 1 Module 1, Unit 2
TV and film storylines/plots	Module 1, *En plus*
Forms of communication	Module 1, Unit 4
Using mobile phones and the internet responsibly	
Opinions on TV programmes/films/types of media	Module 1, Unit 1 Module 1, Unit 2 Module 1, Unit 3 Module 1, Unit 4 Module 1, *En plus*

Advantages/disadvantages of new technology and TV	
Computer-related vocabulary	Module 1, Unit 4

Unit 12 – Work choices

Sub-topics	Where in *Studio 2 Vert*
Days of the week	
Time	
People/jobs/places of work	
What people do in their jobs/duties	
Work experience	
Opinions on jobs/positive and negative aspects	
Working conditions/rules	
School subjects and preferences	
Job adverts	
Future plans – career/studies/lifestyle choices	Module 5, Unit 5

Games and other teaching suggestions
Reading aloud
There are many reading activities in the Pupil Book which give scope for further activities.

1. You can use the texts to practise reading aloud. As an incentive, award five points to a pupil who can read a text without any errors. Points could also be given to teams, depending on seating arrangements – tables, rows, sides of the room.
2. Set a challenge – 'I bet no one can read this without a single mistake' or ask a volunteer pupil to predict how many mistakes he/she will make before having a go, then seeing if he/she can do better than predicted.
3. Texts could be read round the class with pupils simply reading up to a full stop and then passing it on to someone else in the room. They enjoy this activity if it is fast. Alternatively, pupils can read as much or as little as they want before passing it on.
4. You can also read a text, pause, and have the pupils say the next word.

Reading follow-up
Motivation and participation can be enhanced by dividing the class into two teams and awarding points. Once they know a text very well, pupils should be able to complete a sentence from memory, hearing just the beginning. Move from a word to a phrase to a sentence: i.e. you say a word, the pupils give the word in a short context and then in a longer context.
1. You read aloud and stop (or insert the word 'beep') for pupils to complete the word or sentence.
2. You read aloud and make a deliberate mistake (either pronunciation or saying the wrong word). Pupils put up their hands as soon as they spot a mistake.
3. *Hot potato*: Pupils read a bit and pass it on quickly to someone who may not be expecting it.
4. *Marathon*: A pupil reads aloud until he/she makes a mistake. Pupils have to put up their hands as soon as they hear a mistake. A second pupil then takes over, starting at the beginning again and trying to get further than the previous pupil.
5. *Random reading*: You read a phrase at random and the pupils have to say the next bit.
6. You can play music and get the pupils to pass an object round the class. When the music stops, the person with the object has a turn. Let a pupil control the music, facing away from the class.

Mime activities
Mimes are a motivating way to help pupils to learn words.
1. You say a word, for example a job, sport or hobby, or an adjective, and the pupils mime it. This can be done silently with the whole class responding. Alternatively, it can be done as a knockout game starting with six volunteers at the front who mime to the class as you say each word. Any pupil who does the wrong mime or who is slow to react is knocked out. Impose a two-minute time limit.
2. Pupils say a word or phrase and you mime it – but only if the pupils say it correctly. This really puts you on the spot and gets the pupils trying very hard. You could also insist that the pupils say it from memory.
3. You mime and pupils say the word or phrase.
4. Send five or six pupils out of the room. They each have to decide on an adjective which sums up their character. They return to the room individually or together, each one miming their character adjective. The remaining pupils then guess the adjective. Get them to use a sentence, e.g. *Daniel est intelligent*.
5. *Envoyé spécial*: One person goes out of the room. The rest of the class decides on a character adjective to mime. The volunteer comes back into the room and has to guess the adjective that the class is miming. Again, encourage the use of whole sentences.
6. *Class knock-down*: As *Envoyé spécial*, but this time everyone in the class can choose different qualities to mime. The volunteer returns to the room with everyone doing his/her own mime. The volunteer points to each pupil and names the character adjective. If the volunteer is correct, the pupil sits down. This works well as a timed or team activity. The aim is to sit your team down as quickly as possible.
7. A version of charades is a good activity at the end of the lesson. Organise two teams, A and B. Have all the adjectives written down on separate cards, masculine forms only. Put the cards in a pile at the front. A volunteer from Team A comes to the front, picks up the first card and mimes it. The rest of the team must not see the word on the card. Anyone from Team A can put up his/her hand and is then invited by the volunteer to say the word. If correct, the volunteer picks up the next card and mimes it. The aim is to get through the whole list as quickly as possible. Note down the time for Team A. Team B then tries to beat that time.

Exploiting the songs
1. Pupils sing along. Fade out certain bits while they continue. When most of them know the song quite well you can pause the audio to let them give you the next line by heart. Then try the whole chorus, followed by a few verses completely from memory.
2. You could try the 'pick up a song' game: you fade the song after a few lines, the pupils continue singing, and then you fade the song up again towards the end and they see whether they have kept pace with the recording.

Translation follow-up
Motivation and participation can be enhanced by dividing the class into two teams and awarding points. Once they know the text very well, you should be able to say any word, phrase or sentence from the text at random for the pupils to translate into English without viewing the text.
1. You translate the text and stop (or insert the word 'beep') for pupils to complete the word or sentence.
2. You translate, making a deliberate mistake. Pupils put up their hands as soon as they spot a mistake.
3. *Hot potato*: A pupil translates a bit and passes it on quickly to someone who may not be expecting it.

4 *Marathon*: A pupil translates until he/she makes a mistake. Pupils have to put up their hands as soon as they hear a mistake. A second pupil then takes over, starting from the beginning again and trying to get further than the previous pupil.

5 *Random translation*: You read a phrase in French at random and the pupils have to translate it.

6 One half of the class has their books open, the other half has them closed. The half with their books open reads a sentence in French at random. The other side has to translate. Do about five, then swap round.

7 You can play music and get the pupils to pass an object round. When the music stops, the person with the object has a turn. Let a pupil control the music, facing away from the class.

Writing follow-up (text dissection)

Whiteboards are a useful tool. They do not need to be issued to every pupil. Pupils can work in pairs or groups, or they can pass the whiteboards on. You could also divide the class into teams, with one whiteboard per team.

After reading a text in some detail:

1 Display some anagrams of key words from the text and ask pupils to write them correctly. You will need to prepare these in advance and check carefully. Award points for correct answers on each board.

2 Display some jumbled phrases from the text, e.g. *foot au je dimanche joue le*. Pupils rewrite the phrase correctly in their exercise books or on the board. They could work in teams, producing one answer per team on paper.

3 Display an incorrect word or phrase in French and ask pupils to spot the mistake and correct it. This can also be done as 'spot the missing word' or 'spot the word that is in the wrong place'.

4 Ask pupils to spell certain words from memory. Differentiate by first reading out a few words in French and then giving a few in English for them also to write out in French.

5 *Mini-dictée*: Read four or five short sentences in French for pupils to write out. Again, this could be a group exercise.

6 Give pupils phrases in English to write out in French.

Comprehension follow-up

1 Ask questions in English about the text.
2 Ask questions in French about the text.
3 True or false?
4 Who … ?

Vocabulary treasure hunt

1 Find the word for …
2 Find (three) opinions.

Grammar treasure hunt

1 Find (three) adjectives.
2 Find (two) feminine adjectives.
3 Find a verb in the *nous* form.
4 Find a plural noun.
5 Find a negative.

A variation on pairwork

Musical pass the mobile phone: One pupil controls the music, facing away from the class. While the music is playing, a toy or old mobile phone is passed from pupil to pupil. As soon as the music stops, the music operator (who is ideally also equipped with a phone) says the first statement of a dialogue. The other pupil who has ended up with the phone replies. They can, if they like, disguise their voice. The music operator tries to guess who is speaking. The game then continues.

Symbols used in these teaching notes

➕ extension material/suggestion for extending an activity

Ⓡ reinforcement material/suggestion for reinforcing language

PLTS example of an activity which supports personal learning and thinking skills development

💭 thinking skills activity (workbooks only)

🖱 ICT activity

Module 1: T'es branché(e)?
(Pupil Book pp. 6–25)

Unit & Learning objectives	PoS* & Framework objectives	Key language	Grammar and other language features
1 La télé (pp. 8–9) Talking about television programmes Using subject pronouns: *je, tu, il, elle*	**2.1a** identify patterns **1.4/Y8** Speaking – (a) classroom exchanges **4.6/Y8** Language – (a) range of questions **4.6/Y8** Language – (b) range of negatives	*Qu'est-ce que tu regardes à la télé? Je regarde … les émissions de sport/les infos*, etc. *Est-ce que tu aimes (les séries)? Oui, j'aime ça. Non, je n'aime pas ça. C'est amusant/génial*, etc.	**G** *–er* verbs (singular) **G** *ne … pas* **G** questions with *Qu'est-ce que* and *Est-ce que*
2 J'ai une passion pour le cinéma (pp. 10–11) Talking about films Using *j'aime, j'adore* and *je déteste*	**1.1/Y8** Listening – understanding on first hearing **1.5/Y8** Speaking – (a) unscripted talks	*Qu'est-ce que tu aimes comme films? J'aime … J'adore … Je déteste … les films fantastiques les dessins animés* etc. *Qui est ton acteur/actrice préféré(e)?* etc. *Mon acteur/actrice préféré(e), c'est …*	**G** adjective agreement **G** present tense of *être* (singular) – pronunciation: stressing all syllables equally – including intensifiers, connectives and opinions to improve writing
3 La lecture (pp. 12–13) Talking about reading Using *un, une* and *le, la, les*	**2.4/Y8** Writing – (b) organising paragraphs **4.3/Y8** Language – gender and plurals	*Qu'est-ce que tu lis, en ce moment? Je lis … un magazine sur les célébrités un roman policier une BD* etc. *C'est bien? À mon avis, c'est … amusant/nul*, etc. *Qui est ton auteur préféré? Mon auteur préféré, c'est …*	**G** the definite article **G** the indefinite article **G** adjective agreement **G** present tense of *avoir* (singular)
4 Que fais-tu quand tu es connecté(e)? (pp. 14–15) Talking about the internet Using the verb *faire*	**1.2/Y8** Listening – new contexts	*Que fais-tu quand tu es connecté(e)? Je fais des achats. Je lis des blogs. J'envoie des e-mails.* etc. *Je trouve ça chouette/ barbant*, etc.	**G** present tense of *faire* (singular)

1 T'es branché(e)?

Unit & Learning objectives	PoS* & Framework objectives	Key language	Grammar and other language features
5 Quand il fait beau, on va au parc (pp. 16–17) Talking about what you do in different weather Using *on*	**5.6** Strategies – reading aloud	*Qu'est-ce qu'on fait quand…* *il fait chaud* *il fait froid* *il fait beau* *il pleut* *on regarde des DVD* *on fait du bowling* etc. *on va au cinéma/parc* *on joue au foot/basket* *on surfe sur Internet* *avec mes copains*	**G** *on* verb forms **G** present tense of *aller* (singular) – getting details right
Bilan et Révisions (pp. 18–19) Pupils' checklist and practice exercises			
En plus: À ne pas rater! (pp. 20–21) Talking about your favourite television programmes, films and books	**2.2d** pronunciation and intonation **2.2g** write clearly and coherently **5.8** Strategies – evaluating and improving	Review of language from the module *mon personnage préféré* *le scénario est drôle* *je recommande (ce film) à tout le monde*	– giving positive feedback
Studio Grammaire (pp. 22–23) Detailed grammar summary and practice exercises			**G** grammatical terms **G** the present tense: – regular *-er* verbs – irregular verbs: *avoir* and *être* – irregular verbs: *aller* and *faire* **G** negatives
À toi (pp. 114–115) Self-access reading and writing at two levels			

* In addition, the following Programmes of Study are covered throughout the module: 1.1–1.4, 2.2a, 2.2c, 2.2d, 3a, 3c, 3d, 3e, 3f, 4a, 4b, 4d, 4e, 4f, 4g. PoS 4c is covered in all Units 4 & 5 and *En plus* sections. See pp. 7–9 for details.

1 La télé (Pupil Book pp. 8–9)

T'es branché(e)? 1

Learning objectives
- Talking about television programmes
- Using subject pronouns: *je, tu, il, elle*

Framework objectives
1.4/Y8 Speaking – (a) classroom exchanges
4.6/Y8 Language – (a) range of questions
4.6/Y8 Language – (b) range of negatives

FCSE links
Unit 1: Meeting people (Sports and hobbies)
Unit 6: Leisure (Sports/hobbies)
Unit 11: Media (Free time activities; Types of TV programme and films; Opinions on TV programmes/films/types of media)

Grammar
- *–er* verbs (singular)
- *ne ... pas*
- questions with *Qu'est-ce que* and *Est-ce que*

Key language
Qu'est-ce que tu regardes à la télé?
Je regarde ...
les documentaires
les émissions de sport
les émissions de télé-réalité
les infos
les jeux télévisés
les séries (policières/américaines)
Est-ce que tu aimes (les séries)?
Oui, j'aime ça.
Non, je n'aime pas ça.
C'est ...
amusant, génial, intéressant
ennuyeux, nul, barbant
j'adore, j'aime bien
je n'aime pas, je déteste
je ne regarde pas

PLTS
I Independent enquirers

Cross-curricular
ICT: emailing
English: subject pronouns

Resources
CD 1, tracks 2–3
Cahier d'exercices Vert, page 3
ActiveTeach
p.008 Flashcards
p.008 Grammar
p.008 Grammar practice

Starter 1
Aim
To introduce language for television programmes; To use reading strategies

Write up the following. Say that these are all types of television programme and give pupils two minutes working in pairs to translate them. (You could supply the translations in jumbled order if necessary, for support.)

les émissions de sport
les émissions de télé-réalité
les infos
les séries
les jeux télévisés
les documentaires

Ask pupils to swap answers with another pair. Check answers as a class. Ask the class how they worked out the meaning of the French items. Point out the usefulness of reading strategies such as recognising cognates and using context and logic.

Alternative Starter 1:
Use ActiveTeach p.008 Flashcards to introduce television programme vocabulary.

1 Écoute et écris la bonne lettre. (1–6) (AT 1.2)
Listening. Pupils listen to six conversations and for each one write the letter of the correct type of television programme.

Audioscript — CD 1 track 2

1. – *Qu'est-ce que tu regardes à la télé?*
   – *Je regarde les jeux télévisés.*
2. – *Qu'est-ce que tu regardes à la télé?*
   – *Moi, je regarde les documentaires.*
3. – *Qu'est-ce que tu regardes à la télé, Brian?*
   – *Je regarde les séries.*
4. – *Qu'est-ce que tu regardes à la télé, Lucie?*
   – *Normalement à la télé, je regarde les infos.*
5. – *Qu'est-ce que tu regardes à la télé?*
   – *Je regarde les émissions de sport.*
6. – *Qu'est-ce que tu regardes à la télé?*
   – *Je regarde les émissions de télé-réalité.*

Answers
1 e   2 f   3 d   4 c   5 a   6 b

1 T'es branché(e)? 1 La télé

2 Écoute et note les opinions. (1–6) (AT 1.3)

Listening. Pupils listen to six people being asked whether they like television series. For each speaker, they note the letters of the two opinions expressed.

Audioscript CD 1 track 3

1. – Est-ce que tu aimes les séries, Loïc?
   – Oui, j'aime ça. C'est amusant.
2. – Est-ce que tu aimes les séries, Sacha?
   – Non, je n'aime pas ça. C'est barbant.
3. – Est-ce que tu aimes les séries, Rémy?
   – Oui, j'aime ça. C'est génial.
4. – Est-ce que tu aimes les séries, Opale?
   – Oui, j'aime ça. C'est intéressant.
5. – Est-ce que tu aimes les séries, Aurore?
   – Non, je n'aime pas ça. C'est ennuyeux.
6. – Et toi, Damien? Est-ce que tu aimes les séries?
   – Moi, je ne regarde pas les séries. Je n'aime pas ça. C'est nul.

Answers
1 a,d 2 e,h 3 a,b 4 a,c 5 e,f 6 e,g

Studio Grammaire: regular –er verbs (singular)

Use the *Studio Grammaire* box to cover regular –er verbs in the singular. There is more information and further practice on Pupil Book p. 22.

Give pupils two minutes working in pairs to come up with as many examples of –er verbs as they can.

Studio Grammaire: ne ... pas

Use the *Studio Grammaire* box to cover ne ... pas. There is more information and further practice on Pupil Book p. 23.

Starter 2
Aim
To review language for giving opinions

Write up the following, mixing the order (here listed under the correct column for reference). Give pupils two minutes to copy and complete the grid, writing the phrases expressing a positive opinion in the left-hand column and those expressing a negative opinion in the right-hand column.

☺	☹

C'est intéressant.   C'est nul.
C'est amusant.   Non, je n'aime pas ça.
C'est génial.   C'est barbant.
Oui, j'aime ça.   C'est ennuyeux.

Alternative Starter 2:
Use ActiveTeach p.008 Grammar practice to practise regular –er verbs.

3 Lis les textes. Réponds aux questions en anglais. (AT 3.3)

Reading. Pupils read the texts, then answer the questions in English. Some vocabulary is glossed for support.

Answers
1 Océane 2 Pauline 3 Ryan 4 Océane
5 Ryan 6 Pauline

Studio Grammaire: Qu'est-ce que and Est-ce que

Use the *Studio Grammaire* box to cover the use of *Qu'est-ce que* and *Est-ce que* to ask questions.

1 La télé   T'es branché(e)?

4 En tandem. Fais deux dialogues. Utilise les images. (AT 2.3)
Speaking. In pairs: pupils make up two dialogues, using the framework + picture prompts supplied.

Answers
A ● Qu'est-ce que tu regardes à la télé?
  ■ Je regarde les émissions de télé-réalité.
  ● Est-ce que tu aimes les infos?
  ■ Non, je n'aime pas/je déteste ça. C'est nul.
B ● Qu'est-ce que tu regardes à la télé?
  ■ Je regarde les émissions de sport.
  ● Est-ce que tu aimes les jeux télévisés?
  ■ Oui, j'aime/j'adore ça. C'est intéressant.

R Pupils then make up a dialogue along the same lines with their books closed, providing answers which are true for them.

5 Fais un sondage en classe. Pose les questions à cinq personnes. (AT 2.3–4)

PLTS

Speaking. Pupils do a class survey with five other pupils to find out about their television preferences. A grid they can copy and use to note answers and a list of questions are supplied.

6 Décris tes préférences. Change les phrases soulignées. (AT 4.4)
Writing. Pupils describe what they like, using the framework supplied. The parts they need to change are underlined for reference.

If you have connections with a partner school, pupils could exchange emails on their television preferences with their French peers.

Plenary
Review how to make verbs negative using *ne ... pas*. Ask the class to summarise how *ne ... pas* is used, then give a range of prompts from the unit (e.g. *Est-ce que tu aimes les infos?*) to elicit a negative response (e.g. *Non, je n'aime pas ça. C'est nul.*).

Workbook, page 3

Answers

1 1 (f) les émissions de sport
   2 (b) les séries policières
   3 (d) les documentaires
   4 (c) les jeux télévisés
   5 (e) les émissions de télé-réalité
   6 (a) les infos

2

Positive	Negative
C'est génial.	C'est nul.
C'est intéressant.	Je n'aime pas ça.
J'aime ça.	C'est barbant.
C'est amusant.	C'est ennuyeux.

3 1 Moi, je regarde les documentaires. **J'aime ça.** Mais les émissions de sport, **je n'aime pas ça.**
   2 Je regarde les émissions de télé-réalité, c'est **intéressant**. J'aime aussi les séries policières, c'est **amusant**!
   3 Moi, je regarde les émissions de sport. C'est **génial**. Je n'aime pas les infos. C'est **barbant/ennuyeux**.

2 J'ai une passion pour le cinéma

T'es branché(e)? 1
(Pupil Book pp. 10–11)

Learning objectives
- Talking about films
- Using *j'aime*, *j'adore* and *je déteste*

Framework objectives
1.1/Y8 Listening – understanding on first hearing
1.5/Y8 Speaking – (a) unscripted talks

FCSE links
Unit 1: Meeting people (Sports and hobbies)
Unit 6: Leisure (Sports/hobbies)
Unit 11: Media (Free time activities; Types of TV programme and films; Opinions on TV programmes/films/types of media)

Grammar
- adjective agreement
- present tense of *être* (singular)

Key language
Qu'est-ce que tu aimes comme films?
J'ai une passion pour ...
Je suis/ne suis pas fan de ...
J'aime ...
J'adore ...
Je déteste ...
les comédies
les films d'action
les films d'arts martiaux
les films fantastiques
les films d'horreur
les films de science-fiction
les westerns
les dessins animés
Qui est ton acteur préféré?
Mon acteur préféré, c'est ...
Qui est ton actrice préférée?
Mon actrice préférée, c'est ...
Quel est ton film préféré?
Mon film préféré, c'est ...
intelligent(e)

PLTS
E Effective participators

Resources
CD 1, tracks 4–6
Cahier d'exercices Vert, page 4
ActiveTeach
p.010 Flashcards
p.011 Grammar
p.011 Video 1
p.011 Video worksheet 1
p.011 Learning skills

Starter 1
Aim
To introduce language for talking about cinema; To use reading strategies

Write up the following. Give pupils two minutes to copy the list and number it in their personal order of preference. While they are doing this, do the same thing.

les films fantastiques
les films d'arts martiaux
les films de science-fiction
les films d'horreur
les films d'action
les dessins animés
les westerns
les comédies

Read out your list in order, asking pupils to translate each item. Reward any pupil who had exactly the same order as you.

Alternative Starter 1:
Use ActiveTeach p.010 Flashcards to introduce film vocabulary.

1 C'est quel film? (AT 3.1)
Reading. Pupils match each of the pictures to the correct film type (from **a–h**).

Answers
See answers for exercise 2: pupils listen to the exercise 2 recording to check their answers.

2 Écoute et vérifie. (1–8) (AT 1.1)
Listening. Pupils listen to the recording to check their answers to exercise 1.

Audioscript — CD 1 track 4

1 e – les films d'action
2 a – les films fantastiques
3 f – les dessins animés
4 d – les films d'horreur
5 c – les films de science-fiction
6 b – les films d'arts martiaux
7 g – les westerns
8 h – les comédies

Answers
1 e 2 a 3 f 4 d 5 c 6 b 7 g 8 h

3 C'est quel genre de film? Écoute et note la bonne lettre pour chaque conversation. (1–8) (AT 1.3)
Listening. Pupils listen to eight conversations and for each note the letter of the film type mentioned.

2 J'ai une passion pour le cinéma   T'es branché(e)? 1

Audioscript CD 1 track 5

1 – Qu'est-ce que tu aimes comme films, Arthur?
   – J'aime les films d'arts martiaux.
2 – Et toi, qu'est-ce que tu aimes comme films, Nadia?
   – Moi, j'aime les films d'action. J'adore ça.
3 – Aziza, qu'est-ce que tu aimes comme films?
   – J'aime les films fantastiques.
4 – Qu'est-ce que tu aimes comme films, Roméo?
   – J'aime les comédies.
5 – Qu'est-ce que tu aimes comme films, Lara?
   – J'aime les dessins animés.
6 – Qu'est-ce que tu aimes comme films, Léo?
   – J'aime les films d'horreur.
7 – Qu'est-ce que tu aimes comme films, Mehdi?
   – Moi, j'aime les westerns.
8 – Qu'est-ce que tu aimes comme films, Lidia?
   – Moi, j'aime les films de science-fiction. J'adore ça. C'est génial.

Answers
1 b 2 e 3 a 4 h 5 f 6 d 7 g 8 c

Use the pronunciation box to review and practise giving equal weight to all syllables in French words.

4 Écris les phrases. (AT 4.4)
Writing. Pupils write out complete sentences, using the correct expressions for the picture prompts.

Answers
1 J'adore **les comédies** et j'aime aussi **les films d'action**, mais je déteste **les films d'arts martiaux**.
2 J'adore **les films fantastiques** et j'aime aussi **les films d'horreur**, mais je déteste **les westerns**.
3 J'adore **les dessins animés** et j'aime aussi **les films de science-fiction**, mais je déteste **les films d'horreur**.
4 J'adore **les films d'arts martiaux** et j'aime aussi **les westerns**, mais je déteste **les dessins animés**.

Starter 2
Aim
To review vocabulary for talking about cinema

Give pupils two minutes working in pairs to come up with as many types of films in French as they can.

5 Écoute et lis la conversation. (AT 1.4)
Listening. Pupils listen to the conversation about films, following the text at the same time.

Audioscript CD 1 track 6

– Qu'est-ce que tu aimes comme films?
– J'aime les films fantastiques.
– Mais je n'aime pas les films de science-fiction. Je déteste ça.
– Quel est ton film préféré?
– Mon film préféré, c'est Avatar. C'est cool.
– Qui est ton acteur préféré?
– Mon acteur préféré, c'est Sam Worthington parce qu'il est intelligent.

> **Studio Grammaire: adjective agreement**
> Use the *Studio Grammaire* box to cover adjective agreement. There is more information and further practice on Pupil Book p. 62.

6 En tandem. Fais la conversation de l'exercice 5. Change les mots soulignés. (AT 2.4)
Speaking. In pairs: pupils practise the conversation from exercise 5, changing the underlined words.

7 Lis les textes. Écris le bon prénom. (AT 3.4)
Reading. Pupils read the texts, then answer the questions in English by identifying the person being described each time. *parce que* is glossed for support.

Answers
1 Manu 2 Tiki 3 Manu 4 Élisa 5 Tiki 6 Élisa

> **Studio Grammaire: *être* (present tense singular)**
> Use the *Studio Grammaire* box to cover the present tense of *être* (singular). There is more information and further practice on Pupil Book p. 23.

[R] Write up the subject pronouns *je, tu, il, elle, on* in random order. Ask pupils to close their books and copy these out with the correct form of *être*.

1 T'es branché(e)? 2 J'ai une passion pour le cinéma

8 Prépare un exposé. (AT 2.4)

PLTS E

Speaking. Pupils prepare and give a presentation on their film preferences. A list of points to cover and a framework are supplied. Draw pupils' attention to the tip box on including intensifiers, connectives and opinions using *parce que*. Encourage them to write their presentation out in full first, then make prompt cards with just the key words for each sentence and use these to give the presentation.

When pupils have given their presentation, ask the rest of the class to give constructive feedback.

If you have a native French-speaking assistant, you could use him/her to give pupils practice in talking without prompts on the subject of the cinema. The assistant could also talk about his/her own cinema preferences, covering both English and French films.

Whenever an assistant works with the pupils, encourage him/her to give all explanations necessary for the task in French, using consistently the expressions you yourself use in class, and have perhaps already displayed in the classroom for pupils' reference.

Plenary

Review the phrases for introducing opinions used in this unit and in Unit 1. Then give a prompt, e.g. *'Twilight'*: the first pupil gives an opinion of this type of film, then gives the name of another film as a prompt to the next pupil. Carry on in this way round the class.

Workbook, page 4

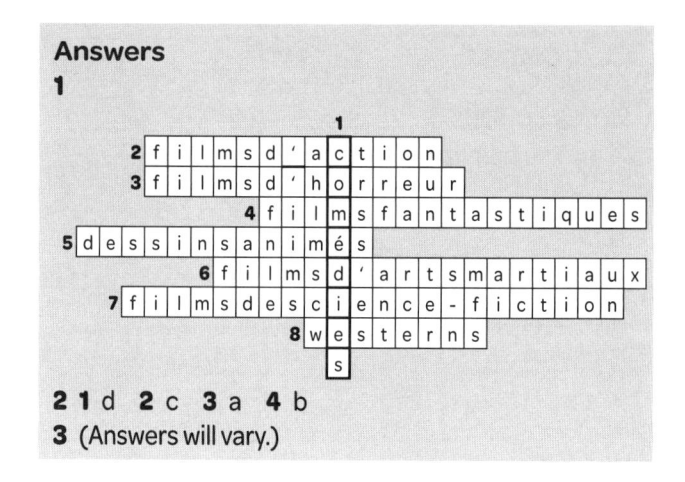

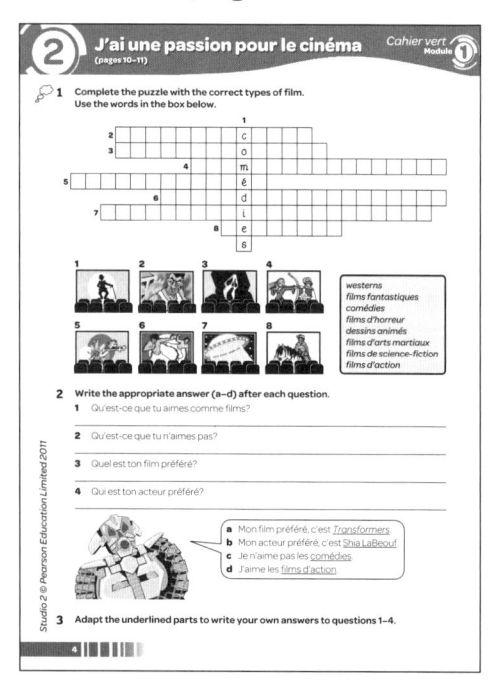

Answers

1

							1								
	2	f	i	l	m	s	d	'	a	c	t	i	o	n	
	3	f	i	l	m	s	d	'	h	o	r	r	e	u	r
				4	f	i	l	m	s	f	a	n	t	a	s	t	i	q	u	e	s
5	d	e	s	s	i	n	s	a	n	i	m	é	s		
				6	f	i	l	m	s	d	'	a	r	t	s	m	a	r	t	i	a	u	x
		7	f	i	l	m	s	d	e	s	c	i	e	n	c	e	-	f	i	c	t	i	o	n
							8	w	e	s	t	e	r	n	s
								s							

2 1 d 2 c 3 a 4 b

3 (Answers will vary.)

Worksheet 1.1 Pronunciation of –er verbs

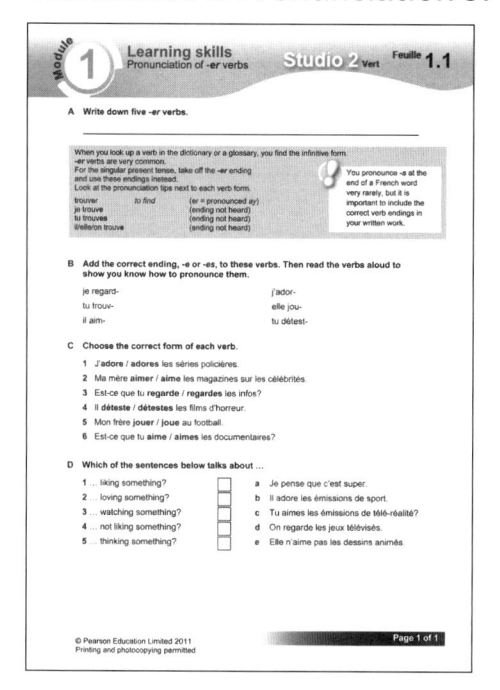

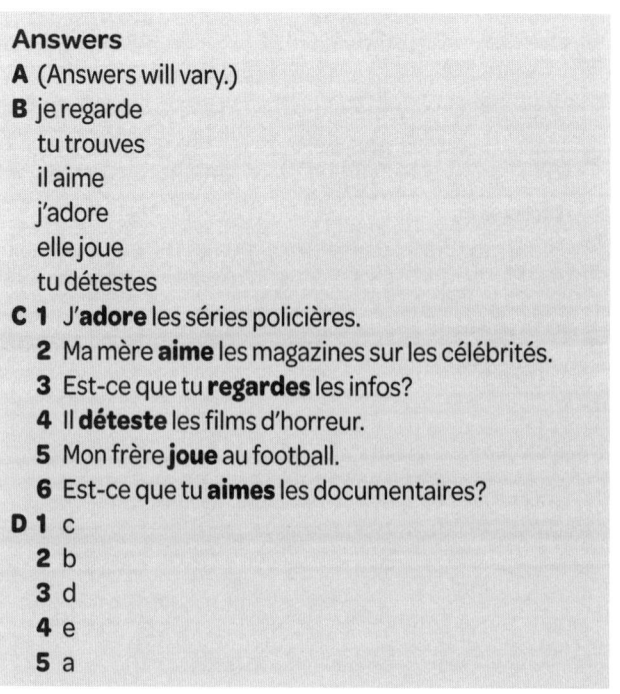

Answers

A (Answers will vary.)

B je regarde
 tu trouves
 il aime
 j'adore
 elle joue
 tu détestes

C 1 J'**adore** les séries policières.
 2 Ma mère **aime** les magazines sur les célébrités.
 3 Est-ce que tu **regardes** les infos?
 4 Il **déteste** les films d'horreur.
 5 Mon frère **joue** au football.
 6 Est-ce que tu **aimes** les documentaires?

D 1 c
 2 b
 3 d
 4 e
 5 a

2 J'ai une passion pour le cinéma   T'es branché(e)? 1

Video

The video component provides opportunities for speaking activities in a plausible and stimulating context. The StudioFR team, whom pupils met in *Studio 1* – Marielle, Samira, Hugo and Alex (and a new member, Mehdi, who joins later in the course) – make video reports on a range of topics to send to StudioGB, their counterpart in the UK. Each video is around three minutes long.

Episode 1: Le ciné club

The team are thinking about starting a cinema club. To help them decide what kind of films to show, they carry out a survey asking young people about their cinema habits and preferences. Video worksheet 1 can be used in conjunction with this episode.

Answers to video worksheet (ActiveTeach)

1 (Answers will vary. Encourage discussion.)

2 A bus, admission, popcorn, cola
  B To open their own cinema club in the studio. It's Alex's idea.
  C Marielle: likes romantic films, never watches science-fiction
  Hugo: likes action films
  Samira: hates action films, prefers comedies
  Alex: likes science-fiction films
  D No, it's pretty much what you would expect.
  E Positive: *j'ai une passion pour …, je suis fan de …*
  Negative: *j'ai horreur de …, je déteste …*
  F To do a survey (*sondage*) about what sorts of films local young people like.

3 A First person: likes comedies and martial-arts films
  Second person: likes horror films (great), hates romantic films (stupid)
  Third person: likes fantasy films (great) and the actress Audrey Tautou (superb)
  Fourth person: likes action films
  Fifth person: likes adventure films (exciting and interesting)
  Sixth person: doesn't like any films at all! (boring)
  B – stupid (near cognate – NC)
  – great
  – frightening
  – superb (NC)
  – exciting
  – interesting (NC)
  – boring
  C First person: occasionally with parents
  Second person: once or twice a month with friends
  D To mark Marielle saying she is scared by the film *Scream!*
  E No, he doesn't like them at all. He prefers TV sports programmes.
  F *Karate Kid, Scream, Twilight, Transformers, Avatar.* They show that young French people like American films.
  G Because their survey simply showed one vote for each type of film, so it was useless.

3 La lecture (Pupil Book pp. 12–13)

T'es branché(e)? 1

Learning objectives
- Talking about reading
- Using *un*, *une* and *le*, *la*, *les*

Framework objectives
2.4/Y8 Writing – (b) organising paragraphs
4.3/Y8 Language – gender and plurals

FCSE links
Unit 1: Meeting people (Sports and hobbies)
Unit 6: Leisure (Sports/hobbies)
Unit 11: Media (Free time activities; Opinions on TV programmes/films/types of media)

Grammar
- the definite article
- the indefinite article
- adjective agreement
- present tense of *avoir* (singular)

Key language
Qu'est-ce que tu lis, en ce moment?
Je lis ...
une BD
un livre sur les animaux
un livre d'épouvante
un magazine sur les célébrités
un roman fantastique
un roman policier
C'est bien?
À mon avis, c'est ...
assez bien
amusant
intéressant
passionnant
ennuyeux
nul
Qui est ton auteur préféré?
Mon auteur préféré, c'est ...

PLTS
R Reflective learners

Resources
CD 1, tracks 7–8
Cahier d'exercices Vert, page 5
ActiveTeach
p.012 Flashcards
p.013 Grammar
p.013 Grammar practice
p.013 Grammar
p.013 Grammar practice
p.013 Class activity
p.013 Grammar skills
p.013 Thinking skills

Starter 1
Aim
To introduce language for talking about books;
To use reading strategies

Write up the following, jumbling the order of the second set. Explain that they are all different kinds of publication. Give pupils two minutes working in pairs to match each type of publication with the appropriate title. If necessary, gloss *roman*.

un magazine sur les célébrités
un livre sur les animaux
un livre d'épouvante
un roman fantastique
un roman policier
une BD

Hello
Animal Farm
Vampire Academy
The Lord of the Rings
The Adventures of Sherlock Holmes
Batman Returns

Hear answers, asking pupils to translate the categories into English.

Alternative Starter 1:
Use ActiveTeach p.012 Flashcards to introduce book vocabulary.

1 C'est quel livre? (AT 3.2)
Reading. Pupils match each of the pictures to the correct book type (from **a–f**).

Answers
See answers for exercise 2: pupils listen to the exercise 2 recording to check their answers.

2 Écoute et vérifie tes réponses. (1–6) (AT 1.2)
Listening. Pupils listen to check their answers to exercise 1. The verb forms *je lis* and *tu lis* are glossed for support.

Audioscript — CD 1 track 7

1 – *Qu'est-ce que tu lis, en ce moment?*
  – *Je lis un roman policier.*
  – *e*
2 – *Qu'est-ce que tu lis, en ce moment?*
  – *Je lis un livre d'épouvante.*
  – *c*
3 – *Qu'est-ce que tu lis, en ce moment?*
  – *Moi, je lis un roman fantastique.*
  – *d*
4 – *Qu'est-ce que tu lis, en ce moment?*
  – *Je lis une BD.*
  – *f*

3 La lecture   T'es branché(e)? 1

5 – Qu'est-ce que tu lis, en ce moment?
  – Moi, en ce moment, je lis un livre sur les animaux.
  – b
6 – Qu'est-ce que tu lis, en ce moment?
  – Je lis un magazine sur les célébrités. C'est génial.
  – a

Answers
1 e **2** c **3** d **4** f **5** b **6** a

> **Studio Grammaire: definite and indefinite articles**
> Use the *Studio Grammaire* box to cover the definite and indefinite articles.

3 Copie le tableau et classe les opinions. Regarde la section *Vocabulaire* si nécessaire. (AT 3.2)
Reading. Pupils copy out the grid and complete it by writing the adjectives in the correct column and translating them into English. They can use the *Vocabulaire* section for reference, if necessary.

Answers

☺	☹	English
amusant		funny
	ennuyeux	boring
intéressant		interesting
	nul	rubbish
assez bien		quite good
passionnant		exciting

4 Écoute et écris le genre de livre et l'opinion. (1–6) (AT 1.4)
Listening. Pupils listen to six conversations and for each write the type of book and the opinion expressed.

Audioscript   CD 1 track 8

1 – Qu'est-ce que tu lis, en ce moment, Antoine?
  – Euh … Je lis un livre sur les animaux.
  – C'est bien?
  – À mon avis, c'est intéressant.
2 – Qu'est-ce que tu lis, en ce moment, Jeanne?
  – En ce moment, je lis un roman fantastique.
  – C'est bien?
  – À mon avis, c'est assez bien.
3 – Qu'est-ce que tu lis, en ce moment, Yvan?
  – Voyons … Je lis un roman policier.
  – C'est bien?
  – À mon avis, c'est passionnant.
4 – Qu'est-ce que tu lis, en ce moment, Luna?
  – Euh, ben moi, en ce moment, je lis une BD.
  – C'est bien?
  – À mon avis, c'est amusant.
5 – Qu'est-ce que tu lis, en ce moment, Tariq?
  – Moi, je lis un magazine sur les célébrités.
  – C'est bien?
  – À mon avis, c'est nul.
6 – Qu'est-ce que tu lis, en ce moment, Emma?
  – Euh … Moi, en ce moment, je lis un livre d'épouvante.
  – C'est bien?
  – À mon avis, c'est ennuyeux.

Answers

	type of book	opinion
1	book about animals	interesting
2	fantasy novel	quite good
3	thriller	exciting
4	comic book	funny
5	magazine about celebrities	rubbish
6	horror story	boring

5 En tandem. Fais deux dialogues. Utilise les images. (AT 2.4)
Speaking. In pairs: pupils make up two dialogues, using the framework + picture prompts supplied.

Answers
A ● Qu'est-ce que tu lis, en ce moment?
  ■ Je lis **un magazine sur les célébrités**.
  ● C'est bien?
  ■ À mon avis, c'est **ennuyeux/nul**.
B ● Qu'est-ce que tu lis, en ce moment?
  ■ Je lis **un livre sur les animaux**.
  ● C'est bien?
  ■ À mon avis, c'est **amusant/passionnant/ intéressant/assez bien**.

1 T'es branché(e)? 3 La lecture

Starter 2

Aim
To review the definite and indefinite articles; To review vocabulary from the unit

Write up the following, omitting the underlined words. Give pupils three minutes to supply the missing articles. If necessary, supply the articles in random order for support.

1 *Je lis un magazine sur les célébrités.*
2 *J'ai un livre sur les animaux.*
3 *Je lis une BD.*
4 *J'aime les romans fantastiques.*

Check answers, asking pupils to translate each completed sentence into English. Remind them as necessary that when you are talking in general about things you like, you have to use the plural form of the definite article.

6 Lis le texte et choisis la bonne réponse. (AT 3.4)

Reading. Pupils read the text and choose the correct option from the two words given each time. Some vocabulary is glossed for support.

Answers
1 livres 2 treize 3 petit 4 parents
5 chocolaterie 6 chocolat

Studio Grammaire: *avoir* (present tense singular)

Use the *Studio Grammaire* box to cover the present tense of *avoir* (singular). There is more information and further practice on Pupil Book p. 23.

R Say different forms of *avoir* and *être* in random order, e.g. *on a*. Pupils say which verb it comes from each time.

Studio Grammaire: adjective agreement

Use the *Studio Grammaire* box to cover adjective agreement. There is more information and further practice on Pupil Book p. 62.

R Write up *grand, gentille, amusante, petit, intelligent, belle.* Ask pupils to say whether each is masculine or feminine and to give the other form in each case.

7 En tandem. Fais le quiz. (AT 2.4)

Speaking. In pairs: pupils do the quiz on reading habits. *pourquoi* is glossed for support.

8 Qu'est-ce que tu lis? Utilise le texte comme modèle. (AT 4.4)

PLTS R

Writing. Pupils write a paragraph on their reading preferences, using the framework supplied. The parts they need to change are underlined for reference.

When they have finished, ask them to read their text through and to make corrections as necessary. Ask them to identify two areas in which they can improve next time they do an extended writing task.

Plenary

Put the class into teams and tell them to study the *Studio Grammaire* boxes on *avoir* (p. 13) and *être* (p. 11) for one minute. Put a sheet of paper for each team at the front of the class. On each paper write *avoir* and the singular subject pronouns in order. Tell pupils to close their books.

Team members take it in turn to come to the front of the class and fill in the present tense singular verb form to match the subject pronoun. They then take the pen back and pass it to the next member of their team. The first team to complete all three verbs correctly is the winner.

Repeat with *être*.

Alternative Plenary:

Use ActiveTeach p.013 Grammar practice to review and practise the verbs *être* and *avoir*.

The teaching notes throughout *Studio 2* suggest a variety of Starters and Plenaries which involve pupils working in teams. You may want to allocate teams at this stage which students can stay in throughout the year. This will save time whenever a team activity comes up. You could also keep an ongoing tally of points won in these activities and award a prize to the team with the highest score at the end of each term/half-term.

3 La lecture   T'es branché(e)? 1

Workbook, page 5

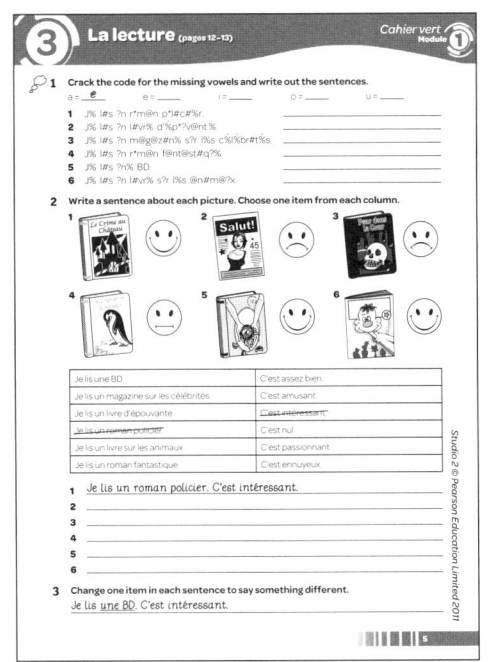

Answers

1 a=@ e=% i=# o=* u=?
1 Je lis un roman policier.
2 Je lis un livre d'épouvante.
3 Je lis un magazine sur les célébrités.
4 Je lis un roman fantastique.
5 Je lis une BD.
6 Je lis un livre sur les animaux.

2 1 *Je lis un roman policier. C'est intéressant.*
2 Je lis un magazine sur les célébrités. C'est nul/ennuyeux.
3 Je lis un livre d'épouvante. C'est nul/ennuyeux.
4 Je lis un livre sur les animaux. C'est assez bien.
5 Je lis un roman fantastique. C'est passionnant/amusant.
6 Je lis une BD. C'est amusant/passionnant.

3 (Answers will vary.)

Worksheet 1.2 Present tense of *avoir* and *être*

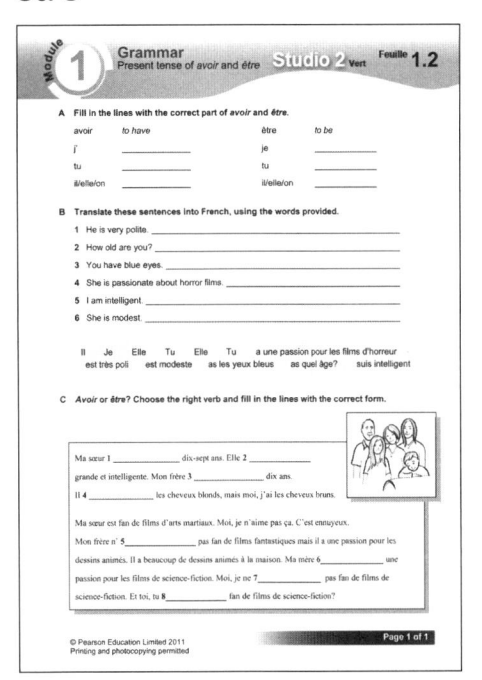

Answers

A avoir *to have*   être *to be*
j'ai   je suis
tu as   tu es
il/elle/on a   il/elle/on est

B 1 Il est très poli.
2 Tu as quel âge?
3 Tu as les yeux bleus.
4 Elle a une passion pour les films d'horreur.
5 Je suis intelligent.
6 Elle est modeste.

C Ma sœur **1 a** dix-sept ans. Elle **2 est** grande et intelligente. Mon frère **3 a** dix ans. Il **4 a** les cheveux blonds, mais moi, j'ai les cheveux bruns.
Ma sœur est fan de films d'arts martiaux. Moi, je n'aime pas ça. C'est ennuyeux. Mon frère n' **5 est** pas fan de films fantastiques mais il a une passion pour les dessins animés. Il a beaucoup de dessins animés à la maison. Ma mère **6 a** une passion pour les films de science-fiction. Moi, je ne **7 suis** pas fan de films de science-fiction. Et toi, tu **8 es** fan de films de science-fiction?

1 T'es branché(e)? 3 La lecture

Worksheet 1.3 Identifying sentences

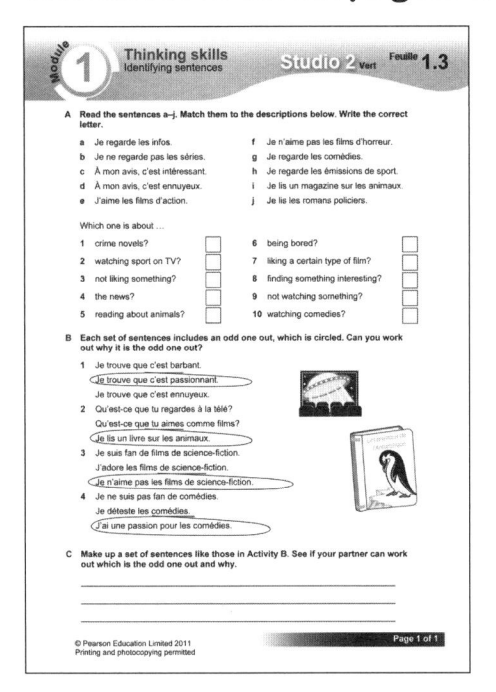

Answers

A 1 j **2** h **3** f **4** a **5** i **6** d **7** e
   8 c **9** b **10** g

B 1 *barbant* and *ennuyeux* are negative, *passionnant* is positive.
   2 The first two are questions, the third is a statement.
   3 The first two like science-fiction films, the third doesn't.
   4 The first two don't like comedies, the third does.

C (Answers will vary.)

4 Que fais-tu quand tu es connecté(e)?

T'es branché(e)? 1 (Pupil Book pp. 14–15)

Learning objectives
- Talking about the internet
- Using the verb *faire*

Framework objectives
1.2/Y8 Listening – new contexts

FCSE links
Unit 1: Meeting people (Sports and hobbies)
Unit 6: Leisure (Sports/hobbies)
Unit 11: Media (Free time activities; Forms of communication; Opinions on TV programmes/films/types of media; Computer-related vocabulary)

Grammar
- present tense of *faire* (singular)

Key language
Que fais-tu quand tu es connecté(e)?
J'envoie des e-mails.
Je fais beaucoup de choses.
Je fais des recherches pour mes devoirs.
Je fais des achats.
Je fais des quiz.
Je joue à des jeux en ligne.
Je lis des blogs.
Je trouve ça ... chouette, pratique, stupide, barbant

PLTS
S Self-managers

Resources
CD 1, tracks 9–10
Cahier d'exercices Vert, page 6
ActiveTeach
p.014 Flashcards
p.014 Grammar
p.015 Video 2
p.015 Video worksheet 2
p.015 Learning skills

Starter 1
Aim
To predict vocabulary in a given topic

Tell pupils that this lesson is about how young French people use the internet. Tell them to keep their books closed. Ask them to predict (in English) which words are likely to come up. Elicit as many as possible.

Then write up the French sentences in exercise 1 (*Je fais des achats*, etc.). Read out the following, asking pupils to find and tell you the French for each one: *I play games online, I read blogs, I shop, I send emails, I do homework research, I do quizzes*.

Point out that anticipating what you are going to read or hear prepares you by giving you a context and this can really help your comprehension.

Alternative Starter 1:
Use ActiveTeach p.014 Flashcards to introduce internet vocabulary.

1 Écoute et écris la bonne lettre. (1–6) (AT 1.3)
Listening. Pupils listen to six conversations and for each one note the letter of the activity mentioned.

Audioscript CD 1 track 9

1 – Que fais-tu quand tu es connecté?
– Je fais beaucoup de choses. Je lis des blogs, par exemple.

2 – Que fais-tu quand tu es connectée?
– Moi, je fais beaucoup de choses. J'envoie des e-mails.

3 – Que fais-tu quand tu es connectée?
– Quand je suis connectée, je fais des achats.

4 – Que fais-tu quand tu es connecté?
– Euh, je fais beaucoup de choses quand je suis connecté. Je joue à des jeux en ligne, par exemple.

5 – Que fais-tu quand tu es connecté?
– Je fais beaucoup de choses. Je fais des quiz ...

6 – Que fais-tu quand tu es connecté?
– Quand je suis connectée, je fais des recherches pour mes devoirs.

Answers
1 d **2** e **3** a **4** f **5** c **6** b

Studio Grammaire: *faire* (present tense singular)
Use the *Studio Grammaire* box to cover *faire* in the present tense (singular). There is more information and further practice on Pupil Book p. 23.

R Pupils in pairs take it in turn to prompt with a present tense singular form of *faire* in French and to respond in English. They then move on to prompting in English and responding in French.

1 T'es branché(e)? 4 Que fais-tu quand tu es connecté(e)?

Use the pronunciation box to remind pupils how to sound French when saying cognates.

Read together through *Stratégie 1* on Pupil Book p. 25, covering techniques for improving pronunciation. Encourage pupils to try out the techniques for themselves.

2 Écris correctement les mots en désordre. Trouve le sens en anglais. (AT 3.2)

Reading. Pupils solve the anagrams. They write out the words and match them with the English meanings.

Answers
1 d'habitude — **d** usually
2 souvent — **e** often
3 tous les soirs — **b** every evening
4 quelquefois — **a** sometimes
5 une fois par semaine — **c** once a week

3 Écoute. Copie et remplis le tableau. (1–6) (AT 1.4)

Listening. Pupils copy out the grid. They listen to six people talking about how they use the internet and complete the grid with the details. The answer options and answer spaces in the grid are colour-coded for support. *pratique* and *barbant* are glossed for support.

Audioscript CD 1 track 10

1 *Moi, tous les soirs, je joue à des jeux en ligne. Je trouve ça chouette.*
2 *Une fois par semaine, je fais des achats. Je trouve ça pratique.*
3 *Souvent, j'envoie des e-mails. Je trouve ça chouette.*
4 *Quand je suis connecté, d'habitude, je lis des blogs. Je trouve ça pratique.*
5 *Quelquefois, je fais des quiz, mais je trouve ça stupide.*
6 *Quelquefois, je fais des recherches pour mes devoirs, mais je trouve ça un peu barbant.*

Answers

	fréquence	activité	opinion
1	c	k	l
2	e	f	m
3	b	j	l
4	a	i	m
5	d	h	n
6	d	g	o

Starter 2

Aim

To review the present tense (singular) of *avoir*, *être* and *faire*

Write up *avoir*, *être*, *faire*. Put the class into pairs. Each pair chooses one of the verbs and writes out all singular forms of the present tense as anagrams, in random order. They swap with another pair and write out the verb forms they receive in the correct order. They then swap with a different pair to check answers.

4 En tandem. Fais trois dialogues. Utilise les images. (AT 2.4)

Speaking. In pairs: pupils make up three dialogues, using the framework + picture prompts supplied.

Answers
A ● Que fais-tu quand tu es connecté(e)?
■ Quelquefois, **j'envoie des e-mails**.
Et souvent, **je joue à des jeux en ligne**.
Je trouve ça **chouette/pratique**.
B ● Que fais-tu quand tu es connecté(e)?
■ Quelquefois, **je fais des achats**.
Une fois par semaine, **je lis des blogs**.
Je trouve ça **chouette/pratique**.
C ● Que fais-tu quand tu es connecté(e)?
■ Quelquefois, **je fais des quiz**.
Une fois par semaine, **je fais des recherches pour mes devoirs**.
Je trouve ça **stupide/barbant**.

5 Lis le texte. Corrige les erreurs dans les phrases en anglais. (AT 3.4)

Reading. Pupils read the text about how young French people use the internet. They then read the sentences summarising it in English and correct the mistakes. *il partage* is glossed for support.

Answers
1 82% of young French people connect to the internet **every day**.
2 A typical young surfer sends emails, **reads blogs** and posts comments.
3 He/She does research for his/her **homework**.
4 He/She prefers sites which talk about cinema, **sport** or culture.
5 Sometimes he/she **buys** things on the internet.
6 He/She plays games or does **quizzes**.

4 Que fais-tu quand tu es connecté(e)? T'es branché(e)? 1

6 Copie et complète le texte avec les bons verbes. (AT 3.4)

Reading. Pupils copy and complete the text using the appropriate verbs. The answers are supplied in random order for support.

Answers
1 fais 2 trouve 3 adore 4 joue 5 suis

➕ Pupils write a paragraph about how they use the internet, using the text in exercise 6 as a model. If they need support, identify with them the sentence openings to use and also the text which needs to change.

PLTS S

Read together through *Stratégie 1* on Pupil Book p. 126, covering the *Look, say, cover, write, check* technique for mastering spelling. Set pupils the challenge of choosing and learning 10 words using this approach, either in the classroom or at home.

Plenary

Review the present tense (singular) of *faire* and the vocabulary of the unit. Write up the following, omitting the underlined text. Put the class into teams and give them three minutes to copy and complete the sentences. They then swap with another team to check answers. Hear answers, asking pupils to translate the completed sentence each time.
1 Je *fais* beaucoup de choses.
2 Que *fais*-tu quand tu es connecté?
3 Il *fait* des achats.
4 Je *fais* des recherches pour mes devoirs.
5 Elle *fait* des quiz.

Workbook, page 6

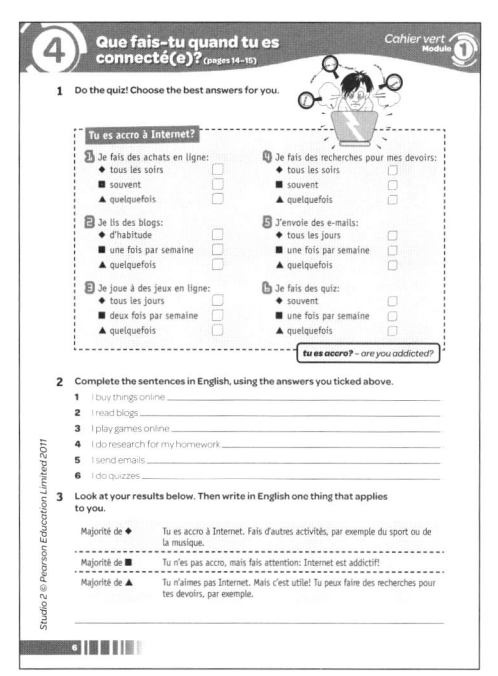

Answers
1 (Answers will vary.)
2 (Answers will vary.)
3 (Answers will vary, based on:)
Mostly ◆
You're addicted to the internet. Do other activities, for example sport or music.
Mostly ■
You're not addicted, but be careful: the internet is addictive!
Mostly ▲
You don't like the internet. But it's useful! You can do research for your homework, for example.

1 T'es branché(e)? 4 Que fais-tu quand tu es connecté(e)?

Worksheet 1.4 Forming longer sentences

Answers

A
et	and
mais	but
surtout	above all
parce que	because
aussi	also
ou	or
quand	when

B une fois par semaine
souvent
quelquefois
tous les soirs

C J'adore les dessins animés **et** j'aime **aussi** les comédies, **mais** je déteste les films d'horreur et les westerns. Mon acteur préféré, c'est Colin Firth, **parce qu**'il est génial. Je n'aime pas Harry Potter, **parce qu**'il est barbant.

D Comics are quite good and blogs are very interesting.

Video

Episode 2: À la radio

Marielle and Alex do a radio interview with Aurore on Radio l'Épine. They tell her about StudioFR and find out what it's like to host a radio programme. Video worksheet 2 can be used in conjunction with this episode.

Answers to video worksheet (ActiveTeach)

1 A It's a visit to a professional radio station to conduct an interview.
  B In part 1, Marielle is being interviewed but in part 2, she is doing the interviewing.
  C French map on the wall, French writing on the posters, a feature about *crêperies* (rare in the UK).

2 A *coucou, salut, bonjour*
  B What do you do? (*Qu'est-ce que tu fais?*)
  C Documentaries and reports about young people (*jeunes*) in Châlons.
  D They send the videos to the UK.
  E One about the voluntary fire service and one about a pancake restaurant (*crêperie*).
  F documentaries, reality shows, music shows
  G No, he says he rarely (*rarement*) listens.
  H – presenter (female)
    – documentaries
    – reports
    – reality TV

3 A Aurore has played some music.
  B Once a week (*une fois par semaine*). Pupils may have heard 'tous les jours' (every day) but that was in Marielle's question.
  C (radio) programme
  D Young people. She uses the word 'jeunes' several times.
  E blogs, forums
  F online

4 A The equipment. She knows he's interested in technology.
  B She doesn't do news (*infos*) or sport. Her colleagues do that.
  C The studio falls into darkness. Alex has been fiddling with the equipment (despite having been told not to).

5 Quand il fait beau, on va au parc (Pupil Book pp. 16–17)

Learning objectives
- Talking about what you do in different weather
- Using *on*

Framework objectives
5.6 Strategies – reading aloud

FCSE links
Unit 1: Meeting people (Sports and hobbies)
Unit 4: Holidays (Weather)
Unit 6: Leisure (Sports/hobbies)
Unit 11: Media (Free time activities)

Grammar
- *on* verb forms
- present tense of *aller* (singular)

Key language
Qu'est-ce qu'on fait quand il (fait beau)?
Quand...
il fait beau
il fait froid
il fait chaud
il pleut
on fait du VTT
on fait du skate
on fait du bowling
on regarde des DVD
on va...
au café, au centre de loisirs, au cinéma, au parc
on joue...
au foot, au basket
on surfe sur Internet
avec mes copains

PLTS
T Team workers

Resources
CD 1, tracks 11–13
Cahier d'exercices Vert, page 7

ActiveTeach
p.016 Flashcards
p.016 Flashcards
p.016 Grammar
p.016 Grammar practice
p.017 Class activity
p.017 Grammar skills
p.017 Thinking skills

Starter 1
Aim
To review subject pronouns

Write up the following, jumbling the order. Give pupils one minute to translate them into English.

je, tu, il, elle, on

Check answers. Ask pupils to give you some verb forms using any of the pronouns. Prompt with infinitives as necessary, using verbs such as *visiter, retrouver, jouer, regarder, avoir, être, faire*, etc.

Alternative Starter 1:
Use ActiveTeach p.016 Flashcards (both sets) to review weather and activities.

1 Écoute et note les activités. (1–4) (AT 1.3)
Listening. Pupils listen to four people talking about the activities they do in different kinds of weather. For each they note the letters of the two activities mentioned.

Audioscript — CD 1 track 11
1 *Quand il fait chaud, on va au café ou on va au parc.*
2 *Quand il fait froid, on va au cinéma ou on fait du bowling.*
3 *Quand il fait beau, on fait du skate ou on fait du VTT.*
4 *Quand il pleut, on regarde des DVD ou on va au centre de loisirs.*

Answers
1 c,d **2** a,f **3** g,h **4** e,b

> **Studio Grammaire:** *on*
> Use the *Studio Grammaire* box to cover the subject pronoun *on*. There is more information and further practice on Pupil Book p. 23.

2 En tandem. Dis les phrases à tour de rôle. (AT 2.3)

PLTS T

Speaking. In pairs: pupils take it in turn to make up sentences, using the picture prompts supplied. They comment on each other's work, using the guidelines in the tip box. Also draw attention to the second tip box, which gives support in getting the details of the language right.

1 T'es branché(e)? 5 Quand il fait beau, on va au parc

Answers
1 Quand il pleut, on va au cinéma.
2 Quand il fait chaud, on va au parc.
3 Quand il fait froid, on regarde des DVD.
4 Quand il fait beau, on fait du skate.
5 Quand il pleut, on fait du bowling.
6 Quand il fait beau, on fait du VTT.

R Pupils in pairs make up sentences of their own like the ones in exercise 2. One pupil talks about the weather; the other completes the sentence with details of the activity. They then swap roles. You could extend the activity by suggesting they come up with illogical things to do each time.

Studio Grammaire: *aller* (present tense singular)
Use the *Studio Grammaire* box to cover the present tense of *aller* (singular). There is more information and further practice on Pupil Book p. 23.

Starter 2
Aim
To review complex sentences

Write up the following, jumbling the order of the words in each sentence. Give pupils three minutes working in pairs to write out the sentences correctly.

1 quand il fait beau, on fait du skate
2 quand il pleut, on va au centre de loisirs
3 quand il fait chaud, on va au parc
4 quand il fait froid, on fait du bowling

Check answers.

Alternative Starter 2:
Use ActiveTeach p.016 Grammar practice to practise *faire* and *aller*.

3 Quelles activités sont mentionnées? Écoute et écris les <u>six</u> bonnes lettres. (AT 1.3)
Listening. Pupils listen to a girl talking about what she does in different kinds of weather. They note the letters of the six activities she mentions.

Audioscript CD 1 track 12

Alors, qu'est-ce qu'on fait quand il pleut? Eh bien, ça dépend. Quelquefois, on va au cinéma ou on regarde des DVD. Souvent, quand il pleut, on va au centre de loisirs et on joue au volley.

Quand il fait beau, normalement, on va au parc. Au parc, on fait du skate ou on joue au foot.

Answers
a, d, b, c, f, h

4 Lis les textes. Écris le bon prénom. (AT 3.4)
Reading. Pupils read the texts about what people do in different kinds of weather, then identify the correct person for each set of pictures.

Answers
1 Nathan 2 Élodie 3 Élodie 4 Élodie
5 Tony 6 Nathan

5 Écoute et chante la chanson. (AT 1.4)
Listening. Pupils listen to the song. They listen again, this time singing along. Some vocabulary is glossed for support.

Audioscript CD 1 track 13

*Quand il pleut, on regarde des DVD.
Nous, on aime bien les dessins animés.*

*Quand il fait beau, on fait du VTT
Ou bien, on fait du skate, surtout en été.*

*Quand je regarde la télé, je préfère les jeux télévisés,
Mais je regarde aussi les infos.
(Bravo!)*

*Quand je suis connectée, je fais des recherches sur les célébrités
Et je poste des photos sur ma page perso.*

*Je tchatte souvent sur MSN.
Je télécharge des chansons, des chansons par douzaine.*

*J'adore faire les choses en ligne.
Mon petit ordi, c'est toute ma vie.
Être connectée, c'est vraiment mon truc préféré.*

6 Trouve dans la chanson l'équivalent des expressions en anglais. (AT 3.4)
Reading. Pupils find in the song in exercise 5 the French for the English phrases given.

Answers
1 on aime bien les dessins animés
2 surtout en été
3 mais je regarde aussi
4 quand je suis connectée
5 je télécharge des chansons
6 c'est vraiment mon truc préféré

5 Quand il fait beau, on va au parc   T'es branché(e)? 1

7 Écris une version de la chanson pour ta bande de copains. (AT 4.4)

Writing. In pairs: pupils write a version of the song for their own group of friends, changing the activity details.

When pupils have finished, ask them to read through their partner's text, noting errors and suggesting improvements. They then produce a second draft, making the corrections and improvements their partner has suggested.

Plenary

Ask the class to explain what *on* means. Put pupils into teams and give them two minutes to write down the *on* form of as many verbs as they can. They swap lists with another team to check each other's answers. The team with the most correct verb forms is the winner.

Workbook, page 7

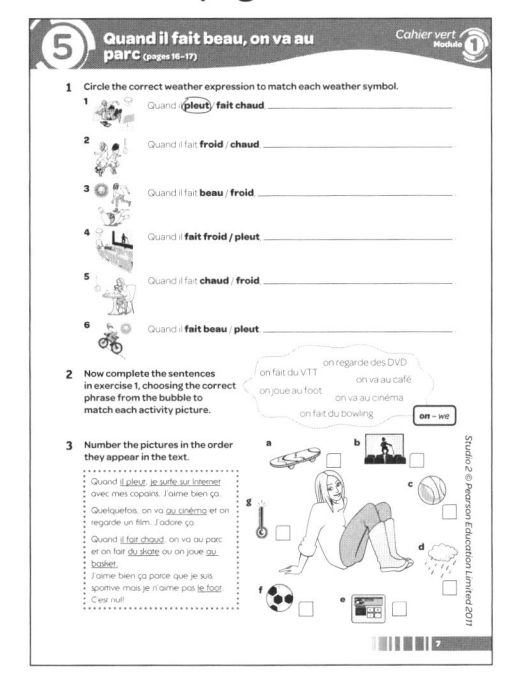

Answers
1 1 *Quand il pleut, on regarde des DVD*.
   2 Quand il fait **chaud, on joue au foot**.
   3 Quand il fait **beau, on fait du bowling**.
   4 Quand il **pleut, on va au cinéma**.
   5 Quand il fait **froid, on va au café**.
   6 Quand il **fait beau, on fait du VTT**.
2 (Answers given for exercise 1.)
3 1 d   2 e   3 b   4 g   5 a   6 c   7 f

Worksheet 1.5 Present tense of *aller* and *faire*

Answers
A 1 Je **vais** au parc tous les jours.
    I go to the park every day.
  2 On **fait** souvent des quiz sur Internet.
    We often do quizzes on the internet.
  3 Ma sœur **va** en ville et elle **fait** des achats.
    My sister goes to town and she does some shopping.
  4 Moi, je **fais** des quiz. Je trouve ça chouette.
    I do quizzes. I find them cool.
  5 Tu **fais** quelquefois des achats en ligne?
    Do you sometimes buy things online?
  6 Arnaud **va** au cinéma une fois par semaine.
    Arnaud goes to the cinema once a week.
B Quand **1 il est** connecté, **2 il fait** beaucoup de choses. D'habitude, **3 il va** sur **son** site préféré où **4 il fait** des quiz. Quelquefois, **5 il va** sur des blogs ou des forums. Souvent, **6 il fait** des achats en ligne. Et **7 il fait** des recherches pour **ses** devoirs tous les soirs.
C 1 Je ne vais pas au cinéma.
  2 Elle n'aime pas les dessins animés.
  3 Il ne fait pas beaucoup de choses.
  4 Tu ne regardes pas les séries.
  5 On ne va pas en ville.

1 T'es branché(e)? 5 Quand il fait beau, on va au parc

Worksheet 1.6 Odd one out!

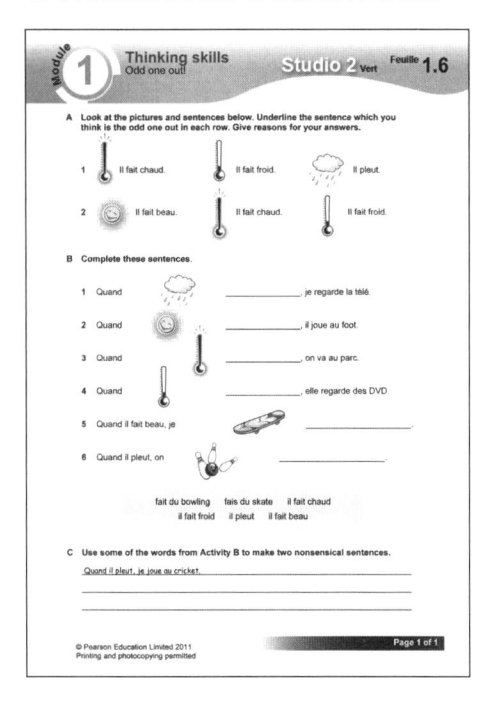

Answers

A (Answers may vary.)
 1 Il pleut (not to do with temperature)
 2 Il fait froid (not nice weather)

B 1 Quand il pleut, je regarde la télé.
 2 Quand il fait beau, il joue au foot.
 3 Quand il fait chaud, on va au parc.
 4 Quand il fait froid, elle regarde des DVD.
 5 Quand il fait beau, je fais du skate.
 6 Quand il pleut, on fait du bowling.

C (Answers will vary.)

Bilan et Révisions (Pupil Book pp. 18–19)

Bilan
Pupils use this checklist to review language covered in the module, working on it in pairs in class or on their own at home. Encourage them to follow up any areas of weakness they identify. There are Target Setting Sheets included in the Assessment Pack, and an opportunity for pupils to record their own levels and targets on the *J'avance* page in the Workbook, p. 12. You can also use the *Bilan* checklist as an end-of-module plenary option.

Révisions
These revision exercises can be used for assessment purposes or for pupils to practise before tackling the assessment tasks in the Assessment Pack.

Resources
CD 1, track 14
Cahier d'exercices Vert, pages 8 & 9

1 Écoute. Copie et remplis le tableau. (1–3) (AT 1.3)
Listening. Pupils copy out the grid. They listen to three conversations about what people watch on television and complete the grid with the details.

Audioscript — CD 1 track 14

1
– Qu'est-ce que tu regardes à la télé, Laura?
– Je regarde les dessins animés et j'aime les séries américaines, mais je ne regarde pas les documentaires et je n'aime pas les émissions de sport.

2
– Qu'est-ce que tu regardes à la télé, Hakim?
– Je regarde les émissions de télé-réalité et j'aime les documentaires, mais je ne regarde pas les infos et je n'aime pas les séries.

3
– Qu'est-ce que tu regardes à la télé, Johnny?
– Je regarde les jeux télévisés et j'aime bien les séries policières, mais je n'aime pas les infos et je ne regarde pas les dessins animés.

Answers

	1 Laura	2 Hakim	3 Johnny
watches	cartoons	reality TV programmes	game shows
likes	American series	documentaries	police series
doesn't watch	documentaries	news	cartoons
doesn't like	sports programmes	series	news

2 En tandem. Fais des conversations. Utilise les images. (AT 2.4)
Speaking. In pairs: pupils make up two conversations, using the framework + picture prompts supplied.

Answers
A ● Que fais-tu quand tu es connecté(e)?
■ Tous les soirs, **je joue à des jeux en ligne**. Une fois par semaine, **je fais des achats**.
● Qu'est-ce que tu lis, en ce moment?
■ Je lis **une BD**.
À mon avis, **c'est amusant/passionnant/intéressant**.

B ● Que fais-tu quand tu es connecté(e)?
■ Tous les soirs, **j'envoie des e-mails**. Quelquefois, **je fais des recherches pour mes devoirs**.
● Qu'est-ce que tu lis, en ce moment?
■ Je lis **un magazine sur les célébrités**.
À mon avis, c'est **nul/ennuyeux**.

3 Lis les textes. Copie et remplis le tableau. (AT 3.4)
Reading. Pupils copy out the grid. They read the three texts about the kinds of films people like and complete the grid with the details.

Answers

	☺	☹
1 Zacharie	action films, comedies	horror films
2 Mélanie	martial arts films, science-fiction films	fantasy films
3 Fouad	cartoons, horror films	westerns

1 T'es branché(e)? Bilan et Révisions

4 Écris les phrases. (AT 4.3)
Writing. Pupils write out the sentences, using the correct words for the picture prompts.

Answers
1 Quand **il pleut**, on **va au centre de loisirs**.
2 Quand **il fait beau**, on **va au parc**.
3 Quand **il fait chaud**, on **joue au football**.
4 Quand **il fait froid**, on **regarde des DVD**.

Workbook, pages 8 and 9

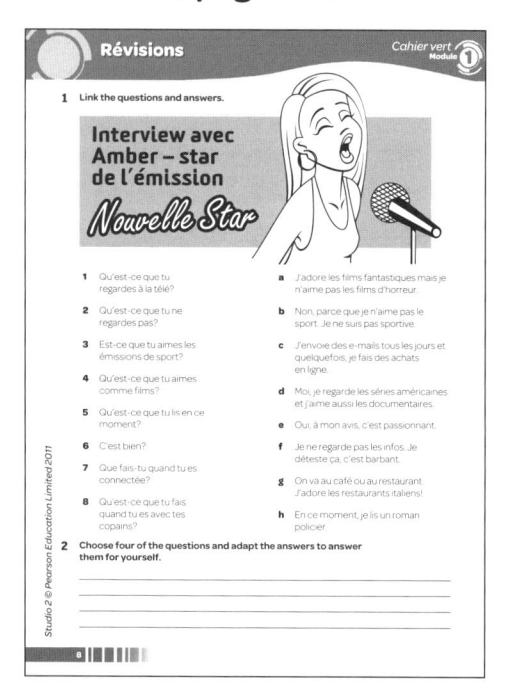

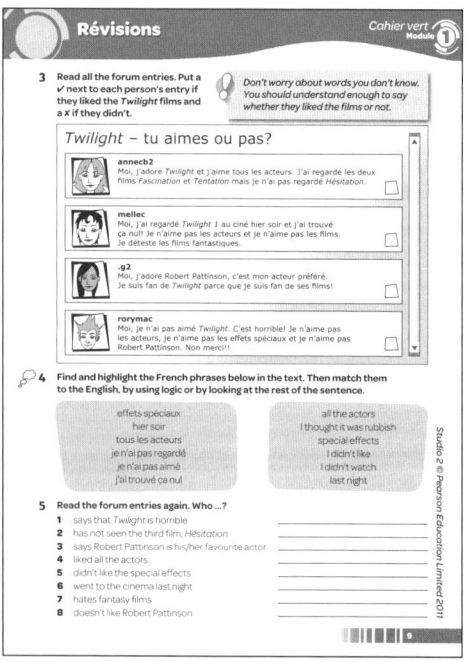

Answers
1 **1** d **2** f **3** b **4** a **5** h **6** e **7** c **8** g
2 (Answers will vary.)
3 annecb2 ✓   mellec ✗   .g2 ✓   rorymac ✗
4 effets spéciaux – special effects
  hier soir – last night
  tous les acteurs – all the actors
  je n'ai pas regardé – I didn't watch
  je n'ai pas aimé – I didn't like
  j'ai trouvé ça nul – I thought it was rubbish
5 **1** rorymac **2** annecb2 **3** .g2 **4** annecb2
  5 rorymac **6** mellec **7** mellec **8** rorymac

T'es branché(e)? 1 — En plus: À ne pas rater! (Pupil Book pp. 20–21)

Learning objectives
- Talking about your favourite television programmes, films and books

Framework objectives
5.8 Strategies – evaluating and improving

FCSE links
Unit 6: Leisure (Sports/hobbies)
Unit 11: Media (TV and film storylines/plots; Opinions on TV programmes/films/types of media)

Key language
Review of language from the module

mon personnage préféré
le scénario est drôle
je recommande (ce film) à tout le monde

PLTS
C Creative thinkers

Resources
CD 1, tracks 15–16

ActiveTeach
p.021 Assignment 1
p.021 Assignment 1: prep

Starter

PLTS C

Aim
To develop reading skills: reading for gist

Give pupils one minute to choose and skim-read one of the texts in exercise 1, then write in English what kind of text it is and what it is about.

Hear answers. Ask pupils what they looked for to help them work out what the text was about. Remind them of the things to look out for when gist reading: pictures, layout (e.g. the names at the end show that these are personal reviews, perhaps in a chatroom), the opening sentences of paragraphs, key nouns (especially proper nouns), adjectives giving opinions (especially at the end of a text). Explain that it is helpful to get the overall gist of any long text in this way before attempting to tackle the detail – this applies to texts in English too.

1 Écoute et lis les textes. (AT 1.4)
Listening. Pupils listen to three people talking about their favourite things (television series, film and book, respectively) and follow the text at the same time. Some vocabulary is glossed for support.

Audioscript — CD 1 track 15

a *Mon émission de télé préférée s'appelle* Glee. *C'est une série et je trouve que c'est passionnant.*

L'action se passe aux États-Unis dans un collège. Mon personnage préféré, c'est Rachel parce qu'elle est jolie et intelligente.

Je pense que le scénario est super. À mon avis, c'est cool. Je recommande cette émission à tout le monde.

b *Mon film préféré s'appelle* Tonnerre sous les tropiques. *C'est une comédie et je trouve que c'est très amusant.*

L'action se passe dans la jungle. Mon personnage préféré, c'est Kirk Lazarus parce qu'il est stupide!

Je pense que le scénario est très drôle. À mon avis, c'est génial. Je recommande ce film à tout le monde.

c *Mon livre préféré s'appelle* Bilbo le hobbit. *C'est un roman fantastique et je trouve que c'est très bien.*

L'action se passe dans la «Terre du Milieu». Mon personnage préféré, c'est Bilbo parce qu'il est gentil et très amusant.

Dans ce livre, j'aime les créatures fantastiques, les dragons, les elfes et les gobelins. À mon avis, c'est passionnant. Je recommande ce livre à tout le monde.

2 Copie et remplis le tableau en anglais pour chaque revue. (AT 3.4)
Reading. Pupils copy out the grid three times. They read the reviews in exercise 1 again and complete a grid for each one with the details in English.

1 T'es branché(e)? En plus: À ne pas rater!

Answers

title	a *Glee*	b *Tonnerre sous les tropiques* (Tropic Thunder)	c *Bilbo le hobbit* (The Hobbit)
genre	series	comedy	fantasy
takes place	USA	jungle	Middle Earth
favourite character	Rachel	Kirk Lazarus	Bilbo
opinion	super, cool	funny, great	exciting

3 Regarde les textes de l'exercice 1. Écris ces phrases. Ensuite, trouve l'anglais pour l'expression. (AT 3.4, AT 4.4)

Writing. Pupils read the texts in exercise 1 again and find in them the expressions indicated by the codes (the letters given are the first letters of all the words in each expression). They then find the English version of each expression, choosing from the options listed.

Answers
1 *Mon film préféré s'appelle ...* **h**
2 Mon émission de télé(vision) préférée s'appelle ... **b**
3 Mon livre préféré s'appelle ... **d**
4 L'action se passe ... **a**
5 Je recommande ce film à tout le monde. **c**
6 À mon avis, c'est ... **g**
7 Mon personnage préféré, c'est ... **f**
8 Je trouve que c'est ... **e**

4 Corrige l'erreur dans chaque phrase. (AT 3.4)

Reading. Pupils read the texts in exercise 1 again, then read the sentences summarising it. They correct the mistake in each sentence.

Answers
1 L'action de *Glee* se passe **aux États-Unis**.
2 Virginie pense que le scénario de *Glee* est **super**.
3 *Tonnerre sous les tropiques* est **une comédie**.
4 Dans *Tonnerre sous les tropiques*, l'action se passe **dans la jungle**.
5 *Bilbo le hobbit* est **un roman fantastique**.
6 Frank **aime** les dragons.

5 Écoute et répète. (AT 1.1)

Listening. Pupils listen to the recording, then repeat the words, to practise the endings –*ant* and –*eux*. The pronunciation tip box gives advice on how to reproduce the sounds accurately.

Audioscript CD 1 track 16

passionnant ... ennuyeux ... intéressant

6 Copie et complète le texte avec les mots de la liste. (AT 3.4)

Reading. Pupils copy and complete the text with the words supplied.

Answers
1 émission 2 série 3 ennuyeux 4 avis
5 recommande

7 Prépare un exposé sur ton livre ou ton film préféré ou ton émission de télé préférée. (AT 2.4)

Speaking. Pupils prepare and give a presentation on their favourite book, film or television programme. A framework is supplied.

When pupils have given their presentation, ask the rest of the class to give constructive feedback. Guidelines on how to rate the performances are supplied.

Plenary

Ask some pupils to say what their favourite programme/film/book is and give a short opinion of it using *À mon avis ...*

En plus: À ne pas rater! T'es branché(e)? **1**

Worksheet 1.7 Mon site Internet préféré

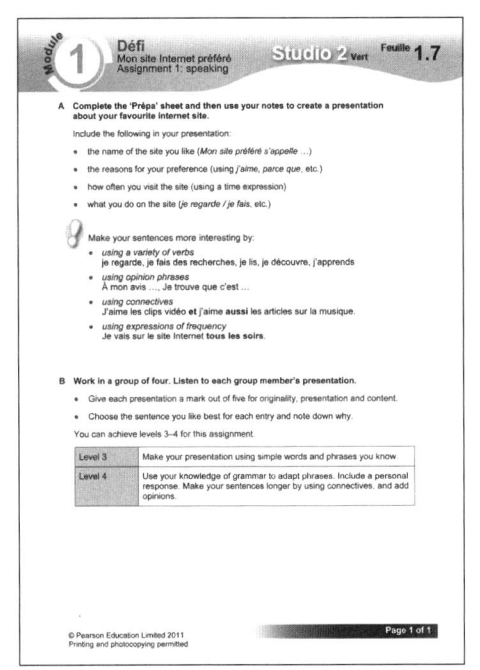

Answers
A Assessed by teacher.

Worksheet 1.8 Mon site Internet préféré. Prépa

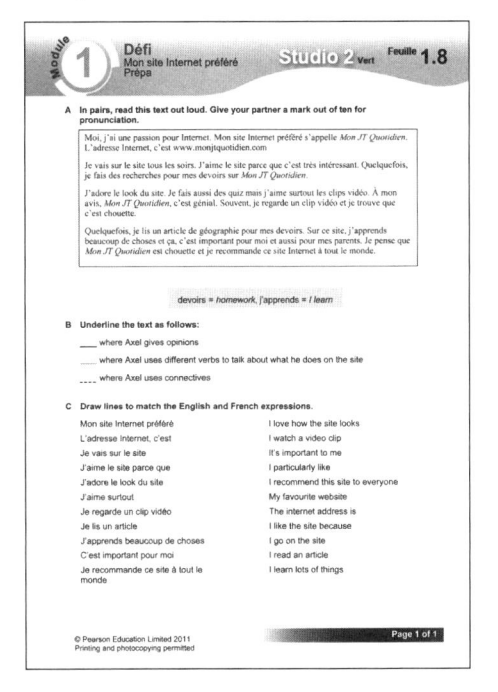

Answers
A Pair work

B Moi, j'ai une passion pour Internet.
Mon site Internet préféré s'appelle *Mon JT quotidien*.
L'adresse Internet, c'est www.monjtquotidien.com
Je vais sur le site tous les soirs.
J'aime le site parce que c'est très intéressant.
Quelquefois, je fais des recherches pour mes devoirs sur *Mon JT Quotidien*.
J'adore le look du site. Je fais aussi des quiz mais j'aime surtout les clips vidéo. À mon avis, *Mon JT Quotidien*, c'est génial.
Souvent, je regarde un clip vidéo et je trouve que c'est chouette.
Quelquefois, je lis un article de géographie pour mes devoirs.
Sur ce site, j'apprends beaucoup de choses et ça, c'est important pour moi et aussi pour mes parents.
Je pense que *Mon JT Quotidien* est chouette et je recommande ce site Internet à tout le monde.

C
Mon site Internet préféré	My favourite website
L'adresse Internet, c'est	The internet address is
Je vais sur le site	I go on the site
J'aime le site parce que	I like the site because
J'adore le look du site	I love how the site looks
J'aime surtout	I particularly like
Je regarde un clip vidéo	I watch a video clip
Je lis un article	I read an article
J'apprends beaucoup de choses	I learn lots of things
C'est important pour moi	It's important to me
Je recommande ce site à tout le monde	I recommend this site to everyone

Studio Grammaire (Pupil Book pp. 22–23)

The *Studio Grammaire* section provides a more detailed summary of the key grammar covered in the module, along with further exercises to practise these points. The activities on ActiveTeach pages 22 and 23 are repeated from elsewhere in the module.

Grammar topics
- grammatical terms
- the present tense:
  - regular *–er* verbs
  - irregular verbs: *avoir* and *être*
  - irregular verbs: *aller* and *faire*
- negatives

Grammatical terms

1 Match up the grammatical terms and the definitions.
Pupils match the grammatical terms with their definitions.

Answers
1 adjective – e 2 irregular – f 3 gender – d
4 infinitive – b 5 pronoun – g 6 verb – c
7 tense – h 8 regular – a

The present tense
Regular *–er* verbs

2 Find the French for these verbs.
Pupils write out the French versions of the English verbs listed, choosing from the French verbs supplied.

Answers
1 je déteste 2 je regarde 3 j'adore 4 j'aime
5 je joue

3 Write out *trouver* (to find) and *penser* (to think) according to the rules for *–er* verbs.
Pupils write out the paradigms (singular) of *trouver* and *penser*, applying the rules for *–er* endings.

Answers
1 je trouve   1 je pense
2 tu trouves   2 tu penses
3 il/elle trouve   3 il/elle pense
4 on trouve   4 on pense

4 Choose the correct form of each verb.
Pupils complete the sentences by choosing the correct verb form from the two options given each time.

Answers
1 Qu'est-ce que tu **regardes** à la télé?
2 Je **regarde** les documentaires.
3 Est-ce que tu **aimes** les séries?
4 Oui, **j'adore** ça.
5 Ma sœur aussi **aime** les séries.

Irregular verbs: *avoir* and *être*

5 Complete these sentences using the correct form of *avoir*.
Pupils complete the sentences using the correct form of *avoir* each time.

Answers
1 J'**ai** une passion pour les films.
2 Elle **a** treize ans.
3 Est-ce que tu **as** un ordinateur?
4 Il **a** un ticket.
5 J'**ai** beaucoup de livres.

6 Write out these sentences and underline the part of the verb *être*.
Pupils copy the sentences and underline each *être* verb form.

Answers
1 Je <u>suis</u> intelligent.
2 Quand je <u>suis</u> connecté, je fais des recherches.
3 Charlie <u>est</u> petit et pauvre.
4 Tu <u>es</u> fan de films fantastiques.
5 Elle <u>est</u> fan de romans policiers.

Studio Grammaire   T'es branché(e)? 1

Irregular verbs: *aller* and *faire*

7 Choose the correct verb, then match the sentence to its translation.

Pupils complete the sentences by choosing the correct verb from the two options given each time. They then match the sentence to the correct English translation.

Answers
1 Souvent, je **vais** au parc. – b
2 Quelquefois, tu **fais** du skate. – e
3 Quand il fait froid, il **va** au cinéma. – c
4 Avec mes copains, on **fait** du VTT. – a
5 On **va** au centre de loisirs. – d

Negatives

8 Turn these positive sentences into negative sentences using *ne ... pas*.

Pupils rewrite the sentences, making them negative using *ne ... pas*.

Answers
1 Je n'aime pas les émissions de sport.
2 Tu ne regardes pas la télé.
3 Elle n'aime pas les infos.
4 Il n'est pas fan de films fantastiques.
5 Il ne va pas au cinéma.
6 On ne va pas au centre de loisirs.
7 Tu n'aimes pas les émissions de télé-réalité.
8 Je ne fais pas beaucoup de choses.

Self-access reading and writing

À toi (Pupil Book pp. 114–115)

A Reinforcement

1 Copie les phrases et écris la bonne lettre. (AT 3.3)
Reading. Pupils copy the sentences and for each one write the letter of the matching picture.

Answers
1 a **2** d **3** e **4** b **5** c **6** f

2 Copie et complète le texte. (AT 3.4)
Reading. Pupils copy and complete the text with the correct words to replace the picture prompts. The answers are supplied in random order for support.

Answers
1 j'aime **2** les émissions de sport **3** stupide
4 les infos **5** super

3 Lis les textes. Copie et remplis les cartes d'identité. (AT 3.4)
Reading. Pupils copy out the identity cards. They read the texts and complete the cards with the details.

Answers
Name: Charlie
♥ Loves: American series
✓ Likes: sports programmes
✗ Doesn't like: documentaries
✗ Doesn't watch: reality TV shows
Favourite programme: *Ma famille d'abord*

Name: Ange
♥ Loves: cartoons
✓ Likes: reality TV shows, series
✗ Doesn't like: sports programmes
✗ Doesn't watch: game shows
Favourite programme: *Super Nanny*

B Extension

1 Lis les textes. Copie le tableau. Mets les images dans la bonne colonne. (AT 3.4)
Reading. Pupils copy the grid. They read the texts about what people do on the internet and complete the grid with the letters of the correct pictures.

Answers

	d'habitude	quelquefois
Baudouin	e	d
Katy	b, c	a

2 Lis le texte. C'est vrai (✓) ou faux (✗)? (AT 3.4)
Reading. Pupils read the text, then note whether the sentences in English about it are true (writing ✓) or false (writing ✗).

Answers
1 ✗ **2** ✓ **3** ✓ **4** ✗ **5** ✓ **6** ✗

3 Écris les phrases. (AT 4.3)
Writing. Pupils write out the sentences, replacing the picture prompts with the correct words.

Answers
1 Quand il fait beau, on fait du skate.
2 Quand il fait froid, on regarde des DVD.
3 Quand il fait chaud, on va au parc ou on fait du VTT.

Module 2: Paris, je t'adore!

(Pupil Book pp. 26–45)

Unit & Learning objectives	PoS* & Framework objectives	Key language	Grammar and other language features
1 Paris touristique (pp. 28–29) Saying what you can do in Paris Using *on peut* + infinitive	**2.1d** use previous knowledge **2.2i** reuse language they have met **2.4/Y8** Writing – (a) using text as stimulus **4.5/Y8** Language – (b) range of modal verbs	*Qu'est-ce qu'on peut faire à Paris? On peut... aller à un concert faire les magasins manger au restaurant visiter les monuments,* etc. *À mon avis... c'est vrai/faux Je suis d'accord. Je ne suis pas d'accord.*	**G** *on peut* – using context as a reading strategy
2 Les jeunes Parisiens (pp. 30–31) Saying what you like doing Using *j'aime* + the infinitive	**2.2g** write clearly and coherently **4.4/Y8** Language – developing sentences **4.6/Y8** Language – (a) range of questions	*J'aime... J'adore... Je n'aime pas... Je déteste... aller au cinéma (avec mes amis) faire du roller (au Trocadéro) prendre des photos* etc.	**G** *j'aime* + infinitive – adding variety to opinions (giving dislikes as well as likes, including reasons)
3 Ça, c'est la question! (pp. 32–33) Asking for tourist information Using question words	**2.2e** ask and answer questions **2.1/Y8** Reading – authentic materials **4.6/Y8** Language – (a) range of questions	*C'est où, le musée? C'est ouvert quand? C'est combien, l'entrée? Est-ce qu'il y a une cafétéria?* etc. *horaires d'ouverture de 10h00 à 17h00* etc. *Il y a (une cafétéria). Il n'y a pas de (boutique de souvenirs).*	**G** questions (*Est-ce que* and question words) – register: using *s'il vous plaît/merci* to be polite
4 C'était comment? (pp. 34–35) Saying what you visited and what it was like Using the perfect tense of *visiter*	**2.1b** memorising **2.2i** reuse language they have met **1.2/Y8** Listening – new contexts **4.5/Y8** Language – (a) range of verb tenses (perfect tense) **5.2** Strategies – memorising	*J'ai visité (le musée du Louvre). J'ai acheté des souvenirs. J'ai (beaucoup) dansé. J'ai rencontré un beau garçon/une jolie fille.* etc. *C'était comment? C'était... cool, bizarre, ennuyeux,* etc. *Ce n'était pas mal.*	**G** the perfect tense – improving writing by including sequencing words and qualifiers – pronunciation: *u* and *ou*

2 Paris, je t'adore!

Unit & Learning objectives	PoS* & Framework objectives	Key language	Grammar and other language features
5 Le 14 juillet à Paris (pp. 36–37) Saying what you did Using the perfect tense of *-er* verbs	**3b** sounds and writing **4.6/Y8** – (b) range of negatives **5.6** Strategies – reading aloud	Review of language from the module	**G** past participles **G** the perfect tense (negative) – using *de* after negative verbs – pronunciation: review and practise the past participle ending *-é*
Bilan et Révisions (pp. 38–99) Pupils' checklist and practice exercises			
En plus: Paris, ville magique! (pp. 40–41) Understanding information about tourist attractions	**2.1c** knowledge of language **2.2b** skim and scan **1.3/Y8** Listening – (a) understanding language for specific functions **2.1/Y8** Reading – authentic materials **5.4** Strategies – working out meaning	Review of language from the module	– developing reading strategies – developing listening strategies
Studio Grammaire (pp. 42–43) Detailed grammar summary and practice exercises			**G** the infinitive **G** *on peut* + infinitive **G** *j'aime* + infinitive **G** the perfect tense of *-er* verbs **G** making perfect tense verbs negative
À toi (pp. 116–117) Self-access reading and writing at two levels			

* In addition, the following Programmes of Study are covered throughout the module: 1.1–1.4, 2.2a, 2.2c, 2.2d, 3a, 3c, 3d, 3e, 3f, 4a, 4b, 4d, 4e, 4f, 4g. PoS 4c is covered in all Units 4 & 5 and *En plus* sections. See pp. 7–9 for details.

1 Paris touristique
(Pupil Book pp. 28–29)

Learning objectives
- Saying what you can do in Paris
- Using *on peut* + infinitive

Framework objectives
2.4/Y8 Writing – (a) using text as stimulus
4.5/Y8 Language – (b) range of modal verbs

FCSE links
Unit 1: Meeting people (Places)
Unit 4: Holidays (Activities; Places in a town; Holiday destinations; Descriptions of holidays)
Unit 5: Travel and accommodation (Holiday activities)
Unit 6: Leisure (Places; Locations)

Grammar
- *on peut*

Key language
Qu'est-ce qu'on peut faire à Paris?
On peut ...
aller à un concert
aller au théâtre
faire les magasins
faire un tour en segway
faire une balade en bateau-mouche
manger au restaurant
visiter les monuments
visiter les musées
À mon avis ...
c'est vrai
c'est faux
Je suis d'accord.
Je ne suis pas d'accord.

PLTS
T Team workers

Resources
CD 1, tracks 17–18
Cahier d'exercices Vert, page 13
ActiveTeach
p.028 Flashcards
p.028 Grammar
p.028 Grammar practice

Starter 1
Aim
To review the infinitive

Write up the following verb forms, jumbling the order (answers = 1st row). Give pupils two minutes to identify and write out all the infinitive forms.

aller tchatter avoir faire manger visiter voir

vais suis fait a mangeons visite es arrive envoie allons

Hear answers. Ask the class when the infinitive is used, reviewing structures like *j'aime, je voudrais, je peux,* etc.

Alternative Starter 1:
Use ActiveTeach p.028 Flashcards to introduce Paris activities.

1 Écoute et mets les photos dans le bon ordre. (1–8) (AT 1.2)
Listening. Pupils listen to people talking about activities you can do in Paris and write the letters of the pictures in the order they are mentioned.

Audioscript CD 1 track 17

1 – *Qu'est-ce qu'on peut faire à Paris?*
  – *Alors, ... On peut visiter les monuments ...*
2 – *Et on peut visiter les musées.*
3 – *On peut faire les magasins ...*
4 – *On peut aller au théâtre ...*
5 – *Et on peut aller à un concert.*
6 – *Qu'est-ce qu'on peut faire aussi à Paris?*
  – *Euh ... On peut manger au restaurant.*
7 – *On peut faire un tour en segway!*
8 – *Ah, oui! Cool! Et on peut faire une balade en bateau-mouche.*
  – *Bon, merci. Au revoir.*

Answers
1 d **2** h **3** f **4** g **5** c **6** b **7** e **8** a

2 Jeu de mémoire. Ton/Ta camarade ferme son livre. Tu poses la question et il/elle répond. Puis changez de rôle. Qui peut donner la réponse la plus longue? (AT 2.3)

Speaking. Pupils play a memory game in pairs. Pupil A closes his/her book and answers the question Pupil B asks. They then swap roles. The aim is to give the longest answer. A sample exchange is given.

> ### Studio Grammaire: *on peut* + infinitive
> Use the *Studio Grammaire* box to cover *on peut* + infinitive. There is more information and further practice on Pupil Book p. 42.

R Write up: *you can ... go, eat, have, be*. Pupils write out the French version for all four (e.g. *on peut aller*, etc.).

2 Paris, je t'adore! 1 Paris touristique

3 Lis le quiz. À ton avis, c'est vrai (✓) ou faux (✗)? (AT 3.2)

Reading. Pupils read the quiz and decide whether each statement is true (writing ✓) or false (writing ✗). Some vocabulary is glossed for support.

Answers
Pupils check their own answers by listening to the exercise 5 recording in the next lesson.

Starter 2
Aim
To apply grammatical knowledge; To review the language of the unit

Write up the following, jumbling the order of the second column. Give pupils two minutes working in pairs to match the beginning of each expression (column 1) with the correct ending (column 2).

1	faire une balade	en bateau-mouche
2	manger	au restaurant
3	aller à	un concert
4	visiter les	monuments
5	faire un tour	en segway
6	faire	les magasins
7	aller au	théâtre
8	visiter	les musées

Check answers, asking pupils to translate the completed expressions into English.

Alternative Starter 2:
Use ActiveTeach p.028 Grammar practice to practise *on peut* + infinitive.

4 En tandem. Discute tes réponses au quiz avec ton/ta partenaire. Il/Elle est d'accord? (AT 2.4)

PLTS T

Speaking. In pairs: pupils discuss their answers to the quiz with their partner, saying whether they agree with each other. A sample exchange is supplied. Some vocabulary is glossed for support.

5 Écoute et vérifie. (1–6) (AT 1.3)
Listening. Pupils listen to check their answers to exercise 3. For Level 4, ask pupils questions about the additional information given by the speakers.

Audioscript CD 1 track 18

Alors, que sais-tu de Paris? C'est vrai ou c'est faux?

1 – À Paris, on peut aller au cinéma.
  C'est vrai. Il y a beaucoup de cinémas à Paris.
2 – À Paris, on peut manger au McDonald's.
  C'est vrai. Il y a soixante-six restaurants MacDo à Paris!
3 – À Paris, on peut visiter le Vatican.
  C'est faux! Le Vatican n'est pas à Paris. C'est à Rome, en Italie.
4 – À Paris on peut aller à la plage.
  C'est vrai! En été, il y a une plage à Paris, au bord de la Seine!
5 – À Paris on peut voir les Alpes.
  C'est faux! Les Alpes sont dans l'est de la France, près de la Suisse, de l'Italie et de l'Allemagne.
6 – À Paris, on peut visiter les égouts.
  C'est vrai! Beaucoup de touristes à Paris visitent les égouts. Beurk! Et toi? Tu voudrais faire ça?

Answers
3 and 5 are false. The rest are true.

6 Lis les textes. Trouve le bon texte pour chaque photo. (AT 3.4)
Reading. Pupils read the texts, then match each of them to the correct photo. Some vocabulary is glossed for support. Draw attention to the tip box on using context as a reading strategy.

Answers
1 A 2 C 3 A 4 C 5 B

Pupils choose one of the texts and write a translation in English.

7 Qu'est-ce que c'est? Écris une phrase pour chaque photo de l'exercice 6. (AT 4.3)
Writing. Pupils write a sentence for each of the photos in exercise 6.

Answers
1 *C'est la cathédrale de Notre-Dame.*
2 *C'est la Seine/C'est un bateau-mouche.*
3 *C'est la tour Eiffel.*
4 *C'est les Champs-Élysées.*
5 *C'est la Joconde.*

1 Paris touristique   Paris, je t'adore! 2

8 Choisis une ville que tu connais. Qu'est-ce qu'on peut faire dans la ville? Écris quelques idées pour des touristes français. (AT 4.4)

Writing. Pupils choose a town they know and write some suggestions for French tourists on what they could do there. A sample opening is given and a key language box supplied for support.

Encourage pupils to use words like *comme, par exemple* and *ou* to create more complex sentences, following the examples in the texts in exercise 6, e.g. *À Londres, on peut visiter les monuments, comme la tour de Londres.*

Plenary

Ask pupils to explain how the structure *on peut* is used. Then challenge them as a class to come up with as many things as they can think of to do in London, using *on peut …*

Answers
1 1 a ✓ b ✗ c ✓ d ✗
  2 a ✓ b ✗ c ✗ d ✓
2 Visitez Strasbourg!
  À Strasbourg, on peut:
  faire les magasins
  aller à un concert
  visiter les musées

  Visitez Nice!
  À Nice, on peut:
  aller au théâtre
  faire un tour en segway
  manger au restaurant

Workbook, page 13

2 Les jeunes Parisiens
(Pupil Book pp. 30–31)

Learning objectives
- Saying what you like doing
- Using *j'aime* + the infinitive

Framework objectives
4.4/Y8 Language – developing sentences
4.6/Y8 Language – (a) range of questions

FCSE links
Unit 1: Meeting people (Places)
Unit 4: Holidays (Activities; Places in a town; Holiday destinations; Descriptions of holidays)
Unit 5: Travel and accommodation (Holiday activities)
Unit 6: Leisure (Places; Locations)

Grammar
- *j'aime* + infinitive

Key language
J'aime …
J'adore …
Je n'aime pas …
Je déteste …
aller au cinéma (avec mes amis)
aller aux concerts (rock)
aller voir des matchs (au Parc des Princes)
faire du roller (au Trocadéro)
faire les magasins
prendre des photos
retrouver mes copains

PLTS
R Reflective learners

Cross-curricular
English: possessive adjectives

Resources
CD 1, tracks 19–20
Cahier d'exercices Vert, page 14
ActiveTeach
p.030 Grammar
p.030 Grammar practice
p.031 Learning skills
p.031 Grammar skills
p.031 Thinking skills

Starter 1
Aim
To review *aimer* + infinitive

Give pupils three minutes to write six sentences using *j'aime* + a different infinitive. If necessary, model an answer for support, e.g. *J'aime tchatter sur MSN.*

Hear some answers. Ask the rest of the class to raise their hands if they agree with the statement each time.

1 Écoute et regarde les photos. Qui parle? (1–6) (AT 1.2)
Listening. Pupils listen to six young Parisians talking about what they like to do and identify each of them from the pictures and texts supplied.

Audioscript CD 1 track 19

1 – Bonjour. Qu'est-ce que tu aimes faire à Paris?
 – J'aime aller voir des matchs au Parc des Princes.
2 – Et toi? Qu'est-ce que tu aimes faire à Paris?
 – Moi? Euh... J'aime faire les magasins.
3 – Salut! Qu'est-ce que tu aimes faire à Paris?
 – Alors ... J'aime retrouver mes copains.
4 – Pardon. Qu'est-ce que tu aimes faire à Paris?
 – J'aime faire du roller au Trocadéro.
5 – Et toi? Qu'est-ce que tu aimes faire à Paris?
 – Euh ... J'aime prendre des photos.
6 – Bonjour. Qu'est-ce que tu aimes faire à Paris?
 – J'aime aller au cinéma avec mes amis.

Answers
1 Clarisse 2 Nadia 3 Malik 4 Lucas
5 Émilie 6 Théo

2 En tandem. Choisis une personne de l'exercice 1 en secret. Ton/Ta camarade devine qui tu es. (AT 2.3)
Speaking. In pairs: pupils take it in turn to choose a person from exercise 1 in secret and to guess who it is. A sample exchange is given and a tip box on possessive adjectives supplied for support.

Studio Grammaire: *j'aime/je n'aime pas* + infinitive
Use the *Studio Grammaire* box to cover *j'aime/je n'aime pas* + infinitive. There is more information and further practice on Pupil Book p. 42.

R Pupils work in pairs. Pupil A names a person in exercise 1 and makes a thumbs up/thumbs down gesture. Pupil B responds with the appropriate sentence, e.g. *J'aime/Je n'aime pas faire les magasins.*

2 Les jeunes Parisiens   Paris, je t'adore!

3 Écoute et remplis le tableau. Il y a deux activités par personne. (1–4) (AT 1.4)

Listening. Pupils copy out the table. They listen and complete the table by writing in two activities for each person: one he/she likes and one he/she dislikes.

Audioscript CD 1 track 20

1
- Pardon. Qu'est-ce que tu aimes faire à Paris?
- J'aime aller aux concerts. J'aime les concerts rock!
- Et qu'est-ce que tu n'aimes pas faire?
- Je n'aime pas faire les magasins!
- Bon, merci.

2
- Bonjour. Qu'est-ce que tu aimes faire à Paris?
- Moi, j'aime faire du skate.
- Et qu'est-ce que tu n'aimes pas faire?
- Euh … Je n'aime pas visiter les monuments!

3
- Et toi? Qu'est-ce que tu aimes faire à Paris?
- J'aime prendre des photos. J'adore ça!
- Qu'est-ce que tu n'aimes pas faire à Paris?
- Je n'aime pas aller au théâtre. C'est ennuyeux!

4
- Salut! Qu'est-ce que tu aimes faire à Paris?
- Alors, moi, j'aime aller voir des matchs de foot!
- Et qu'est-ce que tu n'aimes pas faire?
- Euh … Je n'aime pas manger au restaurant. Je préfère acheter un hamburger au kiosque!

Answers

	aime ☺	n'aime pas ☹
1	c	e
2	h	d
3	g	f
4	b	a

Starter 2
Aim
To review *j'aime/je n'aime pas* + infinitive

Give pupils three minutes to write out six sentences: three on what they like doing (using *j'aime*) and three on what they don't like doing (using *je n'aime pas*). Supply infinitives as prompts for support, if necessary.

Alternative Starter 2:
Use ActiveTeach p.030 Grammar practice to practise *j'aime* + infinitive.

4 Écris des phrases pour chaque personne de l'exercice 3. (AT 4.3)

Writing. Using their (corrected) answers to exercise 3 for reference, pupils write two sentences about what each of the speakers likes and dislikes.

Answers
1 J'aime aller aux concerts rock. Je n'aime pas faire les magasins.
2 J'aime faire du skate. Je n'aime pas visiter les monuments.
3 J'aime prendre des photos. Je n'aime pas aller au théâtre.
4 J'aime aller voir des matchs de foot. Je n'aime pas manger au restaurant.

5 En tandem. Fais des conversations. (AT 2.4)

Speaking. In pairs: pupils make up four dialogues, using the framework + picture prompts supplied. A sample dialogue is given.

Answers
1 ● Qu'est-ce que tu aimes faire à Paris, Emma?
  ■ J'aime aller aux concerts rock.
  ● Qu'est-ce que tu n'aimes pas faire?
  ■ Je n'aime pas visiter les musées.
2 ● Qu'est-ce que tu aimes faire à Paris, Abdel?
  ■ J'aime faire du roller (au Trocadéro).
  ● Qu'est-ce que tu n'aimes pas faire?
  ■ Je n'aime pas aller au cinéma (avec mes amis).
3 ● Qu'est-ce que tu aimes faire à Paris, Flavie?
  ■ J'aime manger au restaurant.
  ● Qu'est-ce que tu n'aimes pas faire?
  ■ Je n'aime pas faire les magasins.
4 ● Qu'est-ce que tu aimes faire à Paris, Jérôme?
  ■ J'aime prendre des photos.
  ● Qu'est-ce que tu n'aimes pas faire?
  ■ Je n'aime pas aller au théâtre.

6 Lis le texte et complète les phrases en anglais. (AT 3.4)

Reading. Pupils read the text and complete the sentences summarising it in English.

Answers
1 taking photos
2 to (pop) concerts
3 visiting museums
4 the *Parc des Princes* (stadium)
5 a supporter
6 it's boring
7 going to the cinema

2 Paris, je t'adore! 2 Les jeunes Parisiens

7 Imagine que tu habites à Paris. Qu'est-ce que tu aimes faire? Qu'est-ce que tu n'aimes pas faire? Écris des phrases. (AT 4.3–4)

Writing. Pupils imagine that they live in Paris and write sentences about what they like/don't like doing. Draw their attention to the tip box on adding variety to their opinions, by using dislikes as well as likes and including reasons.

PLTS R

Ask pupils, when they have finished, to read over their work. They should aim to correct any errors and to identify two areas of improvement to work on in their next extended piece of writing, e.g. verb forms, infinitive after *J'aime,* inclusion of reasons, etc.

Ask pupils to memorise the texts they wrote in exercise 7 and do a mini-presentation to the class.

Plenary

Ask pupils to summarise how verbs of opinion like *aimer, adorer* and *détester* are used. Then say sentences featuring these from the unit: in some of these make grammatical errors – e.g. *je détester* or *j'aime pas* or *j'adore regarde*, etc. Pupils put up their hands to identify and correct an error.

Workbook, page 14

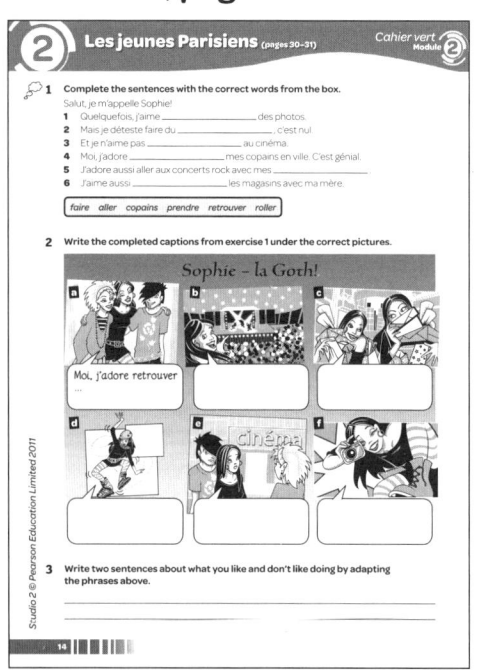

Answers

1
1. Quelquefois, j'aime **prendre** des photos.
2. Mais je déteste faire du **roller**, c'est nul.
3. Et je n'aime pas **aller** au cinéma.
4. Moi, j'adore **retrouver** mes copains en ville. C'est génial.
5. J'adore aussi aller aux concerts rock avec mes **copains**.
6. J'aime aussi **faire** les magasins avec ma mère.

2 a (4) *Moi, j'adore retrouver* mes copains en ville. C'est génial.
  b (5) J'adore aussi aller aux concerts rock avec mes copains.
  c (6) J'aime aussi faire les magasins avec ma mère.
  d (2) Mais je déteste faire du roller, c'est nul.
  e (3) Et je n'aime pas aller au cinéma.
  f (1) Quelquefois, j'aime prendre des photos.

Worksheet 2.1 Infinitives

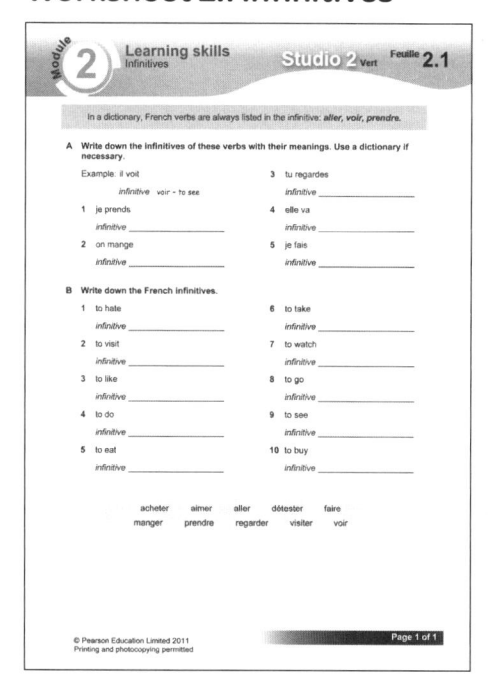

Answers

A
1. *infinitive* prendre – *to take*
2. *infinitive* manger – *to eat*
3. *infinitive* regarder – *to watch*
4. *infinitive* aller – *to go*
5. *infinitive* faire – *to do*

B
1. to hate *détester*
2. to visit *visiter*
3. to like *aimer*
4. to do *faire*
5. to eat *manger*
6. to take *prendre*
7. to watch *regarder*
8. to go *aller*
9. to see *voir*
10. to buy *acheter*

Worksheet 2.2 Expressions with infinitives

Answers

A On peut <u>visiter</u> les monuments.
  On peut <u>visiter</u> les musées.
  On peut <u>aller</u> au théâtre.
  On peut <u>manger</u> au restaurant.
  On peut <u>faire</u> les magasins.

B (Answers will vary.)
  1 J'aime / je n'aime pas / je déteste faire les magasins.
  2 J'aime / je n'aime pas / je déteste prendre des photos.
  3 J'aime / je n'aime pas / je déteste aller au cinéma.
  4 J'aime / je n'aime pas / je déteste aller aux concerts.
  5 J'aime / je n'aime pas / je déteste retrouver mes copains en ville.
  6 J'aime / je n'aime pas / je déteste faire du roller.

Worksheet 2.3 Opinions

Answers

A (NB Order will vary.)
  She doesn't like museums.
  She loves living in Lille.
  She likes going to the cinema.
  She loves going to the park and playing football with her mates.
  She likes rollerblading and meeting her friends at the skatepark.
  She hates going to school.
  Going to rock concerts isn't bad.

B (NB Order will vary.)
  You can go into town and go shopping.
  You can visit the monuments and the museums.
  You can go to the cinema or the theatre.
  You can go to rock concerts.

C (Answers will vary.)

3 Ça, c'est la question!

(Pupil Book pp. 32–33)

Paris, je t'adore! 2

Learning objectives
- Asking for tourist information
- Using question words

Framework objectives
2.1/Y8 Reading – authentic materials
4.6/Y8 Language – (a) range of questions

FCSE links
Unit 1: Meeting people (Time)
Unit 4: Holidays (Holiday destinations; Literature about places to visit)
Unit 5: Travel and accommodation (Holiday activities)
Unit 6: Leisure: (Time)

Grammar
- questions (*Est-ce que* and question words)

Key language
C'est où, le musée?
C'est ouvert quand?
C'est ouvert à quelle heure?
C'est combien, l'entrée?
Est-ce qu'il y a …
une cafétéria/une boutique de souvenirs?
horaires d'ouverture
ouvert tous les jours
sauf le lundi
ouvert du (mardi) au (dimanche)
fermé
de 10h00 à 17h00
tarifs d'entrée
adultes
jeunes
enfants
gratuit
Il y a (une cafétéria).
Il n'y a pas de (boutique de souvenirs).

PLTS
C Creative thinkers

Cross-curricular
ICT: word-processing/design

Resources
CD 1, tracks 21–22
Cahier d'exercices Vert, page 15
ActiveTeach
p.032 Grammar
p.032 Grammar practice

Starter 1
Aim
To review question words

Write up the following, jumbling the order of the second column. Give pupils two minutes to match the French and English versions.

quand?	when?
à quelle heure?	at what time?
combien?	how much?
où?	where?
qu'est-ce que?	what?
comment?	how?
pourquoi?	why?

Hear answers. Ask pupils what other ways you can form questions in French (question intonation on statement; *Est-ce que* … + statement).

1 Écoute et mets les questions dans le bon ordre. (1–6) (AT 1.2)
Listening. Pupils read the questions. They then listen and note the questions in the order they hear them.

Audioscript — CD 1 track 21
S'il vous plaît!/Pardon./Excusez-moi./J'ai une petite question!

Mesdames et messieurs! Silence, s'il vous plaît! Une question à la fois, s'il vous plaît!

1 *C'est où, le musée Carnavalet?*
2 *C'est ouvert quand?*
3 *C'est ouvert à quelle heure?*
4 *C'est combien, l'entrée?*
5 *Est-ce qu'il y a une cafétéria?*
6 *Est-ce qu'il y a une boutique de souvenirs?*

Answers
1 d 2 f 3 c 4 b 5 a 6 e

Studio Grammaire: questions with *Est-ce que* and question words
Use the *Studio Grammaire* box to cover forming questions with *Est-ce que* and question words.

Use the pronunciation box to review and practise making your voice go up at the end of a question.

2 Trouve la bonne réponse à chaque question. (AT 3.4)
Reading. Pupils match the questions and answers. Some vocabulary is glossed for support. Draw attention to the tip box on the 24-hour clock.

Answers
See answers for exercise 3: pupils listen to the exercise 3 recording to check their answers.

56

3 Ça, c'est la question! Paris, je t'adore!

3 Écoute et vérifie. (1–6) (AT 1.3)

Listening. Pupils listen to check their answers to exercise 2.

Read together through the *En France* box on museums in Paris.

Audioscript CD 1 track 22

1 – Pardon. C'est où, le musée Carnavalet, s'il vous plaît?
 – C'est au 23, rue de Sévigné.
2 – C'est combien, l'entrée?
 – C'est 4,50€ pour les adultes et 3,80€ pour les jeunes.
3 – C'est ouvert quand, s'il vous plaît?
 – C'est ouvert tous les jours, sauf le lundi.
4 – Et c'est ouvert à quelle heure?
 – C'est ouvert de dix heures à dix-huit heures.
5 – Est-ce qu'il y a une boutique de souvenirs?
 – Ah non, il n'y a pas de boutique.
6 – Est-ce qu'il y a une cafétéria?
 – Non, mais il y a des restaurants tout près.
 – Merci beaucoup.
 – De rien. Au revoir et bonne journée!

Answers
1 d 2 f 3 c 4 a 5 e 6 b

Starter 2

Aim
To review and practise question forms

Write up the following, omitting the underlined words. Give pupils two minutes working in pairs to fill in the gaps. Supply the answers in random order, if necessary for support.

1 C'est <u>où</u>, le musée?
2 <u>Est-ce qu'</u>il y a un restaurant?
3 C'est ouvert <u>quand/à quelle heure</u>?
4 C'est <u>combien</u>, l'entrée?

Check answers, asking pupils to translate the questions into English.

Alternative Starter 2:
Use ActiveTeach p.032 Grammar practice to practise question words.

4 En tandem. Complète les conversations. (AT 2.3)

Speaking. In pairs: pupils make up four dialogues, using the framework + picture prompts supplied. Draw their attention to the tip box on getting the tone right by including the expressions *s'il vous plaît* and *merci*.

Answers
1 ● **C'est où**, le musée de la Mode, s'il vous plaît?
 ■ C'est dans la rue de Rivoli.
2 ● **C'est ouvert quand**?
 ■ C'est ouvert tous les jours, sauf le lundi.
3 ● **C'est ouvert à quelle heure**?
 ■ C'est ouvert de 11h à 18h.
4 ● **C'est combien, l'entrée**?
 ■ C'est 9€ pour les adultes et 7€ pour les jeunes.

R Pupils choose two of the dialogues and write them out.

5 Lis la publicité pour les catacombes et choisis la bonne réponse. (AT 3.4)

Reading. Pupils read the brochure for the catacombs and complete the sentences by choosing the correct option from the two supplied each time. Encourage pupils to use reading strategies to work out what they need, e.g. context, cognates, using what they know to work out unknown words, etc. Some vocabulary is glossed for support.

Answers
1 Les catacombes, c'est dans **l'avenue Rol-Tanguy**.
2 C'est ouvert tous les jours, sauf **le lundi**.
3 C'est ouvert **de dix heures à cinq heures**.
4 Pour les adultes, l'entrée, c'est **huit euros**.
5 Pour les jeunes, c'est **quatre euros**.
6 **Il n'y a pas de** toilettes.

PLTS C

Pupils choose and research another sight in Paris and design their own brochure on computer.

2 Paris, je t'adore! 3 Ça, c'est la question!

6 Trouve l'équivalent des phrases dans le texte de l'exercice 5. (AT 3.4)

Reading. Pupils find in the catacombs brochure text (exercise 5) the French for the English phrases given.

Answers
1 ouvert du mardi au dimanche
2 enfants: gratuit
3 tarifs d'entrée
4 fermé le lundi
5 horaires d'ouverture
6 de 14 à 26 ans

7 Écris un mini-dialogue au sujet des catacombes. Écris au moins trois questions et trois réponses. (AT 4.4)

Writing. Pupils write a mini-dialogue about the catacombs, including at least three questions and three answers. A sample opening is supplied.

Plenary
Ask pairs to perform their dialogues from exercise 7, with the rest of the class giving feedback on the accuracy of the French and the effectiveness of the delivery (clarity, pronunciation, etc.).

Workbook, page 15

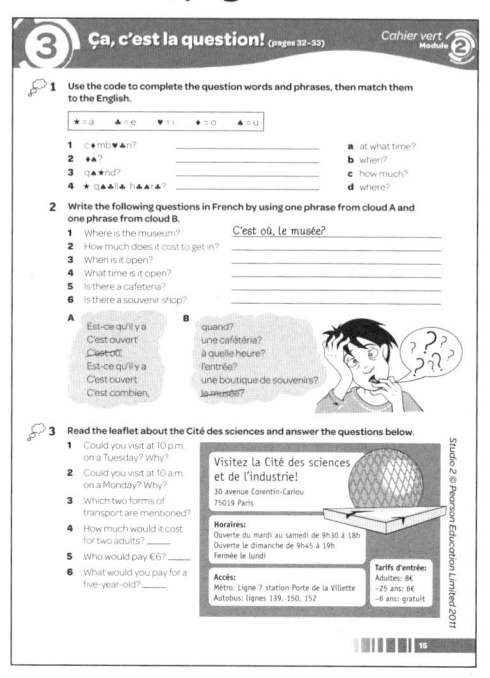

Answers
1 1 combien? – **c** how much?
   2 où? – **d** where?
   3 quand? – **b** when?
   4 à quelle heure? – **a** at what time?
2 1 C'est où, le musée?
   2 C'est combien, l'entrée?
   3 C'est ouvert quand?
   4 C'est ouvert à quelle heure?
   5 Est-ce qu'il y a une cafétéria?
   6 Est-ce qu'il y a une boutique de souvenirs?
3 1 No. It closes at 6 p.m.
   2 No. It's closed on Mondays.
   3 métro/underground and bus
   4 €16
   5 people under 25
   6 nothing/It's free.

4 C'était comment?

(Pupil Book pp. 34–35)

Learning objectives
- Saying what you visited and what it was like
- Using the perfect tense of *visiter*

Framework objectives
1.2/Y8 Listening – new contexts
4.5/Y8 Language – (a) range of verb tenses (perfect tense)
5.2 Strategies – memorising

FCSE links
Unit 4: Holidays (Aspects of holidays; Descriptions of holidays)
Unit 5: Travel and accommodation (Holiday activities)

Grammar
- the perfect tense

Key language
J'ai passé le 14 juillet à Paris.
J'ai acheté des souvenirs.
J'ai (beaucoup) dansé.
J'ai envoyé des cartes postales.
J'ai mangé au restaurant.
J'ai regardé le défilé/le feu d'artifice.
J'ai rencontré un beau garçon/une jolie fille.
J'ai visité ...
le musée du Louvre
la tour Eiffel
les catacombes
l'Arc de Triomphe
le Sacré-Cœur
le Centre Pompidou
C'était comment?
C'était ...
cool, bizarre, ennuyeux, génial, intéressant, marrant, nul
Ce n'était pas mal.

PLTS
S Self-managers

Cross-curricular
ICT: internet research

Resources
CD 1, tracks 23–25
Cahier d'exercices Vert, page 16

ActiveTeach
p.034 Flashcards
p.034 Grammar
p.035 Flashcards
p.035 Class activity
p.035 Video 3
p.035 Video worksheet 3
p.035 Thinking skills

Starter 1
Aim
To introduce the vocabulary of the lesson

Give pupils three minutes to write out the places pictured in exercise 1 on p. 34 of the Pupil Book, in the order in which they would like to visit them, starting with the place that appeals to them most.

Hear some answers. Then identify, by a show of hands, the top three places chosen by the class.

1 Rémi Rapide a visité Paris en 24 heures! Écoute et note les monuments dans le bon ordre. (1–8) (AT 1.2)

Listening. Pupils listen to Rémi Rapide's account of his trip to Paris and note the letters of the pictures in the order they are mentioned.

Audioscript CD 1 track 23

Ouf! Salut! Je m'appelle Rémi Rapide.
1 D'abord, j'ai visité l'Arc de Triomphe.
2 Ensuite, j'ai visité la tour Eiffel.
3 Puis j'ai visité les égouts.
4 Après, j'ai visité le musée du Louvre.
5 Ensuite, j'ai visité le Sacré-Cœur.
6 Puis j'ai visité le Centre Pompidou.
7 Après, j'ai visité la cathédrale de Notre-Dame.
8 Finalement, j'ai visité les catacombes.

Answers
1 b **2** a **3** h **4** c **5** d **6** e **7** f **8** g

Use the pronunciation box to review and practise the sounds *u* and *ou*.

2 Écoute et répète. (AT 1.1, AT 2.1)

Listening. Pupils listen and repeat the words and questions featuring the sounds *u* and *ou*.

Audioscript CD 1 track 24

tu ... du ... musée
ou ... tour ... égouts ... Louvre ... Pompidou
Tu as visité les égouts, le musée du Louvre ou le Centre Pompidou?

3 En tandem. Choisis un monument en secret. Ton/Ta camarade peut deviner en trois questions quel monument tu as visité? (AT 2.3)

Speaking. In pairs: pupils take it in turn to choose a monument in secret and to ask a maximum of three questions to guess what it is. A sample exchange is given.

2 Paris, je t'adore!   4 C'était comment?

> **Studio Grammaire: the perfect tense of –er verbs (singular)**
> Use the *Studio Grammaire* box to cover the perfect tense of –er verbs (singular). There is more information and further practice on Pupil Book p. 43.

Pupils translate the following into French: *He visited the Eiffel Tower. We visited the sewers. I visited the Pompidou Centre. She visited Notre-Dame cathedral.*

4 Imagine que tu as visité Paris en 24 heures. Décris ta visite. Mentionne au moins quatre monuments. (AT 4.3)
Writing. Pupils imagine they have spent 24 hours in Paris and describe their visit, mentioning at least four monuments. A sample opening is supplied. Draw their attention to the tip box on sequencing words.

Pupils research another city on the internet and write about what they did on a 24-hour break there.

> **Starter 2**
> **Aim**
> To introduce adjectives for describing an experience
>
> Write up the following:
>
> | positive | negative |
> |----------|----------|
> | | |
>
> Give pupils three minutes to copy the grid and write out each of the adjectives in exercise 5 (p. 35) in the correct column.
>
> Check answers, asking pupils to translate each adjective into English. For *ce n'était pas mal*, ask them to justify their choice, giving example contexts in English.
>
> **Alternative Starter 2:**
> Use ActiveTeach p.035 Flashcards to practise opinions.

5 Écoute et note le monument (utilise les lettres de l'exercice 1) et l'opinion. (1–8) (AT 1.4)
Listening. Pupils listen to eight people talking about a trip to Paris. For each they note the monument (using the pictures in exercise 1) and the opinion expressed (from **a–h**).

Audioscript   CD 1 track 25

1 – Qu'est-ce que tu as visité à Paris?
– J'ai visité les catacombes.
– C'était comment?
– C'était marrant.
2 – Qu'est-ce que tu as visité?
– Euh ... J'ai visité le musée du Louvre.
– C'était comment?
– C'était intéressant.
3 – Alors, qu'est-ce que tu as visité à Paris?
– J'ai visité l'Arc de Triomphe.
– C'était comment?
– C'était nul! Complètement nul!
4 – Qu'est-ce que tu as visité?
– J'ai visité le Sacré-Cœur.
– C'était comment?
– C'était cool. C'était très cool.
5 – Qu'est-ce que tu as visité à Paris?
– J'ai visité les égouts.
– Les égouts! C'était comment?
– C'était bizarre. Bi-zarre!
6 – Qu'est-ce que tu as visité à Paris?
– Alors, j'ai visité Notre-Dame.
– Ah bon? C'était comment?
– Ce n'était pas mal. Pas mal.
7 – Et toi? Qu'est-ce que tu as visité?
– Moi, j'ai visité la tour Eiffel.
– C'était comment? C'était bien?
– Ah, oui, c'était génial!
8 – Qu'est-ce que tu as visité à Paris?
– Euh ... J'ai visité le Centre Pompidou.
– C'était comment? C'était intéressant?
– Non, c'était un peu ennuyeux.

Answers

	monument	opinion
1	g	C
2	c	D
3	b	F
4	d	B
5	h	G
6	f	H
7	a	A
8	e	E

4 C'était comment?   Paris, je t'adore!

6 En tandem. Fais trois dialogues. Change les mots soulignés. (AT 2.4)
Speaking. In pairs: pupils make up three dialogues, changing the underlined words in the model supplied.

7 Lis les indices. Il/Elle a visité quel monument? Son opinion est positive (✓) ou négative (✗)? (AT 3.4)
Reading. Pupils read the clues and identify the monument being described each time and whether the opinion expressed is positive (writing ✓) or negative (writing ✗). Some vocabulary is glossed for support.

Answers
1. Notre-Dame ✓
2. le musée du Louvre ✗
3. la tour Eiffel ✗
4. le Sacré-Cœur ✗
5. le Centre Pompidou ✓
6. les catacombes ✓

8 Copie et complète la carte postale. (AT 4.3)
Writing. Pupils copy and complete the text of the postcard, replacing the picture prompts with the correct text. A sample opening is supplied. Draw their attention to the tip box on including qualifiers.

Answers
D'abord, j'ai visité **l'Arc de Triomphe**. *C'était* **cool**. *Ensuite, j'ai visité* **la tour Eiffel**. *C'était* **ennuyeux/ barbant**. *Puis j'ai* **visité les égouts**. *Ce n'***était pas mal**. *Après,* **j'ai visité le Centre Pompidou. C'était bizarre**. *Finalement,* **j'ai visité les catacombes. C'était marrant**.

PLTS S

➕ Read together through *Stratégie 2* on Pupil Book p. 45, covering a technique for learning the meaning of French words. Set pupils the challenge of choosing and learning 10 words using this approach, either in the classroom or at home.

Plenary
Play a chain game round the class to review the perfect tense. Each pupil repeats the chain so far and adds an item. If someone makes a mistake or can't add a new item, he/she is out. When the chain is complete, begin a new one. Start the chain off: *À Paris, j'ai visité la tour Eiffel …* The next pupil might add *… et j'ai visité les égouts.*

Workbook, page 16

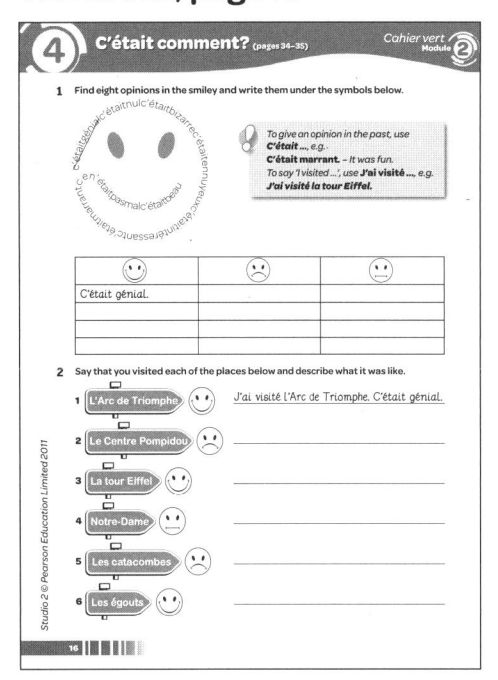

Answers

1

:)	:(	:|
C'était génial.	C'était nul.	C'était bizarre.
C'était intéressant.	C'était ennuyeux.	Ce n'était pas mal.
C'était marrant.		
C'était beau.		

2
1. J'ai visité l'Arc de Triomphe. C'était génial.
2. J'ai visité le Centre Pompidou. C'était nul/ ennuyeux.
3. J'ai visité la tour Eiffel. C'était intéressant/génial/ marrant/beau.
4. J'ai visité Notre-Dame. Ce n'était pas mal./C'était bizarre.
5. J'ai visité les catacombes. C'était nul/ennuyeux.
6. J'ai visité les égouts. C'était intéressant/génial/ marrant/beau.

2 Paris, je t'adore! 4 C'était comment?

Worksheet 2.4 Fact or opinion?

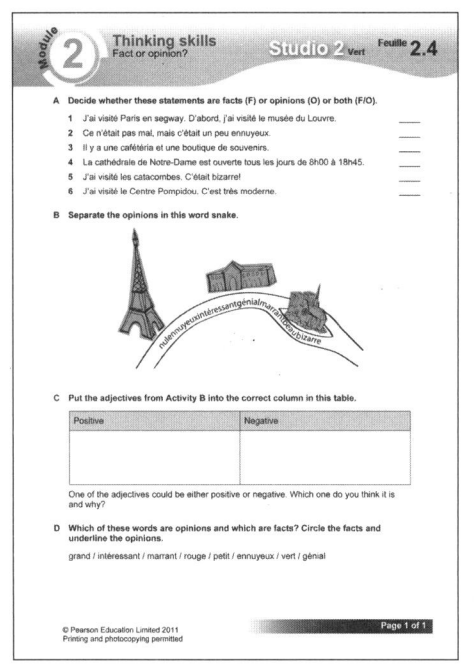

Video
Episode 3: Paris
The team talk about Marielle's trip last year to Paris, in preparation for doing a feature on the city for the StudioGB viewers. Video worksheet 3 can be used in conjunction with this episode.

Answers to video worksheet (ActiveTeach)
1 **A** (Answers will vary.)
  B The places shown are the Eiffel Tower, the Arc de Triomphe, l'Opéra de Paris, Notre-Dame cathedral, the river Seine, Sacré-Cœur cathedral.
  C They are going to film a report on Paris.
2 **A** They have received an email from StudioGB asking for a report on Paris.
  B It's Alex.
  C Marielle.
  D – Hugo: researching online
      – Alex: preparing the images
      – Marielle/Samira: preparing the script
  E Samira – very much so!
  F *fabuleux* – fabulous
      recherches – research
      images – images
      en ligne – on line
      le script – script
3 **A** Because he praises the pictures.
  B – the Eiffel Tower – 11,50€ (for young people, to the third floor)
      – a boat trip – 10€
      – a 'carnet' of métro tickets – 11,60€
  C – She spent a week there.
      – She went by train.
      – She did a boat trip.
      – She visited lots of monuments/museums.
      – She went up the Eiffel Tower.
      – She saw the Notre-Dame cathedral.
      – She met a handsome boy.
      – She went shopping.
      – She travelled to the shops by métro and bought a book of tickets.
  D Pupils may think it has something to do with a ballad, but it means to go for a stroll.
  E Probably meeting a young man – Jonathan. Or maybe the shopping.

Answers
A 1 F
    2 O
    3 F
    4 F
    5 F/O
    6 F/O
B nul
    ennuyeux
    intéressant
    génial
    marrant
    beau
    bizarre
C

Positive	Negative
intéressant	nul
génial	ennuyeux
marrant	
beau	

bizarre could be either – being strange isn't necessarily negative.
D **grand** / intéressant / **marrant** / **rouge** / **petit** / ennuyeux / **vert** / génial
fact = **bold**
opinion = underlined

5 Le 14 juillet à Paris
(Pupil Book pp. 36–37)

Learning objectives
- Saying what you did
- Using the perfect tense of –er verbs

Framework objectives
4.6/Y8 – (b) range of negatives
5.6 Strategies – reading aloud

FCSE links
Unit 4: Holidays (Activities; Descriptions of holidays)
Unit 5: Travel and accommodation (Holiday activities)

Grammar
- past participles
- the perfect tense (negative)

Key language
Review of language from the module

PLTS
E Effective participators

Resources
CD 1, tracks 26–28
Cahier d'exercices Vert, page 17

ActiveTeach
p.036 Flashcards
p.037 Grammar
p.037 Grammar practice
p.037 Class activity
p.037 Video 4
p.037 Video worksheet 4
p.037 Grammar skills
p.037 Learning skills
p.037 Thinking skills

Starter 1
Aim
To review regular –er verbs in the perfect tense;
To apply grammatical patterns

Write up the following, omitting the underlined words. Score through *visiter* to show that it has been used in the example. Give pupils three minutes to write out the complete sentences.

visiter rencontrer acheter envoyer manger

J'ai visité Paris et ...
j'ai mangé au restaurant.
j'ai acheté des souvenirs.
j'ai rencontré des amis.
j'ai envoyé des cartes postales.

Check answers, asking pupils to translate the sentences into English.

1 Trouve la bonne phrase pour chaque photo. (AT 3.2)
Reading. Pupils match the photos and sentences. Some vocabulary is glossed for support.

Answers
See answers for exercise 2: pupils listen to the exercise 2 recording to check their answers.

2 Écoute et vérifie. (1–6) (AT 1.2)
Listening. Pupils listen to check their answers to exercise 1.

Audioscript CD 1 track 26
Je m'appelle Chloé. L'année dernière, j'ai passé le 14 juillet à Paris!
1 f – *J'ai beaucoup dansé.*
2 e – *J'ai regardé le défilé et le feu d'artifice.*
3 a – *J'ai acheté des souvenirs.*
4 c – *J'ai rencontré un beau garçon.*
5 b – *J'ai envoyé des cartes postales.*
6 d – *J'ai mangé au restaurant.*

Answers
1 f 2 e 3 a 4 c 5 b 6 d

Pupils working in pairs take it in turn to prompt with the first half of the sentence (e.g. *J'ai acheté*) and to complete the sentence (*des souvenirs*).

3 En tandem. Copie le tableau. Choisis les images A ou B. Joue au morpion! (AT 2.3)
Speaking. In pairs: pupils copy out the grid. They then choose pictures A or B and play noughts and crosses. A sample exchange is given.

Use the pronunciation box to review and practise the past participle ending –é.

Studio Grammaire: past participles of –er verbs
Use the *Studio Grammaire* box to cover the past participles of –er verbs. There is more information and further practice on Pupil Book p. 43.

63

2 Paris, je t'adore! 5 Le 14 juillet à Paris

Starter 2
Aim
To review the perfect tense; To apply grammatical patterns

Write up the following. Give pupils three minutes to copy and complete the table. If they need more support, supply the present tense forms of *avoir* in random order.

		perfect tense	English
manger	je		
acheter	tu		
visiter	elle	elle a visité	
rencontrer	il		
envoyer	on		we sent
visiter	je		

Check answers. Ask how the perfect tense is formed for these verbs (the appropriate present tense form of *avoir* and the past participle). Ask how the past participle of regular –er verbs is formed (–er removed and replaced by –é).

Alternative Starter 2:
Use ActiveTeach p.036 Flashcards to practise vocabulary for talking about the 14th of July celebrations in Paris.

4 Lis l'e-mail. C'est vrai (✓) ou faux (✗)? (AT 3.5)
Reading. Pupils read the text, then note whether the sentences in French about it are true (writing ✓) or false (writing ✗). *jaloux/jalouse* is glossed for support.

Answers
1 ✓ 2 ✗ 3 ✗ 4 ✓ 5 ✗ 6 ✓

Studio Grammaire: the perfect tense – negative form
Use the *Studio Grammaire* box to cover the negative form of the perfect tense. There is more information and further practice on Pupil Book p. 43.

5 Écoute Raphaël. Qu'est-ce qu'il a fait? (✓) Qu'est-ce qu'il n'a pas fait? (✗) (AT 1.5)
Listening. Pupils listen to Raphaël and look at the pictures, then note which activities he did (writing ✓) and didn't do (writing ✗). *une jolie fille* is glossed for support.

Audioscript CD 1 track 27

1 – Salut, Raphaël! Alors ... Qu'est-ce que tu as fait à Paris le 14 juillet? Tu as regardé le feu d'artifice?
  – Mouais ... J'ai regardé le feu d'artifice.
2 – Tu as aussi regardé le défilé?
  – Oui, j'ai regardé le défilé. C'était ennuyeux.
3 – Le soir, tu as mangé au restaurant?
  – Je n'ai pas mangé au restaurant. J'ai acheté un hamburger au kiosque.
4 – Tu as acheté des souvenirs pour ta famille?
  – Non, je n'ai pas acheté de souvenirs.
5 – Mais tu as envoyé des cartes postales?
  – Non, je n'ai pas envoyé de cartes postales.
  – D'accord ...
6 – Mais j'ai rencontré une jolie fille!
  – Ah, bon?
  – Oui. Elle s'appelle Chloé. Elle habite à Lyon. Elle est très sympa ...

Answers
1 ✓ 2 ✓ 3 ✗ 4 ✗ 5 ✗ 6 ✓

6 Écris des phrases pour Raphaël. (AT 4.3)
Writing. Using the pictures in exercise 5 for reference, pupils write sentences for Raphaël, saying what he did and didn't do. A sample opening is given. Draw attention to the tip box on the use of *de* after a negative.

Answers
1 J'ai regardé le feu d'artifice.
2 J'ai regardé le défilé.
3 Je n'ai pas mangé au restaurant.
4 Je n'ai pas acheté de souvenirs.
5 Je n'ai pas envoyé de cartes postales.
6 J'ai rencontré une jolie fille.

Pupils write out sentences 1, 2 and 6 making them negative.

7 Écoute et lis le rap. Puis lis le rap à voix haute. (AT 1.5, AT 2.5)
Listening. Pupils listen to the rap, reading it at the same time. They then read the rap aloud. Some vocabulary is glossed for support.

5 Le 14 juillet à Paris — Paris, je t'adore!

PLTS E

Pupils compose new pairs of lines for the rap. You could support them by giving them rhyming pairs of words, e.g. *restaurant/amusant; égouts/Centre Pompidou; MacDo/beau; Sacré-Cœur/ennuyeux*. Ask some to read their lines to the class. Encourage constructive comments from the other pupils.

Audioscript CD 1 track 28

Rap parisien

J'suis parisien, je m'appelle Baptiste.
J'habite dans la banlieue, j'suis pas un touriste!
Ce n'est pas trop mal, mais c'est un peu ennuyeux.
Alors, j'ai visité Paris pour changer un peu.

J'ai visité le Louvre et la tour Eiffel,
J'ai admiré la Joconde: elle est très, très belle!
J'ai acheté un jean sur les Champs-Élysées,
Puis j'ai mangé un sandwich dans un petit café.

J'ai visité Notre-Dame, c'était intéressant.
Et au Moulin Rouge, j'ai dansé le cancan!
J'ai voyagé sur la Seine en bateau-mouche.
Tu vois, faut pas me juger sur mon sweat à capuche!

Plenary

Review past participles. Put the class into teams. Give the teams two minutes to write down as many different past participles as they can, giving the infinitive for each one. The teams swap and mark each other's answers: tell them to award two points for each correct participle. The team with the most points is the winner.

Workbook, page 17

Answers

1 1 (e) J'ai passé le 14 juillet à Paris.
   2 (b) J'ai acheté des souvenirs.
   3 (f) J'ai regardé le défilé.
   4 (d) J'ai envoyé des cartes postales.
   5 (g) J'ai rencontré une jolie fille.
   6 (c) J'ai beaucoup dansé.
   7 (a) J'ai mangé au restaurant.

2 1 Je n'ai pas passé le 14 juillet à Paris.
   2 Je n'ai pas acheté de souvenirs.
   3 Je n'ai pas regardé le défilé.
   4 Je n'ai pas envoyé de cartes postales.
   5 Je n'ai pas rencontré de jolie fille.
   6 Je n'ai pas beaucoup dansé.
   7 Je n'ai pas mangé au restaurant.

Worksheet 2.5 Perfect tense and negatives

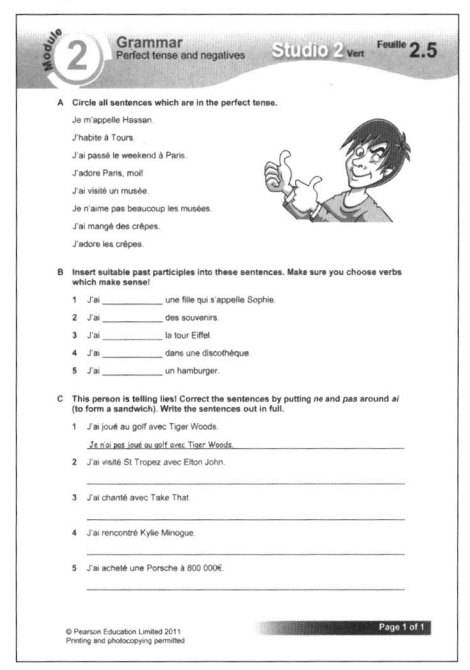

Answers

A Perfect tense sentences are:
   J'ai passé le weekend à Paris.
   J'ai visité un musée.
   J'ai mangé des crêpes.

B 1 J'ai rencontré une fille qui s'appelle Sophie.
   2 J'ai acheté des souvenirs.
   3 J'ai visité la tour Eiffel.
   4 J'ai dansé dans une discothèque.
   5 J'ai mangé un hamburger.

C 1 *Je n'ai pas joué au golf avec Tiger Woods.*
   2 Je n'ai pas visité St Tropez avec Elton John.
   3 Je n'ai pas chanté avec Take That.
   4 Je n'ai pas rencontré Kylie Minogue.
   5 Je n'ai pas acheté une Porsche à 800 000€.

2 Paris, je t'adore! 5 Le 14 juillet à Paris

Worksheet 2.6 Mind mapping – learning vocabulary

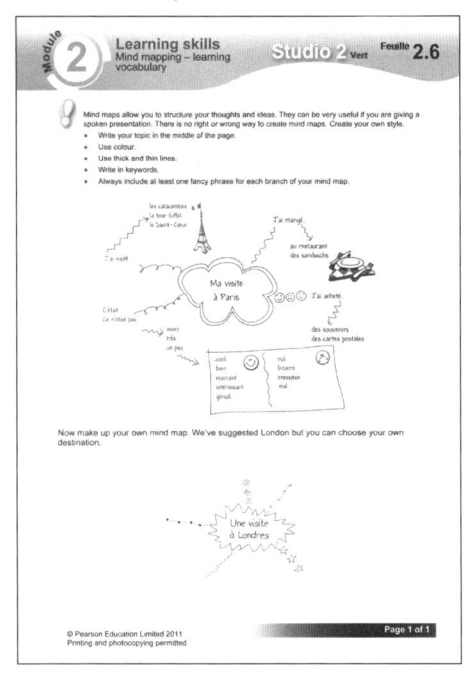

Answers
Assessed by teacher.

Worksheet 2.7 An ideal outing

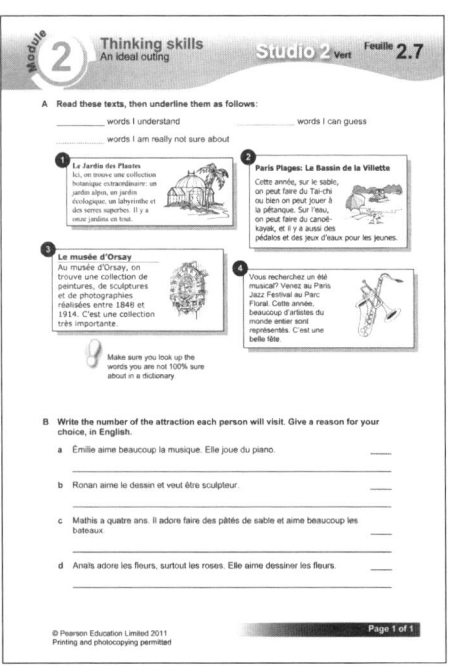

Answers
A (Answers will vary.)
B a 4 Émilie likes music.
  b 3 Ronan loves art.
  c 2 Mathis loves playing on the beach and he loves boats.
  d 1 Anaïs loves flowers.

Video
Episode 4: Paris, je t'aime
The team make a recording of Marielle talking about her trip to Paris last year … and Alex plays a trick on her. Video worksheet 4 can be used in conjunction with this episode.

Answers to video worksheet (ActiveTeach)
1 A Apart from buildings, things included are forms of transport, prices and shops.
  B 'Les Galéries Lafayette' and 'le Printemps' are famous department stores in Paris. 'Le Métro' is the underground system, and 'le Vélib' is the bike-hire system in Paris.
  C (Answers will vary.)
  D Marielle is doing the voiceover for some back projections of films she made.
2 A Ça tourne! – 'It's rolling!'
    Action! – 'Action!' (note the pronunciation)
    Coupé! – 'Cut!'
  B Gare du Nord.
  C – last summer (when Marielle went to Paris)
    – her mother (who she went with)
    – by train (how she got there)
    – in a hotel (where she stayed)
3 A She went to the third floor for 11,50€.
  B fabuleux – fabulous (about Paris in general)
    cool – cool (Eiffel Tower) [She also calls it effrayant – frightening]
    fabuleux – fabulous (about the Peace Wall)
  C It's called the Peace Wall. The word 'paix' (peace) is hard to hear but pupils may have already heard of the wall.
  D It's a museum (musée).
  E She couldn't go in because it's closed on Tuesdays.
  F She went shopping, which is to be expected of Marielle.
  G Souvenirs and postcards.
  H Pupils may think it means 'magazine' but in fact it means 'shop'.
4 A hire bike (vélib)
    river boat (bateau-mouche)
  B The boy she met – Jonathan.
  C They are all giggling and ask her about his ears.
  D Slightly exasperated – the sort of behaviour she has come to expect from Alex. But her reaction is surprisingly mild, considering she has been tricked.
  E 'I'm a good cameraman and an excellent technician!'

Bilan et Révisions (Pupil Book pp. 38–39)

Bilan
Pupils use this checklist to review language covered in the module, working on it in pairs in class or on their own at home. Encourage them to follow up any areas of weakness they identify. There are Target Setting Sheets included in the Assessment Pack, and an opportunity for pupils to record their own levels and targets on the *J'avance* pages in the Workbook, p. 22. You can also use the *Bilan* checklist as an end-of-module plenary option.

Révisions
These revision exercises can be used for assessment purposes or for pupils to practise before tackling the assessment tasks in the Assessment Pack.

Resources
CD 1, track 29
Cahier d'exercices Vert, pages 18 & 19

1 Écoute. Copie et remplis le tableau. (1–5) (AT 1.3)
Listening. Pupils copy out the table. They listen to five people talking about what they did in Paris and complete the table with the details.

Audioscript — CD 1 track 29

1. – Qu'est-ce que tu as fait à Paris?
   – J'ai visité Notre-Dame.
   – C'était comment?
   – C'était beau.
2. – Qu'est-ce que tu as fait à Paris?
   – J'ai visité la tour Eiffel.
   – C'était comment?
   – C'était intéressant.
3. – Qu'est-ce que tu as fait à Paris?
   – J'ai mangé au restaurant.
   – C'était comment?
   – C'était nul.
4. – Qu'est-ce que tu as fait à Paris?
   – J'ai regardé le feu d'artifice.
   – C'était comment?
   – C'était génial!
5. – Qu'est-ce que tu as fait à Paris?
   – J'ai acheté des souvenirs.
   – C'était comment?
   – C'était ennuyeux.

Answers

	activité	☺	☹
1	e	✓	
2	c	✓	
3	d		✓
4	a	✓	
5	b		✓

2 En tandem. Complète les questions et lis le dialogue à voix haute. (AT 2.4)
Speaking. In pairs: pupils complete the questions using the picture prompts and read out the dialogue, taking it in turn to ask and answer the questions.

Answers
● La tour Eiffel, c'est ouvert **quand**, s'il vous plaît?
■ C'est ouvert tous les jours.
● Et c'est ouvert **à quelle heure**?
■ C'est ouvert de neuf heures et demie à six heures et demie.
● C'est **combien**, l'entrée?
■ C'est onze euros cinquante.
● Est-ce qu'il y a **une boutique de souvenirs**?
■ Oui, il y a une boutique de souvenirs.
● Est-ce qu'il y a **une cafétéria**?
■ Oui, il y a une cafétéria et un restaurant.
● Merci. Au revoir.

3 Lis le blog et réponds aux questions en anglais. (AT 3.4)
Reading. Pupils read the blog and answer the questions on it in English.

Answers
1. She loves it.
2. go to a concert; go to the theatre
3. going to see football matches (at the Parc des Princes)
4. *(Any one of:)* taking photos of Paris; rollerblading (at the Trocadéro)
5. shopping – it's boring

2 Paris, je t'adore! Bilan et Révisions

4 Qu'est-ce qu'on peut faire dans ta ville? Qu'est-ce que tu aimes faire? Écris un paragraphe. (AT 4.3–4)

Writing. Pupils write a paragraph on their own town, saying what you can do there and what they like to do. They should adapt Yasmine's text in exercise 3. A list of features to include is supplied.

Pupils wishing to aim for Level 5 could include a reference to something they did last weekend.

Workbook, pages 18 and 19

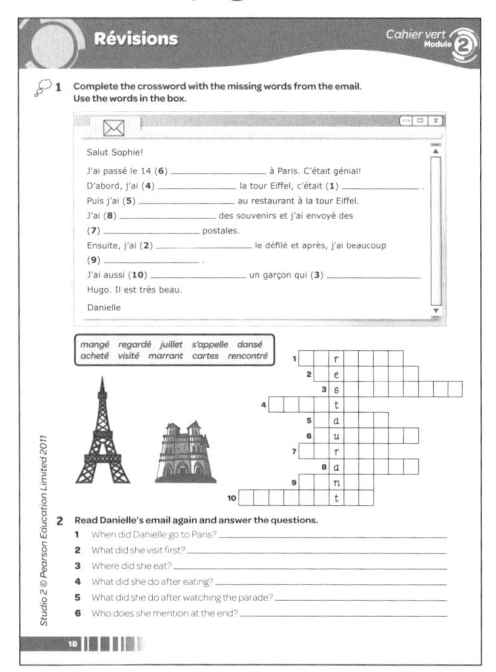

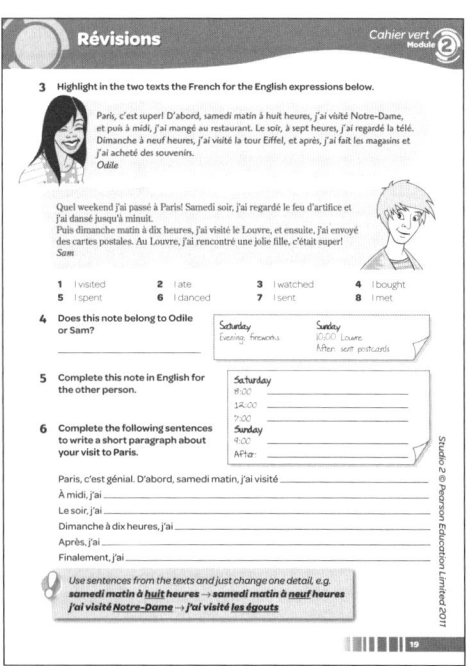

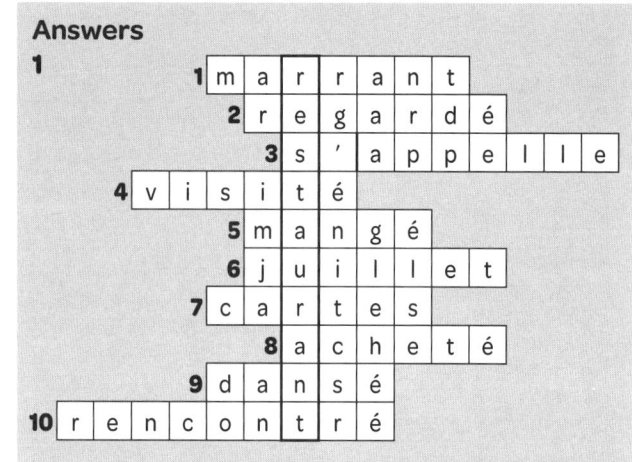

Answers

1

1	m	a	r	r	a	n	t			
2		r	e	g	a	r	d	é		
3			s	'	a	p	p	e	l	l	e
4	v	i	s	i	t	é				
5		m	a	n	g	é				
6		j	u	i	l	l	e	t		
7	c	a	r	t	e	s				
8		a	c	h	e	t	é			
9		d	a	n	s	é				
10	r	e	n	c	o	n	t	r	é	

2
1. on the 14th July
2. the Eiffel Tower
3. at the restaurant at the Eiffel Tower
4. bought souvenirs and sent postcards
5. danced a lot
6. a good-looking boy called Hugo

3 Paris, c'est super! D'abord, samedi matin à huit heures, **j'ai visité** Notre-Dame, et puis à midi, **j'ai mangé** au restaurant. Le soir, à sept heures, **j'ai regardé** la télé.

Dimanche à neuf heures, j'ai visité la tour Eiffel, et après, j'ai fait les magasins et **j'ai acheté** des souvenirs. *Odile*

Quel weekend **j'ai passé** à Paris! Samedi soir, j'ai regardé le feu d'artifice et **j'ai dansé** jusqu'à minuit.

Puis dimanche matin à dix heures, j'ai visité le Louvre, et ensuite, **j'ai envoyé** des cartes postales. Au Louvre, **j'ai rencontré** une jolie fille, c'était super! *Sam*

4 Sam

5 **Saturday**
8:00 visited Notre-Dame
12:00 ate at restaurant
7:00 watched TV
Sunday
9:00 visited Eiffel Tower
After: went shopping/bought souvenirs

6 (Example answer:)
Paris, c'est génial. D'abord, samedi matin, j'ai visité les égouts.
À midi, j'ai mangé au café.
Le soir, j'ai beaucoup dansé.
Dimanche à dix heures, j'ai visité le musée du Louvre.
Après, j'ai fait les magasins.
Finalement, j'ai rencontré un beau garçon/une belle fille.

En plus: Paris, ville magique!
(Pupil Book pp. 40–41)

Learning objectives
Understanding information about tourist attractions

Framework objectives
1.3/Y8 Listening – (a) understanding language for specific functions
2.1/Y8 Reading – authentic materials
5.4 Strategies – working out meaning

FCSE links
Unit 4: Holidays (Literature about places to visit; Descriptions of holidays)
Unit 5: Travel and accommodation (Holiday activities)
Unit 6: Leisure (Sports/hobbies)

Key language
Review of language from the module

PLTS
I Independent enquirers

Cross-curricular
ICT: word-processing

Resources
CD 1, tracks 30–32
ActiveTeach
p.041 Assignment 2
p.041 Assignment 2: prep

Starter
Aim
To practise reading strategies

Use exercise 1 on p. 40 of the Pupil Book.

1 Regarde la page web. Il s'agit de quoi? (AT 3.4)
Reading. Pupils skim-read the webpage to get the gist of what it is about. Draw their attention to the tip box on how to do this.

Answers
the Museum of Magic

2 Relis la page web et choisis la bonne lettre. (AT 3.4)
Reading. Pupils read the webpage in detail and identify in it which buttons you would click to access the different features listed in English. Draw their attention to the tip box on reading strategies.

Answers
1 F **2** E **3** D **4** A **5** C **6** H **7** G **8** B

3 Lis le texte et réponds aux questions en anglais. Utilise le Mini-dictionnaire, si nécessaire. (AT 3.4)

PLTS I

Reading. Pupils read the text and answer the questions on it in English. Draw their attention to the tip box on working out when and how to use reference resources. *la prestidigitation* is glossed for support.

Answers
1 A 'Magic Birthday' to celebrate your child's birthday at the *musée de la Magie*.
2 *Any three of:* visiting the museum; a magic show; a magic lesson; a magical present; a room for the birthday tea
3 Wednesdays, Saturdays and Sundays, except during school holidays

4 Écoute le reportage. Il s'agit de quoi? (AT 1.4)
Listening. Pupils listen to the report on rollerblading sessions in Paris and summarise it in English. Draw their attention to the tip box on listening strategies. Some vocabulary is glossed for support.

Audioscript CD 1 track 30

– Bonjour et bienvenue à Radio Jeunes Paris! Natasha, tu aimes le roller, n'est-ce pas?
– Ah, oui, j'adore faire du roller! Pourquoi?
– Parce que j'ai des informations sur une grande randonnée en roller à Paris.
– Génial! C'est quand, cette grande randonnée?
– C'est tous les vendredi soirs.
– Tous les vendredi soirs? À quelle heure?
– Ça commence à vingt-et-une heures trente.
– À vingt-et-une heures trente. D'accord. Et ça part d'où?
– Ça part de la tour Montparnasse.
– Et c'est pour combien de kilomètres?
– C'est pour environ trente kilomètres.
– Trente kilomètres! Il y a combien de participants?
– Il y a environ quinze mille participants.
– Quinze mille participants! Cool!
– De temps en temps, il y a aussi un thème pour la randonnée.
– Un thème? Quelle sorte de thème?

2 Paris, je t'adore! En plus: Paris, ville magique!

– *Par exemple, le thème pour le printemps, c'est blanc. Il faut porter quelque chose de blanc.*
– *Alors, il faut porter un tee-shirt blanc ou un jean blanc, par exemple?*
– *Oui. Alors, ça t'intéresse?*
– *Ah, oui, je vais y aller vendredi prochain! Tu viens?*

> **Answers**
> a mass rollerblading event in Paris (on Friday evenings)

5 Écoute à nouveau. Mets les phrases dans le bon ordre. (AT 1.4)

Listening. Pupils listen to the exercise 4 recording again and put the English phrases summarising it in the order they are mentioned. Draw their attention to the tip box on using prediction as a listening strategy.

Audioscript CD 1 track 31

As for exercise 4.

> **Answers**
> f, d, c, a, b, e

6 Écoute à nouveau et choisis la bonne réponse. (AT 1.4)

Listening. Pupils listen a third time and complete the sentences by choosing from the two options supplied in each one. Some vocabulary is glossed for support.

Audioscript CD 1 track 32

As for exercise 4.

> **Answers**
> 1 La randonnée en roller, c'est tous les **vendredi soirs**.
> 2 Ça commence à **21h30**.
> 3 Ça part de **la tour Montparnasse**.
> 4 La distance, c'est environ **30 kilomètres**.
> 5 Il y a environ **quinze mille** participants.
> 6 Au printemps, il faut porter des vêtements **blancs**.

7 Écris une page web pour la randonnée en roller. (AT 4.4)

Writing. Pupils write a webpage to advertise the rollerblading sessions described in exercises 4–6. A list of details to include is given and a sample opening supplied. This can be done on computer, making the writing of a second draft easier.

Plenary

Ask the class what they know about Paris now compared to what they knew before doing Unit 2.

Then ask them to tell you in French as much as they can about either the *Musée de la Magie* or the *Grande Randonnée en roller*.

Worksheet 2.8 Une attraction touristique

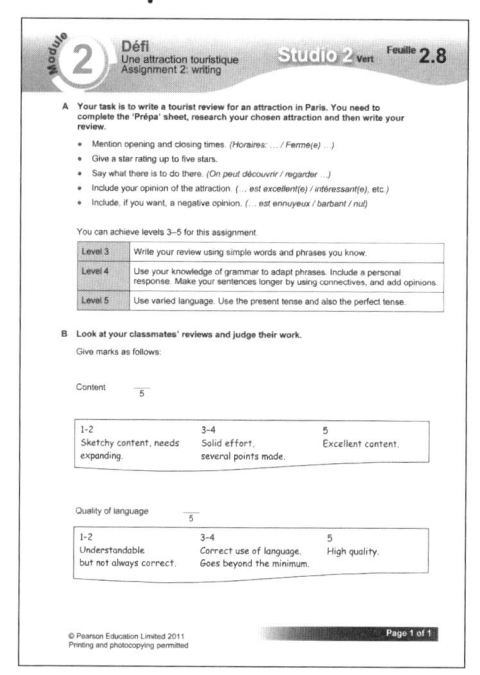

> **Answers**
> Assessed by teacher.

Worksheet 2.9 Une attraction touristique. Prépa

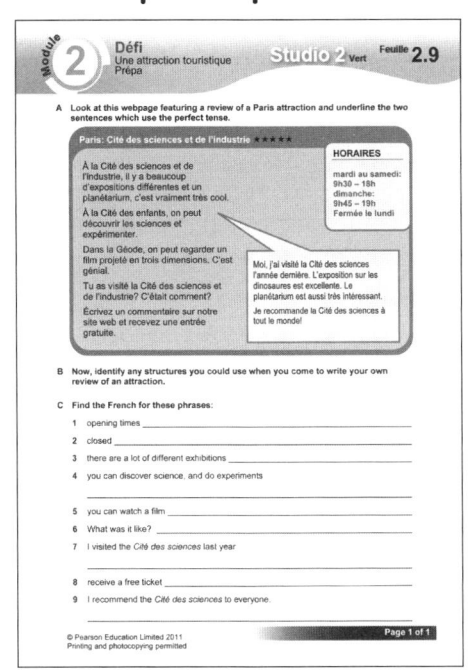

Answers

A The two sentences which use the perfect tense are:
Tu as visité la Cité des sciences et de l'industrie?
Moi, j'ai visité la Cité des sciences l'année dernière.

B (Answers will vary.)

C 1 horaires
   2 fermée
   3 il y a beaucoup d'expositions différentes
   4 on peut découvrir les sciences et expérimenter
   5 on peut regarder un film
   6 C'était comment?
   7 J'ai visité la Cité des sciences l'année dernière.
   8 recevez une entrée gratuite
   9 Je recommande la Cité des sciences à tout le monde.

Studio Grammaire (Pupil Book pp. 42–43)

Paris, je t'adore! 2

The *Studio Grammaire* section provides a more detailed summary of the key grammar covered in the module, along with further exercises to practise these points. The activities on ActiveTeach pages 42 and 43 are repeated from elsewhere in the module.

Grammar topics
- the infinitive
- *on peut* + infinitive
- *j'aime* + infinitive
- the perfect tense of *–er* verbs
- making perfect tense verbs negative

The infinitive

1 Find the six infinitives in the shapes and write each one next to the correct English translation.

Pupils identify the French for the English infinitives listed, choosing from the list of verb forms supplied.

Answers
1 aller (to go)
2 faire (to do or make)
3 manger (to eat)
4 prendre (to take)
5 regarder (to watch)
6 voir (to see)

on peut + infinitive

2 Unjumble the sentences and underline the infinitive in each one. Then translate the sentences.

Pupils write out the jumbled sentences correctly and underline the infinitive in each one. They then translate the sentences into English.

Answers
1 *On peut manger au restaurant. (You can eat in a restaurant.)*
2 On peut faire les magasins. (You can go shopping.)
3 On peut aller à un concert. (You can go to a concert.)
4 On peut visiter les musées. (You can visit the museums.)
5 On peut faire un tour en segway. (You can go on a tour by segway.)
6 On peut voir la tour Eiffel. (You can see the Eiffel Tower.)

j'aime + infinitive

3 Use the symbols and pictures to write sentences.

Pupils write sentences using the picture prompts.

Answers
1 J'aime retrouver mes copains.
2 Je n'aime pas faire les magasins.
3 J'adore aller voir des matchs (de foot).
4 Je déteste faire du roller.
5 Je n'aime pas aller au cinéma (avec mes amis).
6 J'aime prendre des photos.
7 *Pupils' own answers.*

The perfect tense of *–er* verbs

4 Find six past participles in the Louvre Pyramid and use them to complete the sentences below. Then translate the sentences.

Pupils find the past participles hidden in the words and use them to complete the sentences. They then translate the sentences.

Answers
1 dansé 2 visité 3 mangé 4 acheté 5 regardé
6 envoyé

1 I danced at the disco.
2 You visited the Eiffel Tower.
3 He ate in a restaurant.
4 She bought lots of souvenirs.
5 We watched the fireworks.
6 I sent lots of postcards.

Studio Grammaire Paris, je t'adore! 2

5 Copy and complete these perfect tense verbs.

Pupils copy out and complete the perfect tense verb paradigms.

Answers

chanter (to sing)	jouer (to play)	écouter (to listen)
j'ai chanté	j'ai joué	j'ai écouté
tu as chanté	tu as **joué**	tu **as écouté**
il a **chanté**	il a joué	il a écouté
elle a chanté	elle **a** joué	elle a écouté
on a chanté	on a joué	on **a écouté**

Making perfect tense verbs negative

6 Rewrite the sentences in exercise 4 to make them negative.

Pupils rewrite the sentences in exercise 4, making them negative.

Answers
1 *Je n'ai pas dansé à la discothèque.*
2 Tu n'as pas visité la tour Eiffel.
3 Il n'a pas mangé au restaurant.
4 Elle n'a pas acheté beaucoup de souvenirs.
5 On n'a pas regardé le feu d'artifice.
6 Je n'ai pas envoyé beaucoup de cartes postales.

Paris, je t'adore! 2 — À toi (Pupil Book pp. 116–117)

Self-access reading and writing

A Reinforcement

1 Qu'est-ce qu'on peut faire à Paris? Écris ta recommandation pour chaque célébrité. (AT 4.3)

Writing. Pupils write a recommendation on what you can do in Paris for each celebrity pictured. A framework is supplied for support.

Answers
1 On peut manger au restaurant.
2 On peut faire les magasins.
3 On peut aller à un concert.
4 On peut visiter les monuments et les musées.
5 On peut faire une balade en bateau-mouche.
6 On peut aller au théâtre.

2 Décode les phrases. Puis trouve la bonne image pour chaque phrase. (AT 3.2, AT 4.3)

Writing. Pupils decode the sentences, using the information supplied. They then match each sentence to the correct picture.

Answers
1 J'aime faire du roller. (d)
2 Je n'aime pas faire les magasins. (c)
3 J'adore aller au cinéma. (f)
4 Je déteste aller voir des matchs de foot. (b)
5 J'aime retrouver mes copains. (e)
6 Je n'aime pas prendre des photos. (a)

3 Lis la publicité. C'est vrai (✓), faux (✗) ou pas mentionné (PM)? (AT 3.3)

Reading. Pupils read the advert for the Paris sewers, then note whether the sentences in English summarising it are true (writing ✓), false (writing ✗) or contain information not mentioned in the text (writing PM).

Answers
1 ✓ 2 ✗ 3 ✗ 4 ✓ 5 ✓ 6 PM

B Extension

1 Écris une publicité pour une attraction dans ta région. Fais des recherches sur Internet ou invente les informations. (AT 4.3–4)

Writing. Pupils write an advert for an attraction in their area, looking for information online or inventing the information.

If pupils are aiming for Level 5, they could include comments from visitors featuring the perfect tense and *c'était*.

2 Copie et complète l'e-mail avec les bons verbes. (AT 3.5)

Reading. Pupils copy and complete the email using the correct verbs. The answers are supplied in random order for support.

Answers
1 visité 2 acheté 3 mangé 4 regardé 5 dansé 6 rencontré

3 Imagine que tu as passé un weekend à Paris. Qu'est-ce que tu as fait? C'était comment? Écris une carte postale. (AT 4.4–5)

Writing. Pupils imagine that they have spent a weekend in Paris and write a postcard saying what they did and how it was. A framework and a sample opening are supplied for support.

If pupils are aiming for Level 5, they could include the present tense, to say what they like doing or usually do.

Module 3: Mon identité (Pupil Book pp. 46–65)

Unit & Learning objectives	PoS* & Framework objectives	Key language	Grammar and other language features
1 Mon caractère (pp. 48–49) Talking about personality Adjectival agreement	**2.2e** ask and answer questions **2.2f** initiate and sustain conversations **2.2i** reuse language they have met **2.2j** adapt previously learned language **1.2/Y8** Listening – new contexts **1.5/Y8** Speaking (b) using simple idioms **4.3/Y8** Language – gender and plurals **4.4/Y8** Language – developing sentences	*Je suis/Tu es/Il est/Elle est … Je ne suis pas … drôle égoïste intelligent(e)* etc. *mon frère ma sœur mes parents mon meilleur ami ma meilleure amie*	**G** adjective agreement **G** possessive adjectives (*mon/ton*) **G** the present tense of *être* (singular)
2 Ma bande de copains (pp. 50–51) Talking about friendships More practice with the pronoun *on*	**2.2i** reuse language they have met **2.3/Y8** Reading – text features: emotive **2.4/Y8** Writing – (a) using text as stimulus **4.2/Y8** Language – increasing vocabulary	*Tu fais quoi avec tes copains/copines? On écoute de la musique. On va en ville. On rigole. On parle de films. Je fais beaucoup de choses. On s'entend très bien.*	**G** *on* verb forms – developing writing skills: longer sentences
3 Quelle musique écoutes-tu? (pp. 52–53) Talking about music Giving opinions	**2.1b** memorising **2.2j** adapt previously learned language **1.1/Y8** Listening – understanding on first hearing **1.4/Y8** Speaking – (b) unscripted conversations	*Quelle musique écoutes-tu? J'écoute du R'n'B/rap/pop-rock,* etc. *J'aime la musique de X. Je n'aime pas la musique de X. Mon groupe/chanteur préféré, c'est … Ma chanteuse préférée, c'est … J'adore les mélodies,* etc.	**G** the present tense of *venir* (singular) – pronunciation: sounding French
4 Mon style (pp. 54–55) Talking about clothes Using the near future tense	**4.1/Y8** Language – sounds/spelling exceptions **4.5/Y8** Language – (a) range of verb tenses (near furture tense) **4.6/Y8** Language – (a) range of questions **5.1** Strategies – patterns	*Qu'est-ce que tu vas porter à la fête? Je vais porter des baskets/un jean,* etc. *beige, blanc(he), bleu(e),* etc. *Ce weekend, je vais … manger au restaurant jouer au foot* etc.	**G** adjective agreement **G** the near future tense – developing writing skills: longer sentences

3 Mon identité

Unit & Learning objectives	PoS* & Framework objectives	Key language	Grammar and other language features
5 Le weekend dernier (pp. 56–57) Talking about last weekend Using the perfect tense	**2.1c** knowledge of language **3b** sounds and writing **4.5/Y8** Language – (a) range of verb tenses (perfect tense) **5.3** Strategies – English/other languages	*Le weekend dernier… je suis allé(e) au stade j'ai mangé des frites j'ai écouté de la musique* etc.	**G** the perfect tense – checking your work – pronunciation of *–é* in past participles
Bilan et Révisions (pp. 58–59) Pupils' checklist and practice exercises			
En plus: L'identité régionale (pp. 60–61) Talking about different regions in France	**2.1d** use previous knowledge **3.2/Y8** Culture – (b) customs/traditions **5.4** Strategies – working out meaning **5.8** Strategies – evaluating and improving	Review of language from the module	– developing reading strategies: using questions – presentation skills – checking your work
Studio Grammaire (pp. 62–63) Detailed grammar summary and practice exercises			**G** adjectives **G** possessive adjectives **G** the near future tense **G** the perfect tense with *avoir* **G** the perfect tense with *être*
À toi (pp. 118–119) Self-access reading and writing at two levels			

* In addition, the following Programmes of Study are covered throughout the module: 1.1–1.4, 2.2a, 2.2c, 2.2d, 3a, 3c, 3d, 3e, 3f, 4a, 4b, 4d, 4e, 4f, 4g. PoS 4c is covered in all Units 4 & 5 and *En plus* sections. See pp. 7–9 for details.

3 Mon identité

1 Mon caractère (Pupil Book pp. 48–49)

Learning objectives
- Talking about personality
- Adjectival agreement

Framework objectives
1.2/Y8 Listening – new contexts
1.5/Y8 – Speaking (b) using simple idioms
4.3/Y8 Language – gender and plurals
4.4/Y8 Language – developing sentences

FCSE links
Unit 1: Meeting people (Personal information; Physical/character descriptions)

Grammar
- adjective agreement

- possessive adjectives (*mon/ton*)
- the present tense of *être* (singular)

Key language
Je suis …
Tu es …
Il est …
Elle est …
Je ne suis pas …
drôle, égoïste, intelligent(e)
paresseux/paresseuse
patient(e), pénible
sportif/sportive
sympa, timide
mon frère
ma sœur
mes parents
mon meilleur ami
ma meilleure amie

PLTS
C Creative thinkers

Resources
CD 2, tracks 2–4
Cahier d'exercices Vert, page 23

ActiveTeach
p.048 Flashcards
p.048 Grammar
p.048 Grammar practice
p.048 Grammar
p.048 Grammar practice
p.049 Class activity
p.049 Grammar skills

Starter 1

PLTS C

Aim
To review adjective agreement; To identify patterns and work out rules

Write up the following. Give pupils, in pairs, three minutes to read through the sentences and work out any rules they can on adjective agreement.

Anna est intelligente et drôle.
Ben n'est pas drôle, mais il est égoïste.
Luke et Harry sont patients.
Sam, est-il intelligent? Oui, intelligent et patient.
Sarah et sa sœur ne sont pas patientes et Sarah n'est pas égoïste.

Hear answers, asking pupils to give examples of the adjectives each time. (Most adjectives add to the masculine form: –e to produce the feminine form; –s the masculine plural; –es the feminine plural. Adjectives ending in –e in the masculine form don't change in the feminine singular; they add –s in the masculine plural.) Ask pupils to predict the form of adjectives like *drôle* in the feminine plural (*drôles*).

Alternative Starter 1:
Use ActiveTeach p.048 Flashcards to introduce adjectives of personality.

1 Écoute. C'est qui? (1–9) (AT 1.2)
Listening. Pupils listen to nine people describing themselves. They identify the speaker each time, using the pictures and text.

Audioscript — CD 2 track 2

1 *Je suis sportif.*
2 *Je suis patiente.*
3 *Je suis drôle.*
4 *Je suis intelligent.*
5 *Je suis égoïste.*
6 *Je suis sympa.*
7 *Je suis paresseux.*
8 *Je suis pénible.*
9 *Je suis timide.*

Answers
1 Hugo 2 Alyzée 3 Samira 4 Harris 5 Marielle
6 Olivia 7 Frank 8 Arthur 9 Éva

Studio Grammaire: adjective agreement
Use the *Studio Grammaire* box to cover adjective agreement, including a range of different endings/adjectives which don't change. There is more information and further practice on Pupil Book p. 62.

3 Mon identité   1 Mon caractère

R Write up adjectives from the grammar box. Pupils identify whether each is masculine or feminine, or could be either.

2 Copie les textes. Écris correctement les mots en désordre. (AT 3.3)
Reading. Pupils copy and complete the texts, unjumbling the words supplied as anagrams.

Answers
1 sympa   2 intelligente   3 timide   4 paresseuse
5 sportif   6 drôle   7 égoïste   8 pénible

3 Écoute et note les lettres des adjectifs de l'exercice 1. (1–4) (AT 1.3)
Listening. Pupils listen and note the adjectives mentioned, using sentences **a–i** in exercise 1.

Audioscript CD 2 track 3

1 – Décris ton caractère, Julie.
 – Je suis très patiente et je suis aussi assez sportive.
 – Je suis un peu timide, mais je ne suis pas drôle.
2 – Décris ton caractère, Adnan.
 – Je suis très intelligent et je suis aussi assez sympa.
 – Je suis un peu paresseux, mais je ne suis pas égoïste.
3 – Décris ton caractère, Tariq.
 – Je suis très drôle et je suis aussi assez sympa.
 – Je suis un peu sportif, mais je ne suis pas égoïste.
4 – Décris ton caractère, Zahra.
 – Je suis très sympa et je suis aussi assez patiente.
 – Je suis un peu paresseuse, mais je ne suis pas pénible.

Answers
1 g, b, i, a   2 d, c, h, f   3 a, c, b, f   4 c, g, h, e

4 Décris un membre de ta famille. Fais une liste de cinq adjectifs. (AT 4.2)
Writing. Pupils describe a member of their family, listing five adjectives. A sample opening is supplied.

Studio Grammaire: possessive pronouns (*mon/ton*)
Use the *Studio Grammaire* box to cover the possessive pronouns *mon/ma/mes* and *ton/ta/tes*. There is more information and further practice on Pupil Book p. 62.

Starter 2
Aim
To review adjectives used to describe character

Give pupils three minutes to write a description of themselves using adjectives describing character. They need to include at least two negative statements.

Hear answers. Ask pupils to tell you:
– the rules of agreement for most adjectives
– the rules for adjectives ending in *–e* in the masculine singular
– how *paresseux* is different

Alternative Starter 2:
Use ActiveTeach p.048 Grammar practice to practise adjectives.

5 Associe les descriptions aux dessins. (AT 3.3)
Reading. Pupils match the pictures to the descriptions.

Answers
1 f   2 c   3 a   4 b   5 d   6 e

6 Écoute. Choisis la bonne réponse. (AT 1.1, AT 3.4)
Listening. Pupils listen and complete the sentences by choosing the correct option from the two supplied each time.

Audioscript CD 2 track 4

– Décris ton meilleur ami.
– Mon meilleur ami s'appelle Mathis.
 Il est très sportif et il est aussi assez drôle.
 Il est un peu timide, mais il n'est pas paresseux.
 C'est mon meilleur ami.

Answers
1 Mon meilleur ami est très **sportif**.
2 Il est aussi assez **drôle**.
3 Il est un peu **timide**.
4 Il n'est pas **paresseux**.

1 Mon caractère   **Mon identité** 3

7 Lis l'interview. Complète les phrases en anglais. (AT 3.4)

Reading. Pupils read the interview, then complete the sentences summarising it in English.

Answers

1 Noah is fourteen years old. He lives in Marseille with **his parents and his little sister**.
2 He is intelligent and very **nice** too. He is not **lazy**.
3 He is quite **sporty** and he thinks he is **funny**.
4 His best friend Léo is **funny** but sometimes a bit **annoying**.
5 Léo loves **science-fiction films** and **rugby**.

> **Studio Grammaire:** *être* **(present tense singular)**
>
> Use the *Studio Grammaire* box to cover the present tense of *être* (singular, including *on*). There is more information and further practice on Pupil Book p. 23.

8 En tandem. Fais deux dialogues. (AT 2.4)

Speaking. In pairs: pupils make up two dialogues about their favourite celebrities, using the framework supplied.

9 Écris une interview. Utilise le texte de l'exercice 7 comme modèle. (AT 4.4)

Writing. Pupils write an interview using the text in exercise 7 as a model.

Plenary

Ask the class to summarise the rules of adjective agreement you have covered in the unit and to give examples of any adjectives introduced here that don't follow these patterns.

Put the class into teams. Tell them to close their Pupil Books. Set them the challenge of writing out as many different sentences as they can using *Il est/Elle est* and adjectives from the unit. They swap answers with another team, who award two points for a completely correct answer and one point if it's correct apart from an error in the adjective agreement.

Workbook, page 23

Answers

1   1 paresseux   2 sympa   3 patient   4 timide
    5 pénible   6 égoïste   7 drôle   8 sportif
    9 intelligent

2   **a** Noah   **b** Hugo   **c** Sarah

3

English	Masculine	Feminine
intelligent	intelligent	intelligente
funny	drôle	drôle
kind	sympa	sympa
patient	patient	patiente
lazy	paresseux	paresseuse
sporty	sportif	sportive
shy	timide	timide

3 Mon identité 1 Mon caractère

Worksheet 3.1 Adjectival agreement

Answers

A Adjectives describe **nouns**. Many adjectives add -e in the **feminine** form and -s or -es in the **plural** form. Some **adjectives** follow a different pattern.

B

	masculine	feminine	either
drôle			✓
timide			✓
verte		✓	
sportive		✓	
paresseux	✓		
patiente		✓	
intelligent	✓		
blanc	✓		
égoïste			✓
sympa			✓

C 1 Karima est très gentille. Elle aime la lecture et le cinéma. Elle est patiente et aussi intelligente.
2 Nico est sportif. Il aime le foot et le tennis.
3 Zahia est un peu paresseuse mais elle n'est pas du tout égoïste.
4 Ludo est modeste et il est assez impatient.
5 Mélissa est drôle mais timide.

2 Ma bande de copains (Pupil Book pp. 50–51)

Learning objectives
- Talking about friendships
- More practice with the pronoun *on*

Framework objectives
2.3/Y8 Reading – text features: emotive
2.4/Y8 Writing – (a) using text as stimulus
4.2/Y8 Language – increasing vocabulary

FCSE links
Unit 4: Holidays (Weather)

Grammar
- *on* verb forms

Key language
Tu fais quoi avec tes copains/copines?
On écoute de la musique.
On joue à des jeux vidéo.
On va en ville.
On fait du shopping.
On rigole.
Tu parles de quoi avec tes copains?
On parle de sport.
On parle de mode.
On parle de films.
Je fais beaucoup de choses.
On s'entend très bien.

PLTS
E Effective participators

Resources
CD 2, tracks 5–6
Cahier d'exercices Vert, page 24
ActiveTeach
p.050 Flashcards
p.051 Thinking skills

Starter 1
Aim
To review the *il/elle* form of key verbs

Write up the following. Give pupils three minutes to copy and complete the table. If they need support, supply the irregular verb forms in random order.

infinitive	il/elle ...
écouter	
jouer	joue
parler	
regarder	
faire	
avoir	
aller	
être	

Check answers, asking pupils to confirm how you form the *il/elle* form of the verb from the infinitive (drop –*er* and add –*e*).

1 Associe les phrases aux photos. (AT 3.3)
Reading. Pupils match the sentences to the pictures.

Answers
See answers for exercise 2: pupils listen to the exercise 2 recording to check their answers.

2 Écoute et vérifie tes réponses. (1–8) (AT 1.3)
Listening. Pupils listen to check their answers to exercise 1.

Audioscript — CD 2 track 5

1 – Tu fais quoi, avec tes copains?
 – On écoute de la musique.
 – e
2 – Tu fais quoi, avec tes copains?
 – On joue à des jeux vidéo.
 – b
3 – Tu fais quoi, avec tes copains?
 – On va en ville.
 – g
4 – Tu fais quoi, avec tes copains?
 – On fait du shopping.
 – c
5 – Tu fais quoi, avec tes copains?
 – On rigole.
 – f
6 – Tu parles de quoi, avec tes copains?
 – On parle de sport.
 – d
7 – Tu parles de quoi, avec tes copains?
 – On parle de mode.
 – h
8 – Tu parles de quoi, avec tes copains?
 – On parle de films.
 – a

Answers
1 e **2** b **3** g **4** c **5** f **6** d **7** h **8** a

3 Mon identité 2 Ma bande de copains

> **Studio Grammaire:** *on*
> Use the *Studio Grammaire* box to cover the subject pronoun *on*.

R Pupils write out the French for: we sing, we have, we dance, we surf the net.

3 Écoute. Qu'est-ce qui n'est pas mentionné? (AT 1.4)
Listening. Pupils listen and identify which of the three activities <u>isn't</u> mentioned each time. Some vocabulary is glossed for support.

Audioscript CD 2 track 6

1 – Tu fais quoi avec tes copains, David?
   – Euh ... On joue à des jeux vidéo.
   – Et tu parles de quoi avec tes copains?
   – Alors, on parle de musique, en général.
2 – Tu fais quoi avec tes copains ou tes copines, Rachida?
   – Euh ... On va en ville et on rigole. C'est chouette!
   – Et tu parles de quoi avec tes copains?
   – Quelquefois, on parle de sport.
3 – Tu fais quoi avec tes copines, Lara?
   – On fait du shopping.
   – Et tu parles de quoi avec tes copines?
   – On parle de mode, bien sûr!

Answers
1 b 2 a 3 a

4 En tandem. Fais deux dialogues. (AT 2.3)
Speaking. In pairs: pupils make up two dialogues, using the framework + picture prompts supplied.

Answers
A ● Tu fais quoi, avec tes copains ou tes copines?
   ■ On **fait du shopping** ou **on joue à des jeux vidéo**.
   ● Tu parles de quoi, avec tes copains ou tes copines?
   ■ Alors, on parle de **sport** et quelquefois, on parle de **films**.
B ● Tu fais quoi, avec tes copains ou tes copines?
   ■ On **va en ville** ou **on écoute de la musique**.
   ● Tu parles de quoi, avec tes copains ou tes copines?
   ■ Alors, on parle de **mode** et quelquefois, on parle de **musique**.

Starter 2
Aim
To review weather vocabulary

Write up the following. If necessary, explain that they are all sentences describing the weather. Give pupils three minutes to do a quick sketch for each one.

1 *Il fait chaud.*
2 *Il fait froid.*
3 *Il y a du soleil.*
4 *Il y a du vent.*
5 *Il pleut.*
6 *Il neige.*

Ask pupils to swap with a partner and check each other's sketches. Then check answers as a class, asking pupils to translate each sentence into English. Ask pupils to explain what *il fait chaud* means literally, and how this structure is different from English (the verb used is *faire*, not *être* as you would expect from a literal translation).

Alternative Starter 2:
Use ActiveTeach p.050 Flashcards to practise activities with friends.

5 Écris un dialogue. Utilise le modèle de l'exercice 4. (AT 4.3)
Writing. Pupils write a dialogue using the one in exercise 4 as a model.

6 C'est qui? Natasha ou Maxime? (AT 3.4)
Reading. Pupils read the two texts. They then match the correct name (Natasha or Maxime) to each set of picture prompts. Some vocabulary is glossed for support.

Answers
1 Maxime 2 Natasha 3 Natasha 4 Maxime
5 Maxime 6 Natasha

+ Pupils translate the texts into English orally round the class.

7 Écris les mots dans le bon ordre. (AT 4.3)
Writing. Pupils write out the jumbled sentences in the correct order.

2 Ma bande de copains   Mon identité   3

Answers
1 S'il fait beau, on va en ville.
2 Quand il pleut, on écoute de la musique.
3 Quand il fait chaud, on fait du vélo.
4 S'il pleut, on fait du shopping.
5 S'il fait chaud, on joue au football.

8 Prépare un exposé pour ta classe. (AT 2.4)

Speaking. Pupils prepare and give a presentation on what they do with their friends. A framework is supplied for support. Draw their attention to the tip box on using *quand* and *si* to introduce details that will make their sentences more interesting.

PLTS E

When pupils have given their presentation, ask the rest of the class to give constructive feedback. Draw their attention to the tip box on what to look for and how to deliver feedback.

Plenary

Review how *on* is used, asking for examples of the *on* form of verbs in the unit (*on écoute, on joue, on va,* etc.).

Put the class into teams. Give them three minutes to recall all the activities with friends that were covered in the unit, using *on*. At the end of the time, they swap lists with another team and check each other's work, awarding two points for a completely correct sentence and one for a sentence with a minor error. The team with the most points wins.

Workbook, page 24

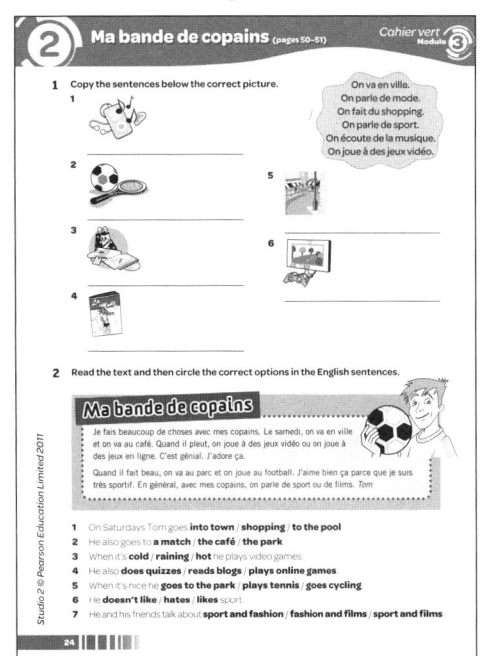

Answers
1 1 On écoute de la musique.
   2 On parle de sport.
   3 On fait du shopping.
   4 On parle de mode.
   5 On va en ville.
   6 On joue à des jeux vidéo.
2 1 On Saturdays Tom goes **into town**.
   2 He also goes to **the café**.
   3 When it's **raining** he plays video games.
   4 He also **plays online games**.
   5 When it's nice he **goes to the park**.
   6 He **likes** sport.
   7 He and his friends talk about **sport and films**.

3 Mon identité 2 Ma bande de copains

Worksheet 3.2 Friendships

Answers

A 1 *Manu*: On parle de sport.
2 *Olivia*: On fait du shopping.
3 *Aurélie*: On écoute de la musique.
4 *Laurène*: On parle de mode.
5 *Lucas*: On rigole.
6 *Nathan*: On regarde des DVD.

B 1 Lucas
2 Laurène
3 Manu
4 Aurélie
5 Nathan
6 Olivia

C 1 Claims to be shy but has lots of friends.
2 Plays in the park when it's raining.
3 Stays in and watches DVDs when the weather is nice outside.
4 Goes to the cinema every day even though it's very expensive.
5 Plays table tennis often but doesn't like it.

Mon identité 3

3 Quelle musique écoutes-tu?
(Pupil Book pp. 52–53)

Learning objectives
- Talking about music
- Giving opinions

Framework objectives
1.1/Y8 Listening – understanding on first hearing
1.4/Y8 Speaking – (b) unscripted conversations

FCSE links
Unit 1: Meeting people (Sports and hobbies)
Unit 6: Leisure (Sports/hobbies)
Unit 11: Media (Free time activities)

Grammar
- the present tense of *venir* (singular)

Key language
Quelle musique écoutes-tu?
J'écoute du R'n'B.
J'écoute du rap.
J'écoute du jazz.
J'écoute du pop-rock.
J'écoute de la musique classique.
J'écoute beaucoup d'artistes différents.
J'aime la musique de X.
Je n'aime pas la musique de X.
Mon groupe préféré, c'est ...
Mon chanteur préféré, c'est ...
Ma chanteuse préférée, c'est ...
J'adore la chanson ...
les mélodies
les paroles

PLTS
I Independent enquirers

Cross-curricular
Music: justifying preferences
Maths: averages

Resources
CD 2, tracks 7–9
Cahier d'exercices Vert, page 25
ActiveTeach
p.052 Flashcards
p.053 Thinking skills

Starter 1
Aim
To introduce the vocabulary for different types of music

Write up the following. Give pupils three minutes to give their personal opinion of each music type by giving a mark out of ten (in French).

R'n'B, pop-rock, rap, musique classique, jazz

Hear some answers. Then ask the class to work out their average score for all five types. Establish who has the broadest musical interests in the class by identifying the pupil with the highest average score.

Alternative Starter 1:
Use ActiveTeach p.052 Flashcards to introduce music vocabulary.

1 Écoute. Qui parle? (1–8) (AT 1.2)
Listening. Pupils listen to eight people talking about the kind of music they listen to. They use the sentences in the speech bubbles to identify the speaker each time.

Audioscript — CD 2 track 7

1 – *Quelle musique écoutes-tu?*
– *J'écoute du jazz.*
2 – *Quelle musique écoutes-tu?*
– *J'aime la musique de Usher.*
3 – *Quelle musique écoutes-tu?*
– *J'écoute du pop-rock.*
4 – *Quelle musique écoutes-tu?*
– *J'écoute du rap.*
5 – *Quelle musique écoutes-tu?*
– *J'écoute beaucoup d'artistes différents.*
6 – *Quelle musique écoutes-tu?*
– *J'écoute de la musique classique.*
7 – *Quelle musique écoutes-tu?*
– *J'écoute du R'n'B.*
8 – *Quelle musique écoutes-tu?*
– *Euh ... Je n'aime pas la musique de Alicia Keys ...*

Answers
1 Irina 2 Marie 3 Simon 4 Yann 5 Abdel
6 Flavie 7 Aurore 8 Esteban

Use the pronunciation box to encourage pupils to sound as French as possible, even when the words they are using are cognates.

2 Fais un sondage en classe. (AT 2.2)
PLTS I

Speaking. Pupils do a survey with other pupils in the class to find out about their music preferences. A grid they can copy to note answers and a sample exchange are given.

3 Mon identité 3 Quelle musique écoutes-tu?

3 Lis les textes. Trouve l'équivalent des expressions en anglais. (AT 3.4)
Reading. Pupils read the texts. They then find in them the French for the English phrases given.

Answers
1 Mon groupe préféré, c'est …
2 Ma chanteuse préférée, c'est …
3 Mon chanteur préféré, c'est …
4 Je n'aime pas les paroles.
5 J'adore la chanson …
6 J'adore les mélodies.
7 J'écoute beaucoup d'artistes différents.
8 c'est triste

➕ Pupils write some simple opinions, saying whether they agree with the views of each of the people in exercise 3.

4 Écoute et complète le texte pour Élisa. (AT 1.4)
Listening. Pupils listen and complete the gap-fill text about Élisa.

Audioscript CD 2 track 8

Moi, j'écoute du rap et du R'n'B.
Mon chanteur préféré, c'est Jay Sean.
J'aime aussi la musique de Mary J Blige.
C'est super!

Answers
1 rap 2 R'n'B 3 chanteur 4 la musique
5 super

Starter 2
Aim
To review language for discussing music preferences

Give pupils three minutes to complete these sentences:

Mon chanteur préféré, c'est … Il est …
Ma chanteuse préférée, c'est … Elle est …
Mon groupe préféré, c'est … J'aime …
Je n'aime pas … parce que …

Hear answers, asking another pupil each time to say whether or not they agree with the opinion expressed.

5 Lis le texte. Quelles sont les trois phrases correctes? (AT 3.4)
Reading. Pupils read the text. They then read the six sentences in English and identify which three of them are correct.

Answers
2, 5, 6

6 Quelle musique écoutes-tu? Écris un paragraphe. (AT 4.4)
Writing. Pupils write a paragraph on the music they listen to. A framework is supplied.

When they have finished, pupils swap texts with a partner and check each other's work. They identify but don't correct errors. They then do a second draft of their own paragraph.

> **Studio Grammaire:** *venir* **(present tense singular)**
> Use the *Studio Grammaire* box to cover the present tense of *venir* (singular, including *on*).

7 Écoute et chante la chanson. (AT 1.4)
Listening. Pupils listen to the song. They listen again, this time singing along.

Audioscript CD 2 track 9

Veux-tu venir (x 2)
Au concert? (x 2)

Qui vient avec nous? (x 2)
Qui c'est qui joue? (x 2)

Mon frère vient.
Ton frère vient?
Ma sœur aussi.
Ta sœur aussi?

C'est ma chanteuse préférée (x 2)
Beyoncé. (x 2)
Tes parents viennent? (x 2)
Mais non, tu rigoles! (x 2)

Ça coûte combien? (x 2)
Je t'invite, donc rien! (x 2)

Alors, je viens. (x 2)
Ça va être bien! (x 2)

3 Quelle musique écoutes-tu?   Mon identité 3

Plenary
Review the language for giving and justifying opinions about music. Ask pupils to come up with a list of singers and bands: write these on the board. Use the names as prompts in random order, asking a different pupil each time to give and justify an opinion on the singer/band.

Workbook, page 25

Answers
1 J'écoute du jazz.
2 J'écoute du rap.
3 J'écoute de la musique classique.
4 J'adore les mélodies.
5 J'aime la musique d'Ellie Goulding.
6 Je n'aime pas la musique des Black Eyed Peas.
7 Mon groupe préféré, c'est Gorillaz.
8 Mon chanteur préféré, c'est Raphaël.
2 1 ✗ 2 ✗ 3 ✓ 4 ✗ 5 ✗ 6 ✓ 7 ✓ 8 ✗
3 (Possible answer:)
Mon groupe préféré, c'est JLS parce que j'aime les paroles. J'écoute beaucoup d'artistes différents.

Worksheet 3.3 Odd one out!

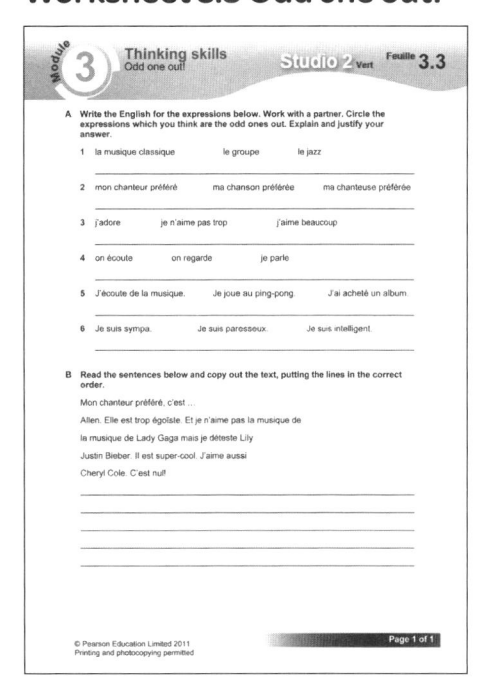

Answers
A The odd one out is in bold, but answers will vary. Other answers with valid reasons may be accepted.
1 classical music   **group / band**   jazz
(not a type of music)
2 favourite singer (male)   **favourite song**
favourite singer (female)
(not a singer)
3 I love   **I don't like much**   I like a lot
(not positive)
4 we listen   we watch   **I speak**
(I, not we)
5 I listen to music.   I play table tennis.
I bought an album.
(perfect, not present, tense)
6 I'm nice.   **I'm lazy**.   I'm intelligent.
(not positive)

B Mon chanteur préféré, c'est Justin Bieber. Il est super-cool. J'aime aussi la musique de Lady Gaga mais je déteste Lily Allen. Elle est trop égoïste. Et je n'aime pas la musique de Cheryl Cole. C'est nul!

3 Mon identité

4 Mon style (Pupil Book pp. 54–55)

Learning objectives
- Talking about clothes
- Using the near future tense

Framework objectives
4.1/Y8 Language – sounds/spelling exceptions
4.5/Y8 Language – (a) range of verb tenses (near future tense)
4.6/Y8 Language – (a) range of questions
5.1 Strategies – patterns

FCSE links
Unit 1: Meeting people (Clothes and colours)
Unit 6: Leisure (Clothes)
Unit 7: Celebrations (Clothes)

Grammar
- adjective agreement
- the near future tense

Key language
Qu'est-ce que tu vas porter à la fête?
Je vais porter …
des baskets, des bottes
des chaussures (de skate)
une chemise
un jean, une jupe, un pantalon
un pull, un sweat à capuche
un tee-shirt, une veste
les vêtements
beige, blanc(he), bleu(e)
marron, noir(e)
orange, vert kaki
Ce weekend, je vais …
manger au restaurant
aller en ville
jouer au foot
faire du camping
aller au cinéma
faire de la rando

PLTS
T Team workers

Resources
CD 2, tracks 10–11
Cahier d'exercices Vert, page 26
ActiveTeach
p.054 Flashcards
p.054 Grammar
p.054 Grammar practice
p.054 Video 5
p.054 Video worksheet 5
p.055 Grammar
p.055 Grammar practice
p.055 Video 6
p.055 Video worksheet 6
p.055 Learning skills
p.055 Grammar skills

Starter 1
Aim
To review colours; To review adjective agreement

Write up the following: black, white, khaki, beige, orange, blue, brown.

Remind pupils that colours are adjectives and that adjectives agree with the nouns they accompany. Give pupils three minutes to look at the text in exercise 1 and write down in French the masculine singular form of all the colours.

Check answers (*noir, blanc, vert kaki, beige, orange, bleu, marron*). Ask pupils what happens to adjectives ending in –*e* in the masculine form when they're used with a feminine noun (they don't change). Ask in what way *blanc* and *marron* are unusual (*blanc* becomes *blanche* in the feminine form and *marron* doesn't change).

1 Fais correspondre les vêtements et les images. (AT 3.1)
Reading. Pupils match the names of the clothing items with the pictures.

Answers
a un jean
b un sweat à capuche orange
c un pantalon vert kaki
d un pull beige
e une jupe marron
f une veste noire
g une chemise bleue
h des bottes noires
i des baskets blanches
j des chaussures de skate

Studio Grammaire: adjective agreement
Use the *Studio Grammaire* box to cover adjective agreement (colours). There is more information and further practice on Pupil Book p. 62.

4 Mon style Mon identité 3

R Pupils choose four items of clothing and four colours and write out phrases in French, taking care to make the adjectives agree (e.g. *une jupe blanche*).

2 Écoute et écris les lettres des vêtements mentionnés. (1–6) (AT 1.3)

Listening. Pupils listen and write the letters of the clothes mentioned (using pictures **a–j** in exercise 1).

Audioscript CD 2 track 10

1 – Qu'est-ce que tu vas porter à la fête?
   – Je vais porter un pull beige et une jupe marron.
2 – Qu'est-ce que tu vas porter à la fête?
   – Je vais porter un sweat à capuche orange et un pantalon vert kaki.
3 – Qu'est-ce que tu vas porter à la fête?
   – Je vais porter un jean et des baskets blanches.
4 – Qu'est-ce que tu vas porter à la fête?
   – Je vais porter une veste noire.
5 – Qu'est-ce que tu vas porter à la fête?
   – Je vais porter une chemise bleue et des bottes noires.
6 – Qu'est-ce que tu vas porter à la fête?
   – Je vais porter des chaussures de skate!

Answers
1 d,e 2 b,c 3 a,i 4 f 5 g,h 6 j

3 Qu'est-ce que tu vas porter à la fête? Choisis trois vêtements. Ensuite, fais un sondage. (AT 2.3)

Speaking. Pupils decide on three items of clothing they are going to wear to a party. They then carry out a survey in the class, asking each other what they are going to wear. A grid they can copy to note answers and a sample exchange are given.

Starter 2
Aim
To review vocabulary for clothes

Pupils work in pairs. They take it in turn to do a quick sketch of an item of clothing from the unit and to name it in French. Tell them to keep count of how many items they successfully name as a pair.

Ask for examples of clothing that they used in the activity. See which pair has the highest score.

Alternative Starter 2:
Use ActiveTeach p.054 Flashcards to practise clothing items.

4 Écoute. Copie et remplis le tableau en anglais. (1–4) (AT 1.4)

Listening. Pupils copy out the table. They listen to four people talking about what they are going to do and what they are going to wear and complete the table with the details in English.

Audioscript CD 2 track 11

1 – Qu'est-ce que tu vas faire ce weekend, Coline?
   – Alors, ce weekend, je vais faire du camping. J'adore ça.
   – Qu'est-ce que tu vas porter?
   – Je vais porter un jean, un pull noir et un chapeau parce qu'il va faire froid!
2 – Qu'est-ce que tu vas faire ce weekend, Akai?
   – Ce weekend, on va aller en ville et on va manger au restaurant.
   – Qu'est-ce que tu vas porter?
   – Je vais porter une chemise verte et un pantalon bleu marine. Je crois que je vais aussi porter une veste.
3 – Qu'est-ce que tu vas faire ce weekend, Mélanie?
   – Je vais faire du shopping en ville avec mes copines.
   – Qu'est-ce que tu vas porter?
   – Je vais porter un jean et un sweat à capuche rouge.
4 – Qu'est-ce que tu vas faire ce weekend, Arthur?
   – Moi, je vais faire de la rando avec ma famille.
   – Qu'est-ce que tu vas porter?
   – Je vais porter un tee-shirt blanc et un short beige. Sportif, hein!

Answers

		Going to do?	Going to wear?
1	Coline	camping	jeans, black jumper, (hat)
2	Akai	go into town, eat in a restaurant	green shirt, navy blue trousers, jacket
3	Mélanie	shopping (in town, with friends)	jeans, red hoodie
4	Arthur	hiking (with family)	white T-shirt, beige shorts

Studio Grammaire: the near future tense (singular)

Use the *Studio Grammaire* box to cover the near future tense in the singular. There is more information and further practice on Pupil Book p. 63.

3 Mon identité 4 Mon style

➕ Ask the class to chant the near future tense of *porter* together several times (*je vais porter, tu vas porter*, etc.), looking at their books. Then get them to close their books and chant it a few times more from memory.

5 Qui va porter quoi? Fais un choix logique. (AT 3.3)

Reading. Pupils match the three text openings for each of the three people (Talia, Renaud and Nicolette) with the most appropriate ending (from **a–c**), using logic to decide what would be the best thing to wear on each occasion.

Answers
Talia – c   **Renaud** – a   **Nicolette** – b

6 Ouah! T'es chic! En tandem, fais des conversations. (AT 2.4)

PLTS T

Speaking. In pairs: pupils make up six dialogues, using the framework + picture prompts supplied. A sample opening is supplied. Draw their attention to the tip box on using *alors*.

Answers
1 Ce weekend, je vais **manger au restaurant**, alors, je vais porter **une chemise blanche**.
2 Ce weekend, je vais **aller en ville**, alors, je vais porter **un sweat à capuche noir**.
3 Ce weekend, je vais **jouer au foot**, alors, je vais porter **des baskets blanches**.
4 Ce weekend, je vais **faire du camping**, alors, je vais porter **un pantalon vert kaki**.
5 Ce weekend, je vais **aller au cinéma**, alors, je vais porter **un jean**.
6 Ce weekend, je vais **faire de la rando**, alors, je vais porter **un pull bleu**.

7 Écris ton blog. Qu'est-ce que tu vas faire et qu'est-ce que tu vas porter, ce weekend? (AT 4.5)

Writing. Pupils write a blog on what they are going to do and wear this weekend. Sample answer openings are given.

Plenary

Ask the class to summarise how the near future tense is formed, then play a game of Verb Tag to practise it.

Put the class into teams and tell them to study the *Studio Grammaire* box on page 55 for one minute. Put a sheet of paper for each team at the front of the class. On each paper write *aller* and the subject pronouns (singular + *on*) in order. Tell pupils to close their books.

Team members take it in turn to come to the front of the class and fill in one of the verbs with the correct form of *aller* and an infinitive. They then take the pen back and pass it to the next member of their team. The first team to complete all the verbs correctly is the winner.

Alternative Plenary:
Use ActiveTeach p.055 Grammar practice to practise the near future tense.

Workbook, page 26

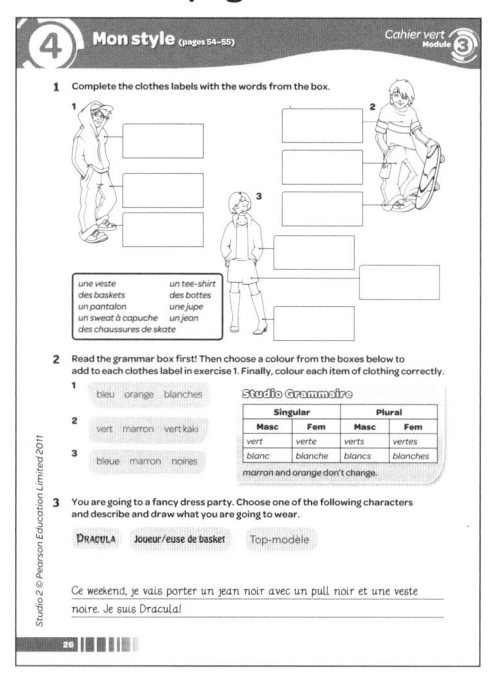

Answers
1 1 un sweat à capuche, un jean, des baskets
 2 un tee-shirt, un pantalon, des chaussures de skate
 3 une veste, une jupe, des bottes
2 1 un sweat à capuche orange, un jean bleu, des baskets blanches
 2 un tee-shirt vert, un pantalon vert kaki, des chaussures de skate marron
 3 une veste marron/bleue, une jupe bleue/marron, des bottes noires
3 (Possible answers:)
Ce weekend, je vais porter un jean noir avec un pull noir et une veste noire. Je suis Dracula!
Ce weekend, je vais porter un tee-shirt bleu, un short bleu et des baskets blanches. Je suis joueur/joueuse de basket.
Ce weekend, je vais porter des bottes rouges, une jupe blanche, une chemise verte et une veste verte. Je suis top-modèle!

4 Mon style Mon identité 3

Worksheet 3.4 Proof reading

Answers

A The four sentences which don't contain any mistakes are:
4 On écoute du R'n'B.
5 Je vais jouer au foot.
7 J'aime jouer au ping-pong.
8 Je regarde souvent la télé.

B Je m'appelle Arthur et j'ai **quatorze** ans. J'habite à Biarritz avec mes **parents** et ma **petite** sœur. Je suis assez **intelligent** et je suis gentil. Je ne suis pas paresseux. Je suis assez drôle et je **pense** que je suis généreux.
J'adore la musique de Rihanna.

C mode – fashion, not mode
baskets – trainers, not baskets
collège – secondary school, not college
pantalon – trousers, not pants
veste – jacket, not vest

Worksheet 3.5 Adjectives and the near future

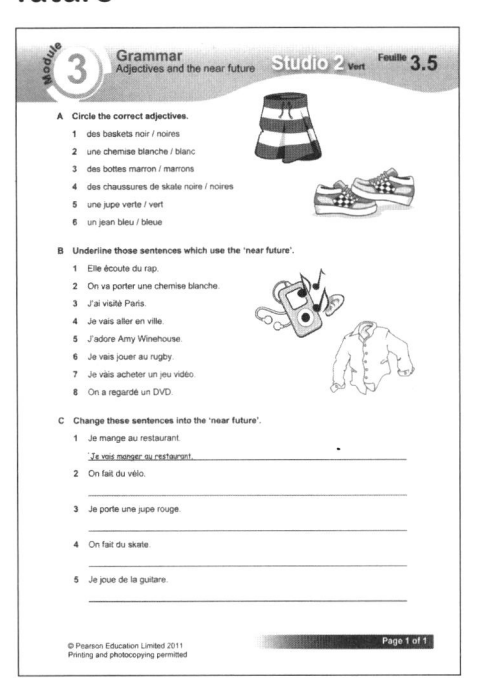

Answers

A 1 des baskets **noires**
  2 une chemise **blanche**
  3 des bottes **marron**
  4 des chaussures de skate **noires**
  5 une jupe **verte**
  6 un jean **bleu**

B The sentences which use the 'near future' are:
  2 On va porter une chemise blanche.
  4 Je vais aller en ville.
  6 Je vais jouer au rugby.
  7 Je vais acheter un jeu vidéo.

C 1 *Je vais manger au restaurant.*
  2 On va faire du vélo.
  3 Je vais porter une jupe rouge.
  4 On va faire du skate.
  5 Je vais jouer de la guitare.

3 Mon identité 4 Mon style

Video
Episode 5: Un nouveau look
Marielle and Samira conduct a survey on fashion, asking people to give their opinion on the best look for Hugo and Alex. Video worksheet 5 can be used in conjunction with this episode.

Answers to video worksheet (ActiveTeach)
1. **A** (Answers will vary.)
   B The girls are interviewing the public about boys' fashions.
   C *style classique* – classic style
   style sportif – sporty style
   style décontracté – casual style
   style skateur – skater style
2. **A** He's not keen on fashion.
   B Alex says 'C'est nul!' (negative), while Marielle says 'J'adore la mode' (positive).
   C They will show members of the public various styles and see which they prefer for Hugo and Alex.
   D He looks quite pleased about it.
   E That their clothes are not very cool.
3. **A** classic style – intelligent but arrogant (words the same in French as in English but pronounced differently)
   skater look – lazy and embarrassing, awful
   B They seem pleased but it's hard to work out why. Discuss it.
   C skater look – adorable, nice (*gentil*)
   sporty look – strong, nice looking (*beau*)
   D Because the girl says Hugo looks like James Bond in the classic look.
   E 'Yuk!'
4. **A** classic style – too fashionable
   casual style – cool
   sporty style – yuk!
   skater style – excellent
   B They agree with it by nodding.
5. **A** He asks what sort of music he is into.
   B The casual style is best, as he likes pop-rock.
   C Because they are going to have to do a fashion show.

Video
Episode 6: Le défilé de mode
The team all try out new fashion looks and comment on them for the StudioGB viewers. Video worksheet 6 can be used in conjunction with this episode.

Answers to video worksheet (ActiveTeach)
1. **A** (Answers will vary.)
   B Each person tries out a different style, presented as a fashion show.
   C This is interesting to discuss. On the face of it, there are no differences, yet somehow it still feels French.
   D (Answers will vary.)
2. **A** 'jean' is the word for 'denim' (*un pantalon en jean, un short en jean*). 'sweat' (short for 'sweat à capuche' – meaning 'hoody') comes from the English word 'sweatshirt'. 'baskets' is the word for trainers and comes from 'basketball shoes'.
   B The English language is influential in the international fashion industry. Many styles and trends come from the USA.
   C 'The style of the summer'. (*Le style de l'été.*)
   D casual (*décontracté*), elegant (*élégant*)
   E The skirt is made of denim (*jean*) and the belt is leather (*cuir*).
3. **A** They are amazed at Marielle's unclassifiable outfit.
   B Because he is lost for words.
   C High heeled.
   D *pantalon, chemise, veste, chaussures, ceinture, jupe*
   E 'veste', because it means 'jacket', not 'vest'.
   F 'I am not fashionable, I AM fashion'.
   G They groan – typical Marielle!
4. **A** Find a James Bond style for Hugo.
   B blue trousers, white shirt, grey jacket, elegant shoes
   C Marielle wore a grey jacket too.
   D She seems quite smitten ('adorable!') and asks Hugo out – or maybe she is pretending for the camera.

5 Le weekend dernier (Pupil Book pp. 56–57)

Mon identité 3

Learning objectives
- Talking about last weekend
- Using the perfect tense

Framework objectives
4.5/Y8 Language – (a) range of verb tenses (perfect tense)
5.3 Strategies – English/other languages

FCSE links
Unit 1: Meeting people (Personal information; Family members; Sports and hobbies)
Unit 6: Leisure (Sports/hobbies)
Unit 11: Media (Free time activities)

Grammar
- the perfect tense

Key language
Le weekend dernier …
je suis allé(e) au stade
je suis allé(e) au parc
je suis allé(e) au café
je suis allé(e) en ville
je suis allé(e) à un concert
je suis allé(e) à la piscine
je suis allé(e) à Paris
je suis allé(e) à la discothèque
j'ai mangé des frites
j'ai écouté de la musique
j'ai regardé un match de foot
j'ai dansé
j'ai joué au tennis
j'ai visité le musée du Louvre
j'ai acheté un jean
j'ai nagé

PLTS
S Self-managers

Cross-curricular
ICT: word-processing; creating a blog

Resources
CD 2, tracks 12–13
Cahier d'exercices Vert, page 27
ActiveTeach
p.056 Grammar
p.056 Grammar practice
p.056 Grammar practice
p.057 Class activity
p.057 Grammar skills

Starter 1
Aim
To practise reading for gist

Give pupils one minute to skim-read the text in exercise 1 and identify what each paragraph is about.

Hear answers. (Answers: **1** Clarisse describes herself and her brother, Rémy; **2** what Clarisse did last night; **3** what Clarisse did last weekend.) Point out the importance of identifying time phrases to help grasp what a text is about. Ask the class to identify the time phrases in paragraphs 2 and 3 and which tense they're used with (*hier soir, le weekend dernier* – perfect tense).

1 Écoute et lis le texte. (AT 1.5)
Listening. Pupils listen to Clarisse and read the text at the same time. Some vocabulary is glossed for support.

Draw pupils' attention to the tip box on the importance of checking accents.

Audioscript CD 2 track 12

Salut! Je m'appelle Clarisse et j'habite à Fontainebleau. Je suis drôle et intelligente et je suis fan de foot! Le foot, c'est ma passion. Mon équipe, c'est le PSG. Mon frère Rémy est très sympa. En général, on s'entend bien et normalement, on regarde les matchs de foot ensemble.

Hier soir, j'ai regardé un match de foot international à la télé. J'ai mangé du popcorn, comme d'hab.

Le weekend dernier, je suis allée au Parc des Princes où j'ai regardé le PSG contre Auxerre. J'ai aimé le match parce qu'il y a eu deux pénalties. Après le match, je suis allée au café où j'ai mangé un sandwich.

2 Relis le texte et mets les images dans le bon ordre. (AT 3.5)
Reading. Pupils read the text in exercise 1 again and put the pictures in the order they're mentioned in the text.

Answers
c, b, a, e, d

3 Trouve l'équivalent des expressions en anglais dans le texte. (AT 3.4)
Reading. Pupils find in the text the French for the English phrases given.

Answers
1 j'ai regardé 2 je suis allé 3 j'ai mangé
4 j'ai aimé

3 Mon identité 5 Le weekend dernier

4 En tandem. Lis le texte à voix haute. Commente la prononciation de ton/ta camarade. (AT 2.5)

Speaking. In pairs: pupils read the text aloud and comment on their partner's pronunciation.

> Use the pronunciation box to review and practise the pronunciation of –é at the end of the past participle.

Studio Grammaire: the perfect tense

Use the *Studio Grammaire* box to cover the perfect tense of regular –er verbs (*je* form) and of *aller* (*je* form). There is more information and further practice on Pupil Book p. 63.

Pupils write three sentences saying what they did last weekend.

Starter 2
Aim
To practise using the correct tense

Write up the following, omitting the underlines. Give pupils ten minutes to write out the text, choosing from the two options given each time.

Hier soir, je regarde/j'ai regardé un match de foot. J'aime/Je suis aimé beaucoup le foot. Le weekend dernier, je joue/j'ai joué au foot avec mes amis. C'est/C'était génial! En général, on joue/on a joué au parc. Après le match, j'ai allé/je suis allé chez mon copain.

Alternative Starter 2:
Use the ActiveTeach p.056 Grammar practice activities to practise the perfect tense with *être*.

5 Écoute et choisis la bonne réponse pour Lucas. (AT 1.5)

Listening. Pupils listen to Lucas and complete the sentences by choosing the correct option from the two given each time.

Audioscript CD 2 track 13

Coucou! Je m'appelle Lucas et je suis fan de musique. J'écoute un petit peu de tout, du R'n'B, du rap, du pop-rock, un peu de reggae, mais je n'aime pas beaucoup le jazz.

Hier soir, j'ai regardé une émission de musique à la télé. C'était pas mal.

Ensuite, j'ai téléchargé le nouvel album de Usher.

Le weekend dernier, je suis allé à Paris Bercy où j'ai vu un concert. J'ai chanté et j'ai dansé. C'était top.

Après le concert, je suis allé au restaurant où j'ai mangé une pizza.

Answers
1 musique 2 musique 3 Usher 4 un concert
5 chanté et j'ai dansé 6 une pizza

6 Trouve la fin de chaque phrase. Écris des phrases complètes. (AT 3.4)

Reading. Pupils match each of the sentence openings with the correct ending, then write out the complete sentences.

Answers
Le weekend dernier, ...
1 **c** je suis allé au stade où j'ai regardé un match de foot.
2 **e** je suis allé au parc où j'ai joué au tennis.
3 **a** je suis allé au café où j'ai mangé des frites.
4 **g** je suis allé en ville où j'ai acheté un jean.
5 **b** je suis allé à un concert où j'ai écouté de la musique.
6 **h** je suis allé à la piscine où j'ai nagé.
7 **f** je suis allé à Paris où j'ai visité le musée du Louvre.
8 **d** je suis allé à la discothèque où j'ai dansé.

7 En tandem. Joue au 'bip' avec ton/ta camarade. (AT 2.4)

Speaking. In pairs: pupils play 'Bip'. One pupil reads out a sentence from exercise 6, replacing a phrase with the word 'bip'; the other pupil identifies the missing phrase. They then swap roles. A sample exchange is given.

8 Écris ton blog. Présente-toi et décris ton weekend. (AT 4.5)

Writing. Pupils write a blog, introducing themselves and describing their weekend. A list of points to cover is supplied. A framework is also given for support. This could be done on computer, to help pupils produce a second draft more easily, and/or could form part of a real class blog.

5 Le weekend dernier Mon identité 3

PLTS S

Read together through *Stratégie 3* on Pupil Book p. 65, covering *faux amis*. Ask pupils to come up with a learning strategy that will help them identify and learn words like this and cognates. Cover (for example) keeping separate lists in a vocabulary notebook, writing them in different colours, coming up with links to remember *faux amis* ('A porter wears a uniform'), etc.

Plenary

Ask the class to summarise how the perfect tense is formed.

Then tell pupils what your passion is, including sentences in the present and perfect tenses, e.g. *Ma passion, c'est jouer au tennis. Je joue tout le temps au tennis. Le weekend dernier, j'ai joué au tennis.* Give pupils two minutes to write out a short text like this about their own passion. (You can write the model up for support if necessary.) Hear answers, asking the rest of the class to give constructive feedback each time.

Workbook, page 27

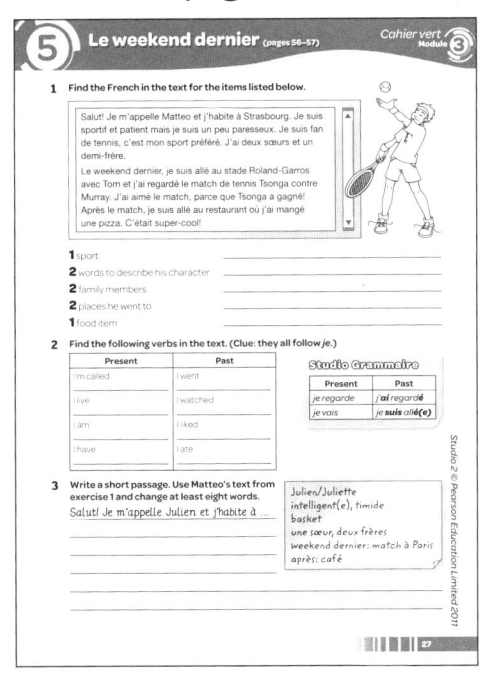

Answers

1 1 sport: tennis
   2 words to describe his character: (any two from:) sportif, patient, paresseux
   2 family members: sœurs, demi-frère
   2 places he went to: stade (Roland-Garros), restaurant
   1 food item: pizza

2

Present	Past
I'm called je m'appelle	I went je suis allé
I live j'habite	I watched j'ai regardé
I am je suis	I liked j'ai aimé
I have j'ai	I ate j'ai mangé

3 (Possible answer:)
Salut! Je m'appelle Julien/Juliette et j'habite à Paris. Je suis sportif(-ve) et intelligent(e) mais je suis un peu timide. Je suis fan de basket, c'est mon sport préféré. J'ai une sœur et deux frères.

Le weekend dernier, je suis allé(e) à Paris et j'ai regardé un match de basket. J'ai aimé le match parce que mon équipe a gagné! Après le match, je suis allé(e) au café où j'ai mangé un sandwich. C'était super-cool!

3 Mon identité 5 Le weekend dernier

Worksheet 3.6 Using more than one tense

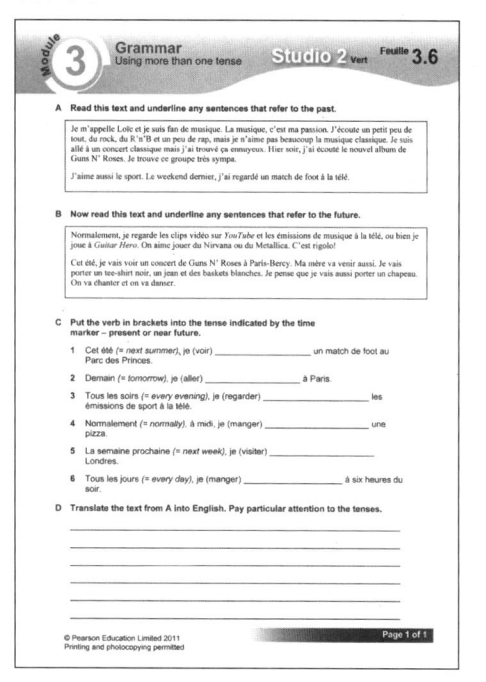

Answers

A Je m'appelle Loïc et je suis fan de musique. La musique, c'est ma passion. J'écoute un petit peu de tout, du rock, du R'n'B et un peu de rap, mais je n'aime pas beaucoup la musique classique. <u>Je suis allé à un concert classique mais j'ai trouvé ça ennuyeux. Hier soir, j'ai écouté le nouvel album de Guns N' Roses.</u> Je trouve ce groupe très sympa.

J'aime aussi le sport. <u>Le weekend dernier, j'ai regardé un match de foot à la télé.</u>

B Normalement, je regarde les clips vidéo sur *YouTube* et les émissions de musique à la télé, ou bien je joue à *Guitar Hero*. On aime jouer du Nirvana ou du Metallica. C'est rigolo!
<u>Cet été, je vais voir un concert de Guns N' Roses à Paris-Bercy. Ma mère va venir aussi. Je vais porter un tee-shirt noir, un jean et des baskets blanches. Je pense que je vais aussi porter un chapeau. On va chanter et on va danser.</u>

C 1 Cet été, je vais voir un match de foot au Parc des Princes.
   2 Demain, je vais aller à Paris.
   3 Tous les soirs, je regarde les émissions de sport à la télé.
   4 Normalement, à midi, je mange une pizza.
   5 La semaine prochaine, je vais visiter Londres.
   6 Tous les jours, je mange à six heures du soir.

D My name is Loïc and I'm a music fan. I'm passionate about music. I listen to a little bit of everything, rock, R'n'B and a bit of rap, but I don't like classical music much. <u>I went to a classical concert but I found it boring. Yesterday evening, I listened to the new Guns N' Roses album.</u> I think that band is really good.
I also like sport. <u>Last weekend I watched a football match on TV.</u>

3 Bilan et Révisions (Pupil Book pp. 58–59)

Bilan
Pupils use this checklist to review language covered in the module, working on it in pairs in class or on their own at home. Encourage them to follow up any areas of weakness they identify. There are Target Setting Sheets included in the Assessment Pack, and an opportunity for pupils to record their own levels and targets on the *J'avance* pages in the Workbook, p. 32. You can also use the *Bilan* checklist as an end-of-module plenary option.

Révisions
These revision exercises can be used for assessment purposes or for pupils to practise before tackling the assessment tasks in the Assessment Pack.

Resources
CD 2, track 14
Cahier d'exercices Vert, pages 28 & 29

1 Écoute. C'est vrai (✓) ou faux (✗)? (1–6) (AT 1.3)
Listening. Pupils listen to the six descriptions and then note whether the sentences in French about them are true (writing ✓) or false (writing ✗).

Audioscript CD 2 track 14

1 – Décris ton caractère, Yara.
   – Je suis un peu paresseuse.
2 – Décris ton caractère, Yoni.
   – Je suis un peu timide.
3 – Décris ton caractère, Malika.
   – Je suis très intelligente et je suis aussi assez sympa.
4 – Décris ton caractère, Antoine.
   – Je suis très sportif et je suis aussi assez intelligent.
5 – Décris ton caractère, Dimitri.
   – Je suis très drôle et je suis aussi assez patient.
6 – Décris ton caractère, Morgane.
   – Je suis un peu paresseuse, mais je ne suis pas pénible.

Answers
1 ✓ 2 ✗ 3 ✓ 4 ✓ 5 ✗ 6 ✗

2 En tandem. Fais des dialogues. Utilise les images. (AT 2.5)
Speaking. In pairs: pupils make up dialogues, using the framework + picture prompts supplied. The questions and sample answer openings are given.

Answers
1 Ce weekend, je vais **faire du bowling**, alors, je vais porter **un tee-shirt rouge, un pantalon vert kaki et une veste bleue**.
2 Ce weekend, je vais **jouer au babyfoot**, alors, je vais porter **une jupe verte et blanche, un sweat à capuche jaune et des chaussures de skate**.
3 Ce weekend, je vais **faire une promenade en barque**, alors, je vais porter **un jean, un pull vert et des baskets blanches**.
4 Ce weekend, je vais **aller au parc d'attractions**, alors, je vais porter **une chemise bleue, un pantalon beige et des bottes noires**.

3 Lis l'e-mail de Jordy et choisis la bonne réponse. (AT 3.4)
Reading. Pupils read Jordy's email and complete the sentences summarising it, choosing the correct option from the two given each time.

Answers
1 Jordy **n'aime pas** la musique classique.
2 Jordy joue **de la guitare**.
3 Frank **joue dans le groupe** avec Jordy.
4 Frank est **sympa**.
5 Jordy **s'entend bien** avec son frère.

4 Écris un paragraphe sur ton meilleur ami/ta meilleure amie. (AT 4.4)
Writing. Pupils write a paragraph about their best friend. A list of features to include and a framework are supplied.

3 Mon identité — Bilan et Révisions

Workbook, pages 28 and 29

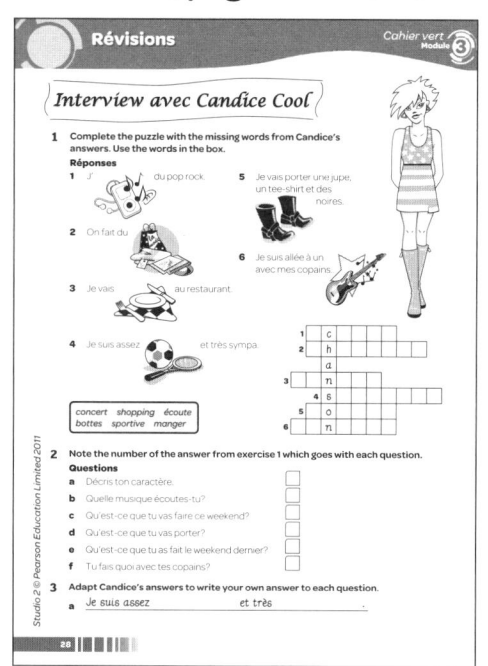

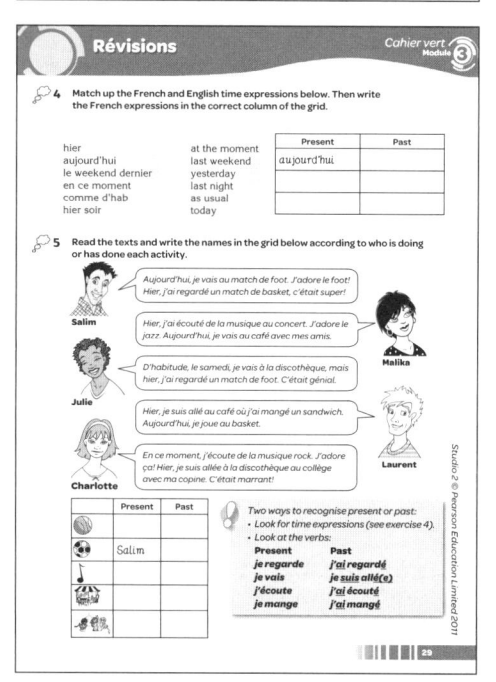

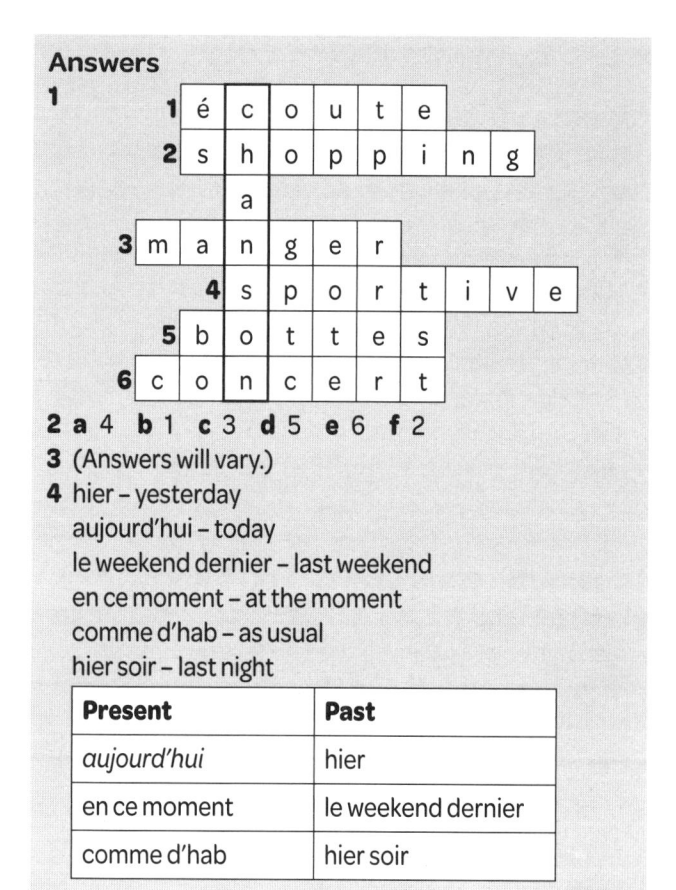

Answers

1

	1	2	3	4	5	6	7
1	é	c	o	u	t	e	
2	s	h	o	p	p	i	n g
		a					
3	m	a	n	g	e	r	
4		s	p	o	r	t	i v e
5	b	o	t	t	e	s	
6	c	o	n	c	e	r	t

2 a 4 b 1 c 3 d 5 e 6 f 2

3 (Answers will vary.)

4 hier – yesterday
aujourd'hui – today
le weekend dernier – last weekend
en ce moment – at the moment
comme d'hab – as usual
hier soir – last night

Present	Past
aujourd'hui	hier
en ce moment	le weekend dernier
comme d'hab	hier soir

5

	Present	Past
basketball	Laurent	Salim
football	Salim	Julie
music	Charlotte	Malika
café	Malika	Laurent
disco	Julie	Charlotte

En plus: L'identité régionale
(Pupil Book pp. 60–61)

Mon identité 3

Learning objectives
- Talking about different regions in France

Framework objectives
3.2/Y8 Culture – (b) customs/traditions
5.4 Strategies – working out meaning
5.8 Strategies – evaluating and improving

FCSE links
Unit 4: Holidays (Holiday destinations; Literature about places to visit)
Unit 7: Celebrations (Celebrations/festivals in target language country)
Unit 10: Region and environment (Description and location of area; Facilities and activities within an area)

Key language
... *est situé dans* ...
On parle ...
Le plat typique, c'est ...
... *est un événement traditionnel*
Le symbole de la région, c'est ...

PLTS
R Reflective learners

Cross-curricular
ICT: internet research

Resources
CD 2, track 15
ActiveTeach
p.061 Assignment 3
p.061 Assignment 3: prep

Starter
Aim
To use reading strategies

Give pupils one minute to work out what the texts in exercise 1 are about.

Check answers. Ask pupils what reading strategies they used to work out new language, covering cognates, context, use of pictures. Remind pupils how useful such strategies are in tackling more challenging texts.

1 Écoute et lis les textes. (AT 1.4)
Listening. Pupils listen to the descriptions of Alsace and Brittany, reading the text at the same time.

Audioscript CD 2 track 15

– L'Alsace est située dans le nord-est de la France.
  En Alsace, on parle l'alsacien.
  Le plat typique, c'est la choucroute.
  Un événement traditionnel alsacien, c'est les marchés de Noël. C'est joli. On peut acheter des cadeaux ou des décorations.
  Le symbole de la région, c'est la cigogne.

– La Bretagne est située dans l'ouest de la France.
  En Bretagne, on parle le breton.
  Les plats typiques, ce sont les crêpes et les galettes. Miam-miam!
  En Bretagne, un événement traditionnel, c'est le fest-noz. C'est une sorte de soirée dansante.
  Le symbole de la région, c'est l'hermine.

2 Copie et remplis les cartes d'identité en anglais. (AT 3.4)
Reading. Pupils copy out the identity cards. They read the texts in exercise 1 again, then complete the cards with the details in English.

Answers
A L'Alsace
  Location: *north-east France*
  Language: *Alsatian*
  Typical dish: *sauerkraut*
  Traditional event: *Christmas markets*
  Symbol of the region: *stork*
B La Bretagne
  Location: *west France*
  Language: *Breton*
  Typical dish: *pancakes (crêpes and galettes)*
  Traditional event: *fest-noz, a sort of dance*
  Symbol of the region: *ermine*

3 Lis le texte et complète les phrases en anglais. (AT 3.5)
Reading. Pupils read the text and complete the sentences summarising it in English. *Dommage!* is glossed for support. Draw pupils' attention to the tip box on using the information in the questions to help work out the answers.

Answers
1 December **2** bought decorations and presents for her family **3** sauerkraut **4** lots of things **5** any storks

3 Mon identité   En plus: L'identité régionale

4 En tandem. A choisit le Pays basque, B choisit la Haute-Savoie. Prépare un exposé oral. (AT 2.4)

Speaking. In pairs: pupil A prepares a presentation on the Pays basque; pupil B prepares a presentation on Haute-Savoie using the framework and prompts supplied. Draw their attention to the tip box on learning a presentation by making notes on prompt cards.

When they have finished, pupils assess each other's work, using the guidelines supplied.

> **Answers**
> A Le Pays basque est situé dans **le sud-ouest de la France**.
>   Au Pays basque, on parle **le basque**.
>   Le plat typique, c'est **la piperade**.
>   Au Pays basque, **la corrida** est un événement traditionnel.
>   Le symbole de la région, c'est **la croix basque**.
> B La Haute-Savoie est située dans **l'est de la France**.
>   En Haute-Savoie, on parle **le savoyard**.
>   Le plat typique, c'est **la fondue savoyarde**.
>   En Haute-Savoie, **le feu d'artifice du quinze août** est un événement traditionnel.
>   Le symbole de la région, c'est **le blason savoyard**.

Pupils choose their own region of France and do research, using books, brochures or the internet, to help them prepare their presentation.

5 Écris ta présentation sur le Pays basque ou la Haute-Savoie. (AT 4.4)

PLTS R

Writing. Pupils write out their oral presentation from exercise 4. A list of features to check is supplied. Pupils then identify two areas in which they could improve, e.g. tense formation, vocabulary, adjective agreement, etc.

> **Plenary**
> Make statements at random about the three French regions covered in the unit: Alsace, Brittany, the Pays basque and Haute-Savoie, e.g. *le plat typique est la galette* (Brittany).
>
> Pupils compete to be the first to identify the region correctly.

Worksheet 3.7 Ta passion, c'est quoi?

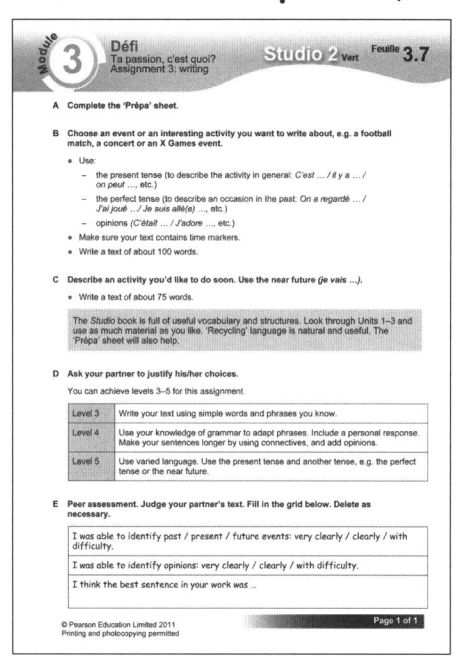

> **Answers**
> Assessed by teacher.

Worksheet 3.8 Ta passion, c'est quoi? Prépa

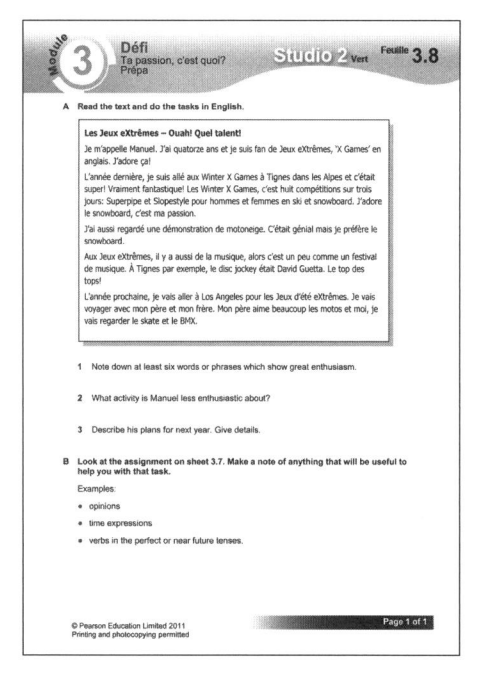

> **Answers**
> A 1 j'adore / c'était super / vraiment fantastique / c'est ma passion / le top des tops / c'était génial
>   2 "motoneige" = snowmobile
>   3 He's going to go to Los Angeles for the summer X Games. He'll go with his father and brother. His father likes motorbikes and he's going to watch skateboarding and BMX.
> B (Answers will vary.)

Studio Grammaire (Pupil Book pp. 62–63)

Mon identité 3

The *Studio Grammaire* section provides a more detailed summary of the key grammar covered in the module, along with further exercises to practise these points. The activities on ActiveTeach pages 62 and 63 are repeated from elsewhere in the module.

Grammar topics
- adjectives
- possessive adjectives
- the near future tense
- the perfect tense with *avoir*
- the perfect tense with *être*

Adjectives

1 Unjumble the adjectives and copy out the phrases.
Pupils unjumble the anagram versions of the colours and write out the complete phrases.

Answers
1 une jupe **bleue**   2 un tee-shirt **vert**
3 une veste **jaune**   4 un jean **blanc**
5 des bottes **noires**   6 des baskets **blanches**

2 Choose the correct adjective to complete each sentence.
Pupils complete the sentences by choosing the correct option from the two given each time.

Answers
1 Il est **sportif**.
2 Elle est **patiente**.
3 Il est **intelligent**.
4 Elle est **sympa**.
5 Il est **paresseux**.

3 Write the correct form of the adjectives in brackets.
Pupils write out the correct form of the adjectives shown in brackets, making sure that it agrees in gender and number each time.

Answers
1 noire   2 bleu   3 verte   4 blanches
5 intelligente   6 bleue   7 rose   8 marron

4 Write your own rule to explain how adjectives work.
Pupils write an explanation of how adjectives agree.

Possessive adjectives

5 Choose the correct possessive adjective, then translate the sentences into English.
Pupils complete the sentences by choosing the correct option from the two given each time. They then translate the sentences into English.

Answers
1 **Mon** meilleur ami est sympa. – My best friend is nice.
2 **Ma** meilleure amie est intelligente. – My best friend is intelligent.
3 **Mon** frère s'appelle Alex. – My brother is called Alex.
4 **Ma** sœur est paresseuse. – My sister is lazy.
5 Comment s'appelle **ta** sœur? – What is your sister called?
6 Avec **mes** copains, on regarde des DVD. – I watch DVDs with my mates.

The near future tense

6 Choose the correct form of the near future tense to fill in the gaps.
Pupils complete the text by choosing the correct form of the near future tense verb from the two options given each time.

Answers
1 je vais faire   2 je vais manger   3 je vais aller
4 Je vais porter   5 tu vas faire

7 Unjumble these sentences and write them out.
Pupils write out the jumbled sentences in the correct order.

Answers
1 Qu'est-ce que tu vas faire, ce weekend?
2 Ce weekend, je vais manger au restaurant.
3 Ce weekend, je vais faire du camping.
4 Qu'est-ce que tu vas porter?
5 Ce weekend, je vais porter un jean.
6 Ce weekend, je vais faire de la rando, alors, je vais porter un short.

101

3 Mon identité   Studio Grammaire

The perfect tense with *avoir*

8 Which three sentences are correct? Correct the two sentences that are wrong.

Pupils identify the three correct sentences and correct the two that have errors in the perfect tense.

> **Answers**
> **Correct:** 1, 4, 5
> **Corrected sentences:**
> 2 J'ai **regardé** des DVD.
> 3 **J'ai** joué au volley avec mes copains.

The perfect tense with *être*

9 Find the five sentences in this word snake.

Pupils write out the five sentences contained in the word snake.

> **Answers**
> Hier soir, je suis allé en ville.
> Le weekend dernier, je suis allé au parc.
> Ensuite, je suis allé au cinéma.
> Puis je suis allé au restaurant.
> Finalement, je suis allé au lit.

10 Translate these sentences into French.

Pupils translate the sentences into French using the perfect tense.

> **Answers**
> 1 J'ai mangé une pizza.
> 2 Je suis allé(e) en ville.
> 3 J'ai regardé un film.
> 4 J'ai joué au ping-pong.
> 5 Je suis allé(e) au cinéma.

3 À toi (Pupil Book pp. 118–119)

Self-access reading and writing

A Reinforcement

1 Associe les phrases aux dessins. (AT 3.2)
Reading. Pupils match the phrases with the pictures.

Answers
1 a 2 h 3 l 4 c 5 e 6 m 7 d 8 i 9 o
10 f 11 g 12 b 13 j 14 k 15 n

2 Écris les phrases. (AT 4.4)
Writing. Using the example as a model, pupils write out the sentences formed by replacing the letters of the pictures from exercise 1 with the correct expressions.

Answers
1 Ce weekend, je vais **jouer au foot**, alors, je vais porter **un short orange** et **un tee-shirt bleu** avec **des baskets**.
2 Ce weekend, je vais **faire du camping**, alors, je vais porter **un jean** et **un pull bleu** avec **des baskets**.
3 Ce weekend, je vais **aller au cinéma**, alors, je vais porter **un pantalon beige** et **un sweat à capuche noir** avec **des bottes noires**.
4 Ce weekend, je vais **manger au restaurant**, alors, je vais porter **une chemise blanche** et **un jean** avec **des bottes noires**.
5 Ce weekend, je vais **faire de la rando**, alors, je vais porter **un tee-shirt bleu** et **un sweat à capuche noir** avec **des baskets**.
6 Ce weekend, je vais **aller à un concert**, alors, je vais porter **une chemise blanche** et **un jean** avec **des bottes noires**.

3 Lis les textes. Copie et remplis le tableau. (AT 3.4)
Reading. Pupils copy out the table. They read the texts and complete the table with the details in English.

Answers

	artist	opinion	other details
Quentin	Lily Allen	doesn't like her music, it's rubbish	likes heavy metal
Guillaume	Katy Perry	likes her music a lot	loves the words and the tunes
Gabrielle	Diam's	is a fan	loves the song *Ma France à moi* (likes the words), likes her look, thinks she's nice and intelligent
	Michael Bublé	doesn't like his music, he's rubbish	sister loves his music, Gabrielle doesn't like the words

B Extension

1 Lis le texte. Mets les titres en anglais dans l'ordre du texte. (AT 3.5)
Reading. Pupils read the text, then list the English titles in the order they are mentioned. *par moments* is glossed for support.

Answers
e, d, a, b, f, c

2 Copie et remplis la carte d'identité pour Mila. (AT 3.4)
Reading. Pupils read the text in exercise 1 again. They then copy and complete the identity card for Mila, in French.

Answers

Prénom: Mila
Âge: 14
Habite: Paris
Caractère: intelligente, sympa, drôle, patiente
Meilleure amie: Chloé (drôle, un peu pénible)
Activité préférée quand il fait beau: aller en ville, faire du shopping
Chanteuse préférée: Lady Gaga

3 Écris un paragraphe pour Yvan. (AT 4.4)
Writing. Using the information on the identity card, pupils write a paragraph about Yvan.

Module 4: Chez moi, chez toi
(Pupil Book pp. 66–85)

Unit & Learning objectives	PoS* & Framework objectives	Key language	Grammar and other language features
1 Là où j'habite (pp. 68–69) Saying where you would like to live Using *j'habite* and *je voudrais habiter*	**2.1e** use reference materials **2.2d** pronunciation and intonation **2.2e** ask and answer questions **2.2g** write clearly and coherently **2.4/Y8** Writing – (a) using text as stimulus **4.5/Y8** Language – (b) range of modal verbs	*J'habite dans … une grande maison un petit appartement une grande ville un petit village* etc. *Je voudrais habiter … à la campagne au bord de la mer dans un vieux château* etc.	**G** *j'habite* and *je voudrais habiter* – pronunciation: –*ieu*– and –*ieil*–
2 Dans mon appart' (pp. 70–71) Describing your home Using prepositions	**2.1a** identify patterns **1.1/Y8** Listening – understanding on first hearing	*Chez moi, il y a … (six) pièces le salon, la cuisine,* etc. *Il n'y a pas de (jardin). dans, devant, derrière, sous, sur le bureau, la machine à laver* etc.	**G** *il y a/il n'y a pas* **G** prepositions
3 À table, tout le monde! (pp. 72–73) Talking about meals Using *du, de la, de l', des*	**2.2b** skim and scan **4.4/Y8** Language – developing sentences **5.4** Strategies – working out meaning	*Pour le petit déjeuner, je prends … du beurre, de la confiture, des céréales,* etc. *Je ne mange rien. D'habitude, on mange … du poisson, de la pizza, des pâtes,* etc. *Le soir, on mange à (six heures).*	**G** the partitive article – developing reading skills: cognates
4 C'est la Chandeleur! (pp. 74–75) Discussing what food to buy Using *il faut* + infinitive	**2.1d** use previous knowledge **1.3/Y8** Listening – (a) understanding language for specific functions **1.3/Y8** Speaking – (b) using language for specific functions	*il faut acheter … un litre de lait un paquet de farine (quatre) tranches de jambon un kilo de bananes six œufs* etc.	**G** *il faut* + infinitive **G** *de* after quantities

Chez moi, chez toi 4

Unit & Learning objectives	PoS* & Framework objectives	Key language	Grammar and other language features
5 Je vais aller au carnaval! (pp. 76–77) Talking about a forthcoming event More practice with the near future	**2.1e** use reference materials **2.2d** use correct pronunciation **2.2k** deal with unfamiliar language **4.5/Y8** Language – (a) range of verb tenses (near future tense) **5.2** Strategies – memorising **5.5** Strategies – reference materials	*je vais …/on va … aller au carnaval boire un coca manger au restaurant participer au défilé porter un costume de (pirate)* etc. *Je vais m'amuser.* etc.	**G** the near future tense – pronunciation: *–qu–* – developing writing skills: using a dictionary
Bilan et Révisions (pp. 78–79) Pupils' checklist and practice exercises			
En plus: Mon chez moi (pp. 80–81) Talking about where you live	**2.2/Y8** Reading – (a) longer, more complex texts **2.4/Y8** Writing – (b) organising paragraphs **3.2/Y8** Culture – (b) customs/ traditions **5.7** Strategies – planning and preparing **5.8** Strategies – evaluating and improving	Review of language from the module	– developing listening skills: predicting – developing writing skills: creating and using a checklist
Studio Grammaire (pp. 82–83) Detailed grammar summary and practice exercises			**G** *je mange* or *je voudrais manger?* **G** the partitive article **G** *prendre* (singular, including *on*) **G** *il faut* + infinitive **G** the near future tense
À toi (pp. 120–121) Self-access reading and writing at two levels			

* In addition, the following Programmes of Study are covered throughout the module: 1.1–1.4, 2.2a, 2.2c, 2.2d, 3a, 3c, 3d, 3e, 3f, 4a, 4b, 4d, 4e, 4f, 4g. PoS 4c is covered in all Units 4 & 5 and *En plus* sections. See pp. 7–9 for details.

4 1 Là où j'habite (Pupil Book pp. 68–69)

chez moi, chez toi

Learning objectives
- Saying where you would like to live
- Using *j'habite* and *je voudrais habiter*

Framework objectives
2.4/Y8 Writing – (a) using text as stimulus
4.5/Y8 Language – (b) range of modal verbs

FCSE links
Unit 2: Home life (Types of accommodation)
Unit 10: Region and environment (Description and location of home; Opinions on different houses)

Grammar
- *j'habite* and *je voudrais habiter*

Key language
J'habite dans …
une grande maison
une petite maison
un grand appartement
un petit appartement
une grande ville
une petite ville
un grand village
un petit village
Je voudrais habiter …
à la campagne
à la montagne
au bord de la mer
dans un vieux château
dans une vieille chaumière
dans une ferme

PLTS
C Creative thinkers

Cross-curricular
English: adjectives

Resources
CD 2, tracks 16–17
Cahier d'exercices Vert, page 33
ActiveTeach
p.068 Flashcards
p.068 Grammar
p.068 Grammar practice
p.069 Learning skills
p.069 Thinking skills

Starter 1

PLTS C

Aim
To focus on the position of adjectives

Write up the following. Give pupils three minutes to translate the phrases into English and to identify which two adjectives behave differently from the others.

un pull rouge	*un film ennuyeux*
un grand sac	*une BD passionnante*
un garçon drôle	*une petite voiture*
des lunettes de soleil moches	*une chanteuse nulle*

Check answers. Ask pupils if they can come up with a rule on the position of adjectives, based on the examples here (adjectives usually come after the noun, not before the noun as in English). Which two adjectives don't follow this rule? (*grand* and *petite* – they come before, not after the noun)

Ask pupils if they remember any other adjectives they saw in Module 2 which come before the noun (*beau – un beau garçon; joli – une jolie fille*).

1 Écoute. C'est qui? (1–6) (AT 1.2)
Listening. Pupils listen to six people talking about where they live. They identify each speaker using the text and pictures.

Audioscript CD 2 track 16

1 – Où habites-tu?
– J'habite dans une grande maison.
2 – Où habites-tu?
– J'habite dans une petite maison.
3 – Où habites-tu?
– J'habite dans un petit appartement.
4 – Et toi? Où habites-tu?
– J'habite dans un grand appartement.
5 – Où habites-tu?
– J'habite dans une grande ville.
6 – Et toi? Où habites-tu?
– J'habite dans un petit village.

Answers
1 *Éva* **2** Jamel **3** Mathieu **4** Cassandra
5 Malika **6** Tristan

2 Associe les images aux phrases. (AT 3.2)
Reading. Pupils match the sentences to the pictures. Some vocabulary is glossed for support.

Answers
1 b **2** c **3** f **4** a **5** e **6** d

1 Là où j'habite   Chez moi, chez toi   4

> **Studio Grammaire: *je voudrais* + infinitive**
> Use the *Studio Grammaire* box to cover *je voudrais* + infinitive. There is more information and further practice on Pupil Book p. 82.

3 Écoute et remplis le tableau en anglais. (1–5) (AT 1.3)

Listening. Pupils copy out the table. They listen to five people talking about where they would like to live and complete the table with the details in English.

Answers

	lives in ...	would like to live ...
1	a big house	in the mountains
2	a small flat	in an old castle
3	a small village	at the seaside
4	a small house	in a farm
5	a big town	in an old cottage/in the country

Pupils listen again and note the reasons given. Encourage them to use these reasons in exercises 4 and 5.

Audioscript CD 2 track 17

1. – Où habites-tu?
   – J'habite dans une grande maison.
   – Où voudrais-tu habiter?
   – Je voudrais habiter à la montagne.
   – À la montagne? Pourquoi?
   – Parce que j'aime faire du ski.

2. – Où habites-tu?
   – J'habite dans un petit appartement.
   – Où voudrais-tu habiter?
   – Je voudrais habiter dans un vieux château.
   – Dans un vieux château? Pourquoi?
   – Parce que j'adore les films d'horreur!

3. – Où habites-tu?
   – J'habite dans un petit village.
   – Où voudrais-tu habiter?
   – Je voudrais habiter au bord de la mer.
   – Au bord de la mer? Pourquoi?
   – Parce que j'aime nager dans la mer!

4. – Où habites-tu?
   – J'habite dans une petite maison.
   – Où voudrais-tu habiter?
   – Je voudrais habiter dans une ferme.
   – Dans une ferme? Pourquoi?
   – Parce que j'aime les animaux.

5. – Où habites-tu?
   – J'habite dans une grande ville.
   – Où voudrais-tu habiter?
   – Je voudrais habiter dans une vieille chaumière, à la campagne.
   – Dans une vieille chaumière, à la campagne? Pourquoi?
   – Parce que je préfère la campagne. C'est plus tranquille.

Starter 2
Aim
To practise *je voudrais* + infinitive; To review vocabulary about where you live

Write up the following: *Je voudrais habiter dans un petit village*. Give pupils three minutes to write three more sentences, using this one as a model, about where they would like to live.

Hear answers. Ask pupils to explain how *je voudrais* is used (it's followed by the infinitive). Ask what is unusual about the adjectives *petit*, *grand* and *vieux* (they come before the noun, not after it like other adjectives).

Alternative Starter 2:
Use ActiveTeach p.068 Grammar practice to practise *je voudrais* + infinitive.

4 En tandem. Fais des dialogues. Change les phrases soulignées. (AT 2.3–4)

Speaking. In pairs: pupils make up dialogues, changing the underlined phrases in the model dialogue.

Use the pronunciation box to review and practise the pronunciation of *–ieu–* and *–ieil–*.

5 Où habites-tu? Où voudrais-tu habiter? Utilise le texte comme modèle. (AT 4.4)

Writing. Pupils write a paragraph on where they live and where they'd like to live, adapting the model supplied.

107

4 Chez moi, chez toi   1 Là où j'habite

6 Lis les textes. C'est qui? Utilise le Mini-dictionnaire si nécessaire. (AT 3.4)
Reading. Pupils read the texts, using the Mini-dictionnaire if necessary, and identify the people being described. Pictures of the people are supplied for support.

Answers
1 the Queen 2 Harry Potter 3 Lisa Simpson
4 Shrek 5 Snow White

7 Choisis une célébrité ou un personnage. Écris des phrases pour décrire où il/elle habite. (AT 4.3–4)
Writing. Pupils choose a celebrity or a character and write sentences to describe where he/she lives.

8 Lis ta description à ton/ta camarade. Il/Elle devine qui c'est. (AT 2.3, AT 1.3)
Speaking. Pupils read their description from exercise 7 to a partner, who tries to work out who it is.

Plenary
Ask the class to summarise how and when *je voudrais* is used. Ask them then to talk about the position of adjectives (generally *after* the noun, but some key adjectives come *before* the noun, e.g. *petit, grand, vieux*).

Put the class into teams. Give them two minutes to write down, with Pupil Books closed, as many ways of finishing the sentence *Je voudrais habiter...* as they can. Tell them that there are 12 ways of finishing it in the unit.

Teams swap and check each other's answers, awarding two points for a completely correct answer and one for an answer with an error, e.g. an adjective in the wrong position. The team with the most points is the winner.

Workbook, page 33

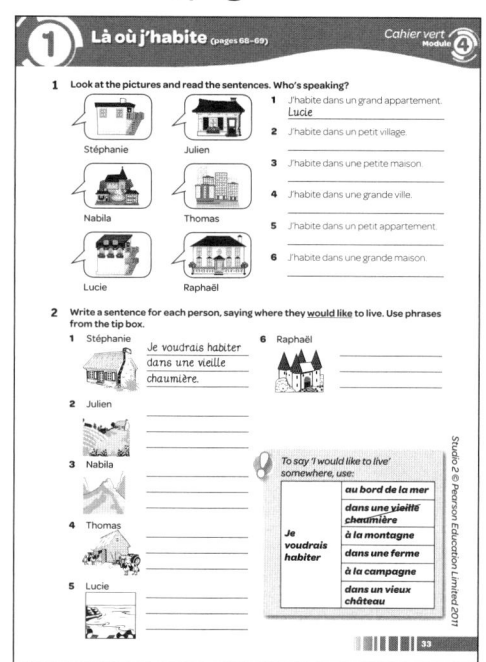

Answers
1 1 Lucie 2 Nabila 3 Julien 4 Thomas
   5 Stéphanie 6 Raphaël
2 1 *Je voudrais habiter dans une vieille chaumière.*
   2 Je voudrais habiter à la campagne.
   3 Je voudrais habiter à la montagne.
   4 Je voudrais habiter dans une ferme.
   5 Je voudrais habiter au bord de la mer.
   6 Je voudrais habiter dans un vieux château.

Worksheet 4.1 Looking up adjectives in a dictionary

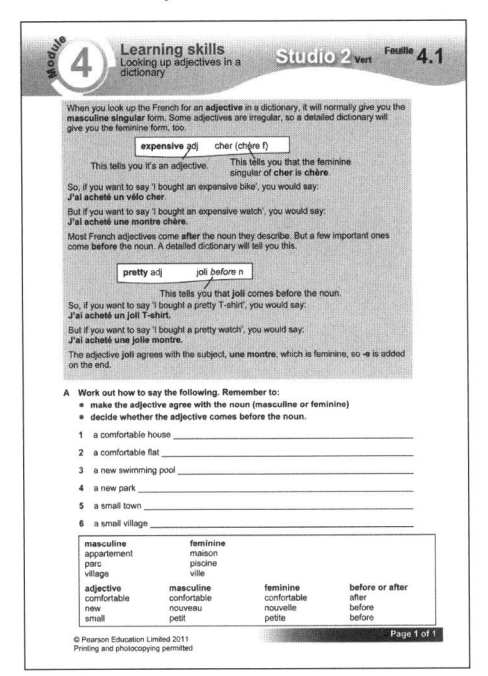

Answers

A
1. une maison confortable
2. un appartement confortable
3. une nouvelle piscine
4. un nouveau parc
5. une petite ville
6. un petit village

Worksheet 4.2 Making deductions

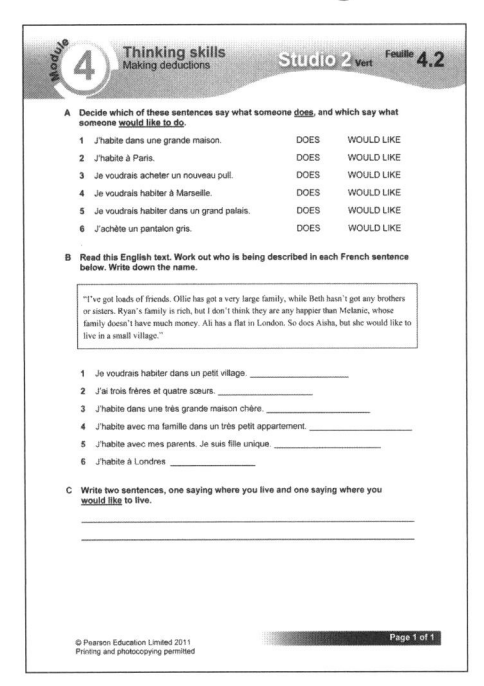

Answers

A
1. DOES
2. DOES
3. WOULD LIKE
4. WOULD LIKE
5. WOULD LIKE
6. DOES

B
1. Aisha
2. Ollie
3. Ryan
4. Melanie
5. Beth
6. Ali (or Aisha)

C (Answers will vary.)

chez moi, chez toi 4

2 Dans mon appart' (Pupil Book pp. 70–71)

Learning objectives
- Describing your home
- Using prepositions

Framework objectives
1.1/Y8 Listening – understanding on first hearing

FCSE links
Unit 2: Home life (Rooms in a house; Description of own room; Household equipment)
Unit 10: Region and environment (Description and location of home)

Grammar
- *il y a/il n'y a pas*
- prepositions

Key language
Chez moi, il y a…
(six) pièces
le salon, le jardin
la cuisine, la salle à manger
la salle de bains
ma chambre
la chambre de (mes parents/ ma sœur/mon frère)
Il n'y a pas de (jardin).
dans, devant, derrière, sous, sur
le bureau, le canapé
le lit, le frigo
l'armoire (f)
la chaise, la machine à laver
le lavabo
la douche, la fenêtre
la table, la télé-satellite

PLTS
I Independent enquirers

Cross-curricular
English: prepositions

Resources
CD 2, tracks 18–20
Cahier d'exercices Vert, page 34
ActiveTeach
p.070 Flashcards
p.070 Class activity
p.071 Flashcards
p.071 Grammar
p.071 Grammar practice
p.071 Video 7
p.071 Video worksheet 7
p.071 Thinking skills

Starter 1
Aim
To review *il y a* and *il n'y a pas (de)*

Write up the following. Ask what *il y a* and *il n'y a pas (de)* mean, to check comprehension. Pupils indicate whether each of the items listed in English is in their own home, writing *il y a* if it is and *il n'y a pas (de)* if it isn't.

il y a   *il n'y a pas (de)*

1 a kitchen
2 4 bedrooms
3 a garden
4 2 bathrooms
5 a dining room
6 a living room

Pupils check answers in pairs.

Alternative Starter 1:
Use ActiveTeach p.70 Flashcards to introduce rooms in a house.

1 Écoute et note les lettres dans le bon ordre. (1–9) (AT 1.2–3)
Listening. Pupils listen and note the letters of the rooms pictured in the order they are mentioned.

Audioscript CD 2 track 18

Salut! Je m'appelle Nadia. Chez moi, il y a sept pièces.

1 *Il y a la cuisine…*
2 *il y a le salon…*
3 *mais il n'y a pas de salle à manger.*
4 *Il y a quatre chambres. Il y a ma chambre…*
5 *la chambre de mes parents…*
6 *la chambre de mon frère…*
7 *et la chambre de ma petite sœur.*
8 *Il y a aussi la salle de bains.*
9 *Oh! Il y a aussi deux jardins. Il y a un petit jardin devant l'appartement et un grand jardin derrière l'appartement.*

Et toi? C'est comment, chez toi?

Answers
1 d 2 a 3 e 4 i 5 g 6 h 7 f 8 c 9 b

Studio Grammaire: *il y a/il n'y a pas de*
Use the *Studio Grammaire* box to cover *il y a/il n'y a pas de*. Point out that *il n'y a pas* is followed by *de* and the article (*le/la*) is dropped, e.g. *Il n'y a pas de salle à manger.*

2 Dans mon appart' Chez moi, chez toi 4

R Write up the following, jumbling the order of the words in each sentence. Pupils write out each sentence in the correct order.

Il n'y a pas de jardin.
Il y a la chambre de mes parents.
Il y a la salle de bains.
Il n'y a pas de salle à manger.

2 En tandem. Décris ton appartement imaginaire. Ajoute une pièce à la fois. (AT 2.2–3)

Speaking. In pairs: pupils list the rooms in an imaginary flat, taking it in turn to add one room at a time. A sample opening is given.

3 Écris une description de ta maison/ ton appartement idéal(e). (AT 4.3)

PLTS I

Writing. Pupils write a description of their ideal house/flat. A framework is supplied, along with a sample opening. Encourage pupils to include at least one detail not given, using a dictionary to look up language they don't know.

Starter 2
Aim
To review/introduce prepositions

Give pupils five minutes to copy out the prepositions in the *Studio Grammaire* box on p.71 and do a quick illustration for each one that will help them remember the meaning.

Alternative Starter 2:
Use ActiveTeach p.071 Flashcards to practise/ introduce prepositions.

4 Où est le tee-shirt? Écoute et mets les images dans le bon ordre. (1–7) (AT 1.3)

Listening. Pupils listen and put the pictures showing the T-shirt in different places in the order they are mentioned.

Audioscript CD 2 track 19

1 – *Maman! MA-MAN!*
 – *Oui!*
 – *Où est mon tee-shirt orange?*
 – *Ton tee-shirt orange? Il est dans l'armoire, non?*
 – *Non. Il n'est pas dans l'armoire!*
2 – *Il est sur la chaise, alors?*
 – *Non. Il n'est pas sur la chaise!*
3 – *Il est peut-être sous le lit?*
 – *Beurk! Qu'est-ce que c'est? Non! Il n'est pas sous le lit!*
4 – *Il est derrière le bureau, alors?*
 – *Derrière le bureau? Mais, non! Il n'est pas derrière le bureau.*
5 – *Mmm ... Il est peut-être dans la machine à laver?*
 – *Dans la machine à laver! Non! Il n'est pas dans la machine à laver!*
6 – *Alors, il est dans le frigo?*
 – *Dans le frigo! C'est marrant, ça. Non, maman, il n'est pas dans le frigo!*
7 – *Ah, voilà! Voilà ton tee-shirt!*
 – *Où ça?*
 – *Là! Devant le canapé.*
 – *Devant le canapé?*
 – *Oui. Devant le canapé ... et sous le chat!*
 – *Oh, non!!*

Answers
1 c 2 a 3 b 4 f 5 d 6 g 7 e

Studio Grammaire: prepositions
Use the *Studio Grammaire* box to cover prepositions.

R Use a soft toy and a box/a book as a prompt to practise prepositions.

5 En tandem. Joue avec ton/ta camarade! (AT 2.3)

Speaking. In pairs: pupils play *Où est mon tee-shirt?*, a variation on Battleships. They copy the playing card and choose three hiding places for their T-shirt by ticking three boxes. They take it in turn to try and guess one of their partner's hiding places. The first person to find all three is the winner.

6 Écoute et lis la chanson. (AT 1.4)

Listening. Pupils listen to the song, reading the text at the same time. Some vocabulary is glossed for support.

Audioscript CD 2 track 20

Quelle pagaille!
Refrain:
Aïe! Aïe! Aïe! Quelle pagaille!
Chez nous, c'est beaucoup trop petit.
Oh! Oh! Oh! Quel chaos!
Mais on aime bien habiter ici.

Dans ma chambre minuscule, j'ai un lit mezzanine,
Avec un bureau et une chaise sous mon lit.
Mais mon armoire est à côté, dans la cuisine.
C'est un peu embarrassant quand je m'habille!
(Refrain)

4 Chez moi, chez toi 2 Dans mon appart'

Dans la salle de bains, entre la douche et les toilettes,
Il y a l'antenne pour la télé-satellite.
Et la machine à laver est devant la fenêtre,
Sous le lavabo car la cuisine est trop petite!
(Refrain)

Dans le salon, il y a très peu de place
Pour nous sur notre petit canapé.
Je ne suis pas contente car le frigo est en face
Et je ne peux pas voir l'écran de la télé!
(Refrain)

7 Chante la chanson! (AT 2.3)
Speaking. Pupils listen to the song again, this time singing along.

Plenary
Review the prepositions covered in the unit. For each preposition, ask a pupil to demonstrate what it means at the front of the class, using a soft toy or other item and a box/book.

Give prompts in French consisting of a preposition + an item of furniture, for pupils to translate into English (e.g. *devant l'armoire*). Then move on to prompting in English for pupils to give preposition + furniture item in French.

Alternative Plenary:
Use ActiveTeach p.071 Grammar practice to review and practise prepositions.

Workbook, page 34

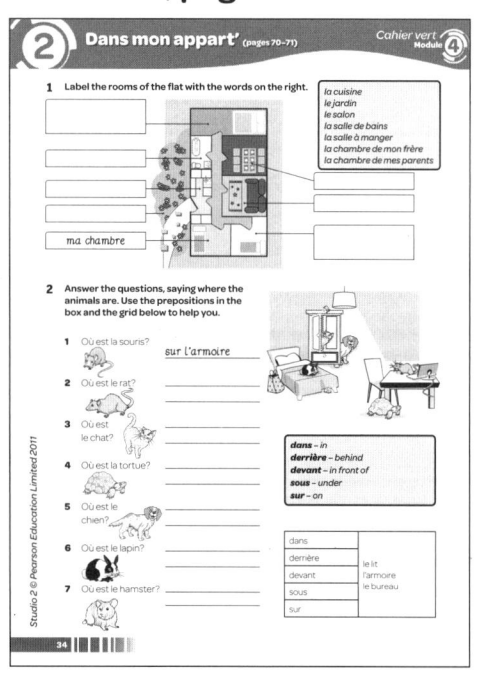

Answers
1. (Rooms labelled as follows:)
   la chambre de mes parents (double bedroom); la salle de bains (bathroom); la cuisine (kitchen); le jardin (garden); *ma chambre (single bedroom – as example)*; la salle à manger (dining room); le salon (living room); la chambre de mon frère (single bedroom)
2.
   1 sur l'armoire
   2 sur le bureau
   3 dans l'armoire
   4 devant le bureau
   5 derrière l'armoire
   6 sur le lit
   7 sous le lit

Worksheet 4.3 Truth and probability

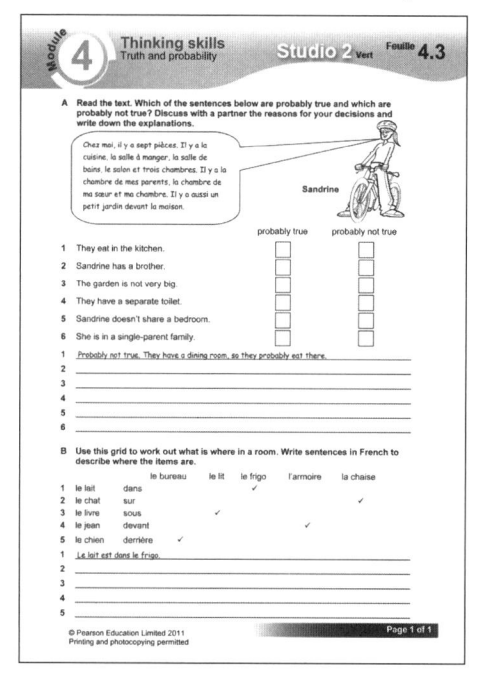

Answers
A 1 *Probably not true, as they have a dining room.*
   2 Probably not true, as she only mentions a sister.
   3 Probably true. She says it's small.
   4 Probably not true, as she lists all seven rooms and doesn't mention a toilet.
   5 Probably true, she mentions her room and her sister's room.
   6 Probably not true, as she mentions her parents.

B 1 *Le lait est dans le frigo.*
   2 Le chat est sur la chaise.
   3 Le livre est sous le lit.
   4 Le jean est devant l'armoire.
   5 Le chien est derrière le bureau.

2 Dans mon appart' **Chez moi, chez toi** **4**

Video

Episode 7: Où est le micro?
Samira, Hugo and Alex search all over Marielle's house for the microphone she has forgotten ... only to find out that Marielle has it in her bag at the studio. Video worksheet 7 can be used in conjunction with this episode.

> **Answers to video worksheet (ActiveTeach)**
> **1 A** (Answers will vary.)
>   **B** The problem is that they have lost the microphone. It turns out it was in Marielle's bag all along.
>   **C** Presumably he is filming it.
> **2 A** 'impossible' and 'casse-pieds'. Both are useful expressions to call someone who is a pain in the neck.
>   **B** Number 1.
>   **C** 'belle' (beautiful) and 'nouvelle' (new).
>   **D** It doesn't seem to be either, actually!
>   **E** Her brother's bedroom, her parents' bedroom and her bedroom.
>   **F** It's pink (*rose*) – her favourite colour.
>   **G** Yes, they find shoes, handbags and clothes (but not the microphone).
>   **H** Samira – issuing orders as usual.
>   **I** *Il n'y a pas de ...*
> **3 A** It might be in her wardrobe (*armoire*).
>   **B** *en face* – opposite
>   *dans* – in
>   *derrière* – behind
>   *à côté* – next to
>   *à droite* – on the right
>   **C** *armoire* – cupboard/wardrobe
>   *rez-de-chaussée* – ground floor
>   *salon* – living room
>   *canapé* – sofa
>   *lave-vaisselle* – dishwasher
>   **D** Because he's commenting on the large number of DVDs instead of searching.
>   **E** She grabs the phone to ring Marielle.
>   **F** [Name] *à l'appareil*.
>   **G** It's next to the living room.
>   **H** Maybe it's in the dishwasher.
>   **I** Yes!

chez moi, chez toi 4
3 À table, tout le monde!
(Pupil Book pp. 72–73)

Learning objectives
- Talking about meals
- Using *du, de la, de l', des*

Framework objectives
4.4/Y8 Language – developing sentences
5.4 Strategies – working out meaning

FCSE links
Unit 7: Celebrations (Food and drink)
Unit 8: Health and fitness (Food and drink vocabulary/menus)
Unit 9: Food and drink (Food and drink vocabulary)

Grammar
- the partitive article

Key language
Pour le petit déjeuner, je prends …
du beurre
du café
du chocolat chaud
du jus d'orange
du lait
du pain
du thé
de la confiture
des céréales
une tartine
Je ne mange rien.
le dîner
D'habitude, on mange …
du poisson
du poulet
de la pizza
de la viande
des fruits
des pâtes
des plats à emporter
Comme dessert, je prends …
du yaourt
une mousse au chocolat
de la glace (à la fraise)
Je suis végétarien(ne).
Le soir, on mange à (six heures).

PLTS
E Effective participators

Cross-curricular
ICT: word-processing

Resources
CD 2, tracks 21–22
Cahier d'exercices Vert, page 35
ActiveTeach
p.072 Flashcards
p.072 Grammar
p.072 Grammar practice
p.073 Grammar skills

Starter 1
Aim
To introduce food/drink vocabulary; To use reading strategies

Use exercise 1 on p. 72 of the Pupil Book as the Starter.

Alternative Starter 1:
Use ActiveTeach p.072 to introduce vocabulary for breakfast items.

1 Copie le bon mot pour chaque numéro. (AT 3.1)
Reading. Pupils label all the food and drink items numbered in the picture, using the key language box for support. Draw pupils' attention also to the tip box on cognates and near-cognates.

Answers
1 des céréales 2 de la confiture 3 du lait
4 du pain 5 une tartine 6 du beurre
7 du jus d'orange 8 du café 9 du thé
10 du chocolat chaud

Studio Grammaire: 'some' (the partitive article)
Use the *Studio Grammaire* box to cover the different words for 'some' (the partitive article). There is more information and further practice on Pupil Book p. 82.

R Pupils write out the vocabulary in exercise 1 using different colours for the masculine, feminine and plural items.

2 Écoute et note les bons numéros pour chaque personne. (1–4) (AT 1.3)
Listening. Pupils listen to four speakers talking about what they eat and drink. They note the items mentioned, using the items **1–10** pictured in exercise 1. Some vocabulary is glossed for support.

Audioscript CD 2 track 21

1 – *Bonjour. Tu t'appelles comment?*
– *Je m'appelle Charlotte.*
– *Bonjour, Charlotte. Je fais un sondage sur le petit déjeuner. Qu'est-ce que tu prends pour le petit déjeuner?*
– *D'habitude, je prends du chocolat chaud et des céréales.*
– *Du chocolat chaud et des céréales. Merci.*
– *De rien. Au revoir.*

3 À table, tout le monde! Chez moi, chez toi 4

2
- Pardon. Tu t'appelles comment?
- Moi, je m'appelle Tariq.
- Je fais un sondage. Qu'est-ce que tu prends pour le petit déjeuner?
- Euh ... Normalement, je prends du pain avec du beurre.
- Du pain avec du beurre ... Bon, merci, Tariq!

3
- Pardon. Tu t'appelles comment?
- Je m'appelle Irina.
- Alors, Irina, qu'est-ce que tu prends pour le petit déjeuner?
- Normalement, je prends un café au lait: du café avec beaucoup, beaucoup de lait!
- Du café avec du lait. Et qu'est-ce que tu manges?
- Je ne mange rien.
- Tu ne manges rien?
- Non.
- D'accord. Merci. Au revoir.

4
- Bonjour. Comment tu t'appelles, s'il te plaît?
- Je m'appelle Maxime.
- Je fais un sondage. Qu'est-ce que tu prends pour le petit déjeuner, Maxime?
- D'habitude, je prends du jus d'orange ...
- Du jus d'orange ... Oui?
- Et une tartine avec de la confiture.
- Et une tartine avec de la confiture. Bon, merci.

Answers
Charlotte: 10, 1
Tariq: 4, 6
Irina: 8, 3
Maxime: 7, 5, 2

3 Fais un sondage en classe. (AT 2.3–4)
Speaking. Pupils do a survey with other pupils in the class to find out what they have for breakfast. A grid they can copy to note answers and a sample exchange (with the text to change underlined) are given.

Pupils make a graph of the results of their survey. This can be done on computer, using a word-processing or spreadsheet package.

Starter 2
Aim
To review the partitive; To review vocabulary for breakfast food/drinks

Write up the following, omitting the underlined text (NB: this is sometimes only part of a word). Tell pupils that these are all items you might eat or drink for breakfast and give them three minutes to write them out, supplying the partitive article/article or completing/supplying the word as appropriate.

de la confiture   *du café*
du chocolat chaud   *du lait*
une *tartine*   *du jus* d'orange
du pain   *du* beurre
du thé   *des* céréales

Read through together the *En France* box on croissants/pains au chocolat.

Alternative Starter 2:
Use ActiveTeach p.072 Grammar practice to practise the partitive article.

4 Écoute et lis. Trouve le bon titre en anglais pour chaque texte. (A–C) (AT 1.4, AT 3.4)
Listening. Pupils listen to three people talking about when they typically have dinner and what they usually eat. They read the text at the same time. They find the best title (from **1–3**) for each speaker. Some vocabulary is glossed for support.

Audioscript   CD 2 track 22

A *Le soir, on mange à huit heures. D'abord, on mange du poulet ou du poisson. Après, on prend du yaourt ou des fruits.*

B *Chez moi, on mange à sept heures et demie. Je ne mange pas de viande parce que je suis végétarienne. Mon frère aussi est végétarien. Mon plat préféré, c'est les pâtes à la sauce tomate. Comme dessert, je prends une mousse au chocolat.*

C *Dans ma famille, on mange à sept heures. D'habitude, on mange à table dans la cuisine. Mais le samedi soir, on mange devant la télé dans le salon. On prend des plats à emporter, de la pizza, par exemple. Après, on mange de la glace. J'adore la glace à la fraise!*

Answers
A 2 **B** 3 **C** 1

4 Chez moi, chez toi   3 À table, tout le monde!

5 Trouve le bon texte pour chaque photo. (AT 3.4)
Reading. Pupils find the correct text (from **A–C** in exercise 4) for each of the food/drink items pictured.

Answers
1 C 2 A 3 C 4 B 5 A 6 A

6 Écris le bon mot pour chaque photo. Utilise *du, de la* ou *des*. (AT 4.2)
Writing. Pupils label the food/drink items pictured in exercise 5, using the correct form of the partitive article.

Answers
1 de la pizza
2 du poisson
3 de la glace (à la fraise)
4 des pâtes (à la sauce tomate)
5 du yaourt
6 du poulet

7 Qu'est-ce que tu prends pour le petit déjeuner? Et pour le dîner? Écris un paragraphe. (AT 4.3–4)
Writing. Pupils write a paragraph on what they have for breakfast and for dinner. A framework is supplied for support. Draw their attention to the tip box, which contains key phrases from the texts in exercise 4 for them to work into their own writing.

PLTS E

Pupils learn their paragraph by heart and give a presentation on their eating habits.

Plenary
Ask the class to summarise the forms of the partitive article and how the partitive is used.

Read out food items from the unit at random: pupils respond with an action for the appropriate partitive article – standing up for *du*, touching their nose for *de la* and touching both ears for *des*.

Workbook, page 35

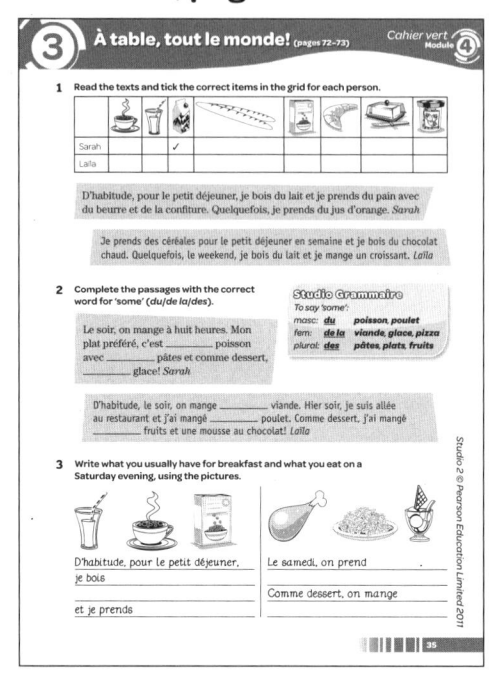

Answers

1

	hot chocolate	orange juice	milk	bread	cereals	croissant	butter	jam
Sarah		✓	✓	✓			✓	✓
Laïla	✓		✓		✓	✓		

2 Le soir, on mange à huit heures. Mon plat préféré, c'est **du** poisson avec **des** pâtes et comme dessert, **de la** glace! *Sarah*

D'habitude, le soir, on mange **de la** viande. Hier soir, je suis allée au restaurant et j'ai mangé **du** poulet. Comme dessert, j'ai mangé **des** fruits et une mousse au chocolat! *Laïla*

3 (Possible answer:)
D'habitude, pour le petit déjeuner, je bois du jus d'orange et du chocolat chaud et je prends des céréales.

Le samedi, on prend du poulet avec des pâtes. Comme dessert, on mange de la glace.

Worksheet 4.4 The partitive article

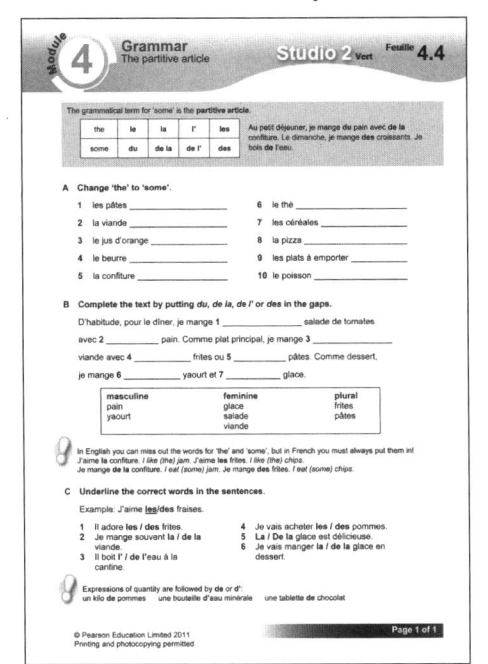

Answers

A
1. des pâtes
2. de la viande
3. du jus d'orange
4. du beurre
5. de la confiture
6. du thé
7. des céréales
8. de la pizza
9. des plats à emporter
10. du poisson

B D'habitude, pour le dîner, je mange **1 de la** salade de tomates avec **2 du** pain. Comme plat principal, je mange **3 de la** viande avec **4 des** frites ou **5 des** pâtes. Comme dessert, je mange **6 du** yaourt et **7 de la** glace.

C
1. Il adore les frites.
2. Je mange souvent de la viande.
3. Il boit de l'eau à la cantine.
4. Je vais acheter des pommes.
5. La glace est délicieuse
6. Je vais manger de la glace en dessert.

4 C'est la Chandeleur!
(Pupil Book pp. 74–75)

Learning objectives
- Discussing what food to buy
- Using *il faut* + infinitive

Framework objectives
1.3/Y8 Listening – (a) understanding language for specific functions
1.3/Y8 Speaking – (b) using language for specific functions

FCSE links
Unit 7: Celebrations (Celebrations/festivals in target language country; Invitations – venue, time, transport; Food and drink)
Unit 8: Health and fitness (Food and drink vocabulary/menus)
Unit 9: Food and drink (Food and drink vocabulary; Shopping for food; Likes and dislikes; Recipes)

Grammar
- *il faut* + infinitive
- *de* after quantities

Key language
il faut acheter ...
un litre de lait
un paquet de farine
(quatre) tranches de jambon
un kilo de bananes
500 grammes de pommes
250 grammes de fraises
une tablette de chocolat
une bombe de crème Chantilly
six œufs

PLTS
T Team workers

Cross-curricular
Food technology: recipes and quantities

Resources
CD 2, tracks 23–24
Cahier d'exercices Vert, page 36
ActiveTeach
p.074 Flashcards
p.075 Video 8
p.075 Video worksheet 8
p.075 Learning skills

Starter 1
Aim
To review food vocabulary

Write up the following, jumbling the order (here: first four are sweet, last two savoury, for reference). Give pupils two minutes to write out the items under the headings *Savoury* and *Sweet*.

une banane, des pommes, du chocolat, des fraises, du jambon, du fromage

Check answers, asking pupils to translate the items into English. Ask them what other foods they could add to both lists.

1 Écoute. Ils préfèrent quelle sorte de crêpes? Écris la bonne lettre. (1–4) (AT 1.3)

Listening. Read through together the *En France* box on *la Chandeleur*, the French version of Pancake Day. Pupils then listen to four people talking about pancakes, and for each speaker identify what pancakes they like, from pictures **a–d**.

Audioscript CD 2 track 23

1 – *Tu préfères quelle sorte de crêpes pour la Chandeleur?*
– *Euh ... Je préfère les crêpes banane-chocolat.*
– *Pourquoi?*
– *Parce que j'adore le chocolat. Et les bananes!*

2 – *Tu préfères manger quelle sorte de crêpes, toi?*
– *Moi, j'aime beaucoup les crêpes aux pommes. Et toi?*
– *Moi aussi, j'aime les crêpes aux pommes!*

3 – *Demain, c'est la Chandeleur. Tu préfères quelle sorte de crêpes?*
– *Moi, j'adore les fraises!*
– *Alors, tu aimes les crêpes aux fraises?*
– *Ah, oui, j'adore les crêpes aux fraises!*

4 – *Tu manges quelle sorte de crêpes pour la Chandeleur?*
– *Moi, je n'aime pas les crêpes sucrées. Je préfère les crêpes salées.*
– *Par exemple, les crêpes jambon-fromage?*
– *Oui, j'adore les crêpes jambon-fromage!*

Answers
1 c **2** d **3** b **4** a

2 En tandem. Tu préfères quelle sorte de crêpes? Discute avec ton/ta camarade. (AT 2.3)

Speaking. In pairs: using the key language supplied, pupils discuss what kind of crêpes they prefer. A framework is supplied, plus a sample exchange, with the words to change underlined.

4 C'est la Chandeleur! Chez moi, chez toi

3 Qu'est-ce qu'il faut acheter pour les crêpes? Écoute et écris les lettres dans le bon ordre. (1–8) (AT 1.3)

Listening. Pupils listen to a conversation in which people discuss what they need to buy to make pancakes. They note the letters of the food/drink items pictured, in the correct order.

Ask pupils what sort of pancakes the speakers are going to make (*des crêpes jambon-fromage et des crêpes banane-chocolat*).

Audioscript CD 2 track 24

1 – Alors, qu'est-ce qu'il faut acheter pour les crêpes?
   – D'abord, il faut acheter un paquet de farine ...
   – Un paquet de farine ...
2 – Un litre de lait ...
   – Un litre de lait ...
3 – Des œufs ...
   – Combien d'œufs?
   – Euh ... six.
   – Six œufs.
4 – Qu'est-ce qu'il faut aussi acheter?
   – Il faut aussi acheter 250 grammes de fromage ...
   – 250 grammes de fromage ...
5 – Quatre tranches de jambon ...
   – Du jambon, quatre tranches ...
6 – Et pour le dessert: un kilo de bananes ...
   – Deux kilos de bananes?
   – Non. Un kilo de bananes.
   – D'accord, un kilo de bananes.
7 – Et une tablette de chocolat ...
   – Une tablette de chocolat. Miam-miam! J'adore le chocolat!
8 – C'est tout?
   – Oui, c'est tout.
   – Ah, non! J'ai oublié. Il faut aussi acheter une bombe de crème Chantilly.
   – Une bombe de crème Chantilly. Alors, il faut aller au supermarché!
   – D'accord. Allons-y!

Answers
1 e 2 c 3 h 4 b 5 d 6 a 7 f 8 g

Studio Grammaire: *il faut* + infinitive
Use the *Studio Grammaire* box to cover *il faut* + infinitive. There is more information and further practice on Pupil Book p. 83.

Starter 2
Aim
To practise *il faut* + infinitive

Give pupils three minutes to write six sentences, each one using *il faut* + a different infinitive. Challenge them to include at least one surprising/illogical/contentious statement, e.g. *il faut être égoïste, il faut écouter du jazz,* etc.

Hear answers, asking pupils to translate their sentences into English. Ask the rest of the class if they agree each time.

Alternative Starter 2:
Use ActiveTeach p.074 Flashcards to practise food vocabulary (pancake ingredients).

4 En secret! Invente une crêpe bizarre! Écris la liste des ingrédients. (AT 4.2–3)
Writing. Without showing their partner, pupils invent a weird pancake and write a shopping list of all the ingredients they need (flour, milk, eggs + filling ingredients). They should aim to use vocabulary they know.

Studio Grammaire: *de* with quantities
Use the *Studio Grammaire* box to cover the use of *de* after quantities.

5 En tandem. Lis ta liste à voix haute. Ton/Ta camarade note les ingrédients. Après, il/elle devine: c'est quelle sorte de crêpe? (AT 1.2, AT 2.3–4, AT 4.3)

PLTS T

Speaking. In pairs: pupils take it in turn to read their list aloud. Their partner notes down the ingredients and tries to work out what kind of pancake it is.

6 Lis les textes et réponds aux questions. C'est Adrien ou Dalila? (AT 3.4)
Reading. Pupils read the two texts, from Adrien and Dalila. They then answer the questions by identifying who is being described each time. *apporter* is glossed for support.

Answers
1 Adrien 2 Adrien 3 Dalila 4 Adrien 5 Dalila
6 Adrien

R Pupils read the texts in exercise 6 again and identify the *il faut* expressions used (*il faut ... acheter, apporter, prendre, apporter*).

4 Chez moi, chez toi   4 C'est la Chandeleur!

7 Écris un e-mail. Invite un copain/une copine à manger. (AT 4.3–4)

Writing. Pupils write an email inviting a friend to dinner, using the texts in exercise 6 as a model. A framework and a list of details to include are supplied.

Plenary

Ask pupils to tell you how *il faut* is used and what it means.

Then tell pupils to imagine they are organising a class party and they have to make a list of things they need to do, using *il faut acheter/apporter* and (where appropriate) the partitive article. Do this as a class, writing suggestions on the board, or put pupils into teams, then hear ideas from each team.

Answers

1 1 (b) 500g de fromage
   2 (f) un litre de lait
   3 (e) une tablette de chocolat
   4 (a) un kilo de bananes
   5 (d) un paquet de farine
   6 (c) quatre tranches de jambon

2 Occasion: birthday
   Time: 8 p.m.
   Going to eat: pancakes (cheese, chocolate, banana)
   Activities after food: watch DVDs or listen to music
   Need to bring: a DVD and some CDs

3 (Possible answer:)
   Demain, c'est mon anniversaire! Tu es invité(e) à manger chez moi à sept heures et demie. On va manger de la pizza: de la pizza au fromage, au jambon, tu peux choisir! Après, on peut aller au cinéma ou jouer sur ma PlayStation. Alors, il faut apporter de l'argent et des jeux de console.

Workbook, page 36

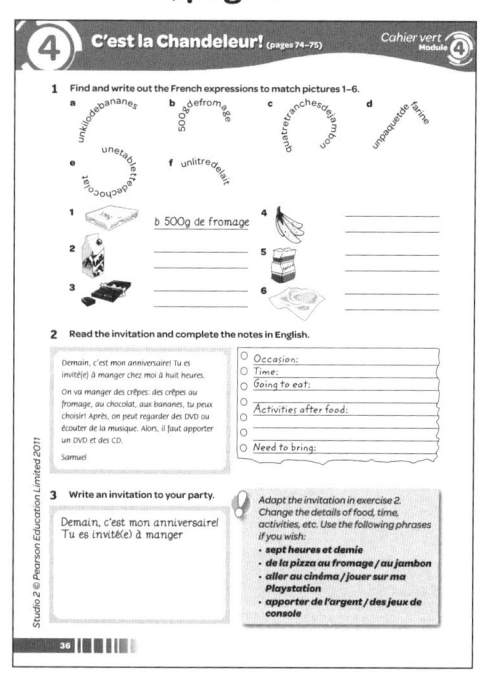

Worksheet 4.5 Having fun with language!

Answers

A Je mange à huit heures
   Du pain et du beurre
   Et des céréales
   C'est génial!
   Je bois du thé
   Ou du café
   Sur le canapé

B (Answers will vary.)

C (Answers will vary.)

4 C'est la Chandeleur! Chez moi, chez toi

Video

Episode 8: Les crêpes

Marielle and Alex find out from Gaëlle, the chef at the Atelier des Crêpes restaurant, how to make crêpes. Video worksheet 8 can be used in conjunction with this episode.

Answers to video worksheet (ActiveTeach)

1. **A** (Answers will vary.)
   B (Answers will vary.)
   C He's permanently hungry.
2. **A** They adore them.
   B Wash your hands and put on an apron (as they do here).
   C 200 grams (flour), a pinch (salt), one litre (milk)
   D So she can remember them.
   E *farine* – flour
   sel – salt
   un œuf battu – beaten egg
   un fouet – whisk
3. **A** Ham, egg, cheese, tomato, mushrooms.
   B 'J'ai faim' – I'm hungry
   C Because Alex is being greedy again.
   D a ladle
   E two minutes
   F By demanding lots of cheese.
   G Alex now wants a chocolate pancake as well.

5 Je vais aller au carnaval!
(Pupil Book pp. 76–77)

Learning objectives
- Talking about a forthcoming event
- More practice with the near future

Framework objectives
4.5/Y8 Language – range of verb tenses (near future tense)
5.2 Strategies – memorising
5.5 Strategies – reference materials

FCSE links
Unit 7: Celebrations (Celebrations/festivals in target language country; Organising a celebration; Activities at a celebration)

Grammar
- the near future tense

Key language
je vais …/on va …
aller au carnaval
boire un coca
chanter et danser (sur le char)
manger au restaurant
participer au défilé
porter un costume de (pirate)
prendre des photos (avec mon portable)
regarder le défilé/le feu d'artifice
Je vais m'amuser.
On va s'amuser.

PLTS
S Self-managers

Resources
CD 2, tracks 25–26
Cahier d'exercices Vert, page 37
ActiveTeach
p.076 Grammar
p.076 Grammar practice
p.077 Class activity
p.077 Grammar skills

Starter 1
Aim
To review the present and near future tenses;
To use grammatical knowledge

Write up the following in two columns, jumbling the order of the sentence endings. Give pupils three minutes to match the sentence openings and endings.

1 *D'habitude, je*
2 *L'année prochaine, il va*
3 *Ce weekend, je*
4 *Normalement, on*

regarde le film avec mes copains.
aller à Nice.
vais porter un costume de vampire.
va à la crêperie.

Check answers, asking pupils to translate the completed sentences into English. Ask them how they worked out which sentence halves went together. Review how the near future tense is formed (*aller* + infinitive).

1 Écoute et lis les e-mails. (AT 1.5)
Listening. Pupils read the two emails, reading the text at the same time. Some vocabulary is glossed for support.

Audioscript — CD 2 track 25

– *La semaine prochaine, je vais aller au Carnaval de Nice. Je vais regarder le défilé avec ma famille et je vais prendre des photos avec mon portable. Après, on va manger au restaurant. Je vais manger des crêpes et je vais boire un coca. Et toi, tu vas aller au carnaval?*

– *Moi aussi, je vais aller au carnaval. Mais cette année, je vais participer au défilé! Le thème de notre char, c'est les films d'horreur. Alors, je vais porter un costume de vampire! Je vais chanter et danser sur le char avec mes amis. On va s'amuser! Le soir, je vais regarder le feu d'artifice avec mon frère.*

2 Regarde les images. C'est Noëmie ou Cassandra? Écris N ou C. (AT 3.5)
Reading. Pupils read the emails in exercise 1 again. They look at the pictures and identify whether each one refers to Noëmie (writing N) or Cassandra (writing C).

Answers
1 N **2** C **3** C **4** N **5** C **6** N

Studio Grammaire: the near future tense
Use the *Studio Grammaire* box to cover the near future tense. There is more information and further practice on Pupil Book p. 83.

5 Je vais aller au carnaval!   **Chez moi, chez toi** **4**

R Pupils identify orally all the verbs in the near future tense in exercise 1.

3 Écris une phrase pour chaque image de l'exercice 2. (AT 4.5)

Writing. Pupils write a sentence for each of the pictures in exercise 2. A key language box is supplied for support.

Answers
1 Je vais aller au carnaval./Je vais regarder le défilé (avec ma famille).
2 Je vais porter un costume de vampire.
3 Je vais regarder le feu d'artifice (avec mon frère).
4 On va/Je vais manger au restaurant./Je vais manger des crêpes et je vais boire un coca.
5 Je vais participer au défilé./Je vais chanter et danser sur le char (avec mes amis).
6 Je vais prendre des photos avec mon portable.

R Pupils translate into English the sentences in the key language box that they didn't use to label the pictures.

Starter 2
Aim
To review the near future tense; To review carnival vocabulary

Write up the following, omitting the underlined words. Give pupils three minutes to complete the sentences with the correct infinitive. Ask them to write out all the singular forms (including *on*) of the near future tense verb in each case. If necessary, supply the infinitives in random order for support.

1 Je vais <u>aller</u> au carnaval.
2 On va <u>boire</u> une limonade.
3 Elle va <u>manger</u> des crêpes.
4 On va <u>participer</u> au défilé.
5 Je vais <u>regarder</u> le feu d'artifice.
6 Il va <u>prendre</u> des photos.

Alternative Starter 2:
Use ActiveTeach p.076 Grammar practice to practise the near future tense.

4 Écoute et note en anglais les deux activités pour chaque personne. (1–4) (AT 1.5)

Listening. Pupils listen to four people talking about what they are going to do and note in English the two activities each person mentions.

Encourage pupils to write their answers in note form. Point out the example, emphasising how little they need to write to show they have understood correctly. Say that this is a very useful skill to develop: not only does it impress examiners, it also gives them more time to listen and work out the answers.

Audioscript   **CD 2 track 26**

Bonjour et bienvenue à Radio Jeunes Nice! Je vais poser à de jeunes Niçois la question suivante: Qu'est-ce que tu vas faire au carnaval de Nice, cette année?

1 – Bonjour. Comment t'appelles-tu?
 – Je m'appelle Romain.
 – Alors, Romain, qu'est-ce que tu vas faire au Carnaval de Nice, cette année?
 – Bon, je vais regarder le défilé avec mes copains.
 – Tu vas regarder le défilé? Et après?
 – Après, on va boire quelque chose. On va boire un coca ou une limonade.
 – D'accord. Merci, Romain.

2 – Salut! Comment tu t'appelles?
 – Moi, je m'appelle Élise.
 – Salut, Élise. Qu'est-ce que tu vas faire au carnaval?
 – Euh … Je vais prendre des photos avec mon portable.
 – Des photos de quoi? Du défilé?
 – Oui, c'est ça.
 – Et le soir, qu'est-ce que tu vas faire?
 – Le soir, je vais regarder le feu d'artifice, avec ma famille.
 – Ah, oui, moi aussi je vais regarder le feu d'artifice. Alors, amuse-toi bien!
 – Merci.

3 – Bonjour. Tu t'appelles comment?
 – Je m'appelle Samir.
 – Alors, qu'est-ce que tu vas faire au carnaval, Samir?
 – Cette année, je vais participer au défilé!
 – Tu vas participer au défilé? Sur un char?
 – Oui.
 – Tu vas porter un costume?
 – Oui, je vais porter un costume de pirate!
 – Un costume de pirate! C'est super, ça!
 – Ah, oui. On va s'amuser!

4 – Et comment t'appelles-tu?
 – Je m'appelle Margot.
 – Salut, Margot. Qu'est-ce que tu vas faire au carnaval, cette année?
 – Moi, je vais chanter et danser sur un char.
 – Tu vas chanter et danser toute seule?
 – Mais, non! Avec mes amis!
 – Ah, d'accord! Et qu'est-ce que tu vas faire après?
 – Après, on va manger. On va manger de la pizza.
 – Alors, bon appétit! Au revoir et merci.

123

4 Chez moi, chez toi — 5 Je vais aller au carnaval!

Answers

	first activity	second activity
1	watch parade	drink cola or lemonade
2	take photos	watch fireworks
3	take part in parade	wear pirate costume
4	sing and dance	eat pizza

5 Trouve la fin de chaque phrase. Écris des phrases complètes. (AT 3.5)

Reading. Pupils match the sentence openings and endings, writing out the complete sentences. *une squelette* is glossed for support.

Answers
À Hallowe'en, ...
1 d je vais aller à une fête chez une copine.
2 c je vais porter un costume de squelette.
3 b je vais prendre des photos de mes copains.
4 f on va manger un hamburger-frites.
5 h on va boire du coca ou de l'Orangina.
6 e on va faire du 'trick or treat'.
7 a on va regarder un film d'horreur en DVD.
8 g on va s'amuser!

Use the pronunciation box to review and practise the pronunciation of –qu–.

6 En tandem. Choisis les images A ou B. Décris ce que tu vas faire à la fête d'Hallowe'en. (AT 2.5)

Speaking. In pairs: pupils choose a set of pictures, A or B, and use these to describe what they are going to do at the Hallowe'en party. A sample opening is given.

7 Imagine que tu vas aller à une fête d'Hallowe'en. Écris un paragraphe. (AT 4.5)

Writing. Pupils imagine that they are going to go to a Hallowe'en party and write a paragraph about their plans. A framework is supplied. Draw pupils' attention to the tip box on improving their writing by including one or two words they have looked up in a dictionary.

PLTS S

Read together through *Stratégie 4* on Pupil Book p. 85, covering different ways to learn vocabulary. Ask pupils to choose two techniques (either from those listed or ones that they've thought up themselves) and use them to learn two different sets of vocabulary from the units in Module 4. Ask them in a subsequent lesson which method they found better and why.

Plenary

Ask the class to summarise how the near future tense is used and formed.

Split the class into boys and girls. The girls use the sentences they wrote in exercise 3 to give prompts in English to the boys (e.g. 'We're going to take part in the parade.'). The boys (with their books closed) respond with the French. Award two points for a completely correct answer, one point for an answer with a minor error. After a few turns, they swap roles. The team with the most points is the winner.

Workbook, page 37

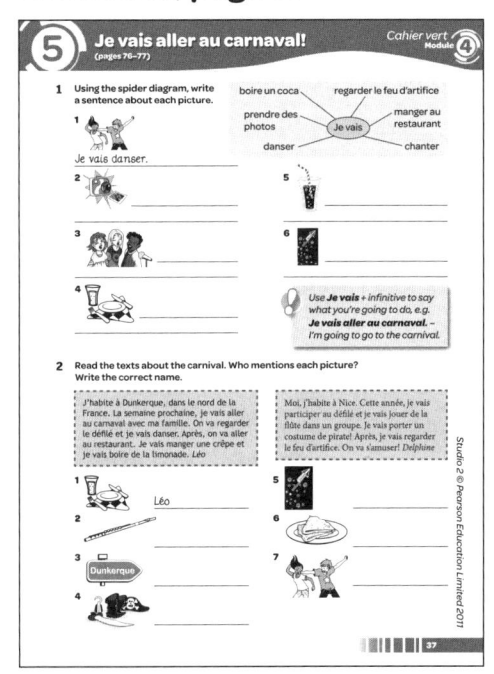

Answers
1 1 Je vais danser.
2 Je vais prendre des photos.
3 Je vais chanter.
4 Je vais manger au restaurant.
5 Je vais boire un coca.
6 Je vais regarder le feu d'artifice.
2 1 Léo 2 Delphine 3 Léo 4 Delphine
5 Delphine 6 Léo 7 Léo

Worksheet 4.6 The near future

Answers

A À Noël, on aime bien être en famille. <u>Cette année, on va manger à midi.</u> <u>Après, on va jouer avec les cadeaux de Noël.</u> <u>Je vais téléphoner avec mon nouveau portable.</u> J'aime bien parler avec mes copains. <u>Le soir, on va regarder des DVD.</u> <u>Je vais aller au lit à 11 heures du soir.</u>
(The other sentences are present tense.)

B Pour la fête la semaine prochaine, je vais porter une jupe noire. D'abord, on va manger des chips et on va boire du coca. Après, on va regarder des DVD. Moi, je vais aller à la maison vers minuit. On va s'amuser!

C (Answers will vary.)

Bilan et Révisions (Pupil Book pp. 78–79)

Bilan
Pupils use this checklist to review language covered in the module, working on it in pairs in class or on their own at home. Encourage them to follow up any areas of weakness they identify. There are Target Setting Sheets included in the Assessment Pack, and an opportunity for pupils to record their own levels and targets on the *J'avance* page in the Workbook, p. 42. You can also use the *Bilan* checklist as an end-of-module plenary option.

Révisions
These revision exercises can be used for assessment purposes or for pupils to practise before tackling the assessment tasks in the Assessment Pack.

Resources
CD 2, track 27
Cahier d'exercices Vert, pages 38 & 39

1 Écoute. Copie et remplis le tableau. (1–6) (AT 1.3)
Listening. Pupils copy out the table. They listen to six conversations and complete the table with the details in English.

Audioscript CD 2 track 27

1. – Qu'est-ce qu'il faut acheter au supermarché?
   – Il faut acheter un paquet de farine…
   – Un paquet de farine…
2. – Un litre de lait…
   – Un litre?
   – Oui.
   – Un litre de lait…
3. – Du jambon…
   – Combien de jambon?
   – Euh… Cinq tranches.
   – Cinq tranches de jambon…
4. – C'est tout?
   – Il faut aussi acheter des pommes.
   – Un kilo?
   – Non, deux kilos.
   – Alors, deux kilos de pommes.
5. – Il faut acheter des œufs?
   – Ah, oui! Il faut acheter des œufs. Six œufs.
   – D'accord. Six œufs.
6. – Et il faut acheter du fromage.
   – 250 grammes?
   – Oui, 250 grammes de fromage.
   – 250 grammes de fromage. OK! Allons-y!

Answers

	what?	how much?
1	c	1 packet
2	a	1 litre
3	d	5 slices
4	e	2 kilos
5	f	6
6	b	250 grams

2 En tandem. Fais des dialogues. Change les phrases soulignées. (AT 2.4)
Speaking. In pairs: pupils make up dialogues. A framework is supplied, with the details to change underlined.

3 Lis l'e-mail. Quelles sont les trois phrases correctes? (AT 3.4)
Reading. Pupils read the email. They then read the sentences in English summarising it and identify the three sentences which are correct. Some vocabulary is glossed for support.

Answers
1, 5, 6

4 Copie et complète le texte. (AT 4.3)
Writing. Pupils copy and complete the text, using the picture prompts.

Answers
a regarder le défilé
b prendre des photos (avec mon portable)
c manger des crêpes
d porter un costume de vampire
e chanter
f danser

Bilan et Révisions — Chez moi, chez toi 4

Workbook, pages 38 and 39

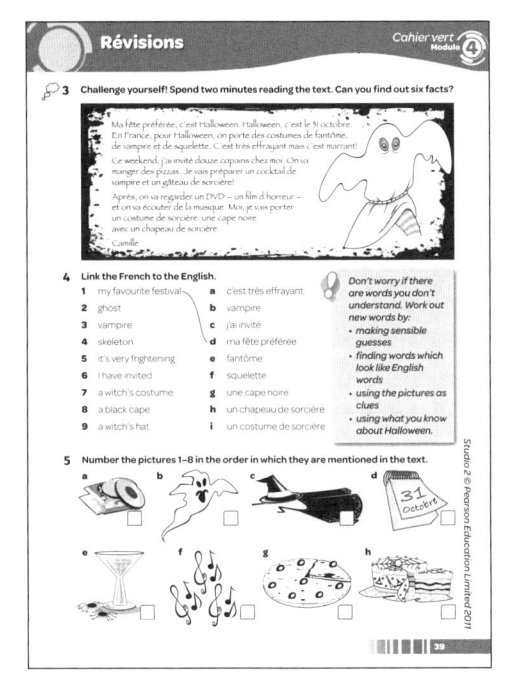

Answers

1. **Un cocktail de vampire**
   Missing: 1 litre lemonade, 1 litre orange juice
   Un gâteau de sorcière
   Missing: 200g butter, 3 eggs

2.
   1. Hallowe'en party
   2. Saturday night
   3. ghost, witch or vampire costume
   4. vampire cocktail
   5. witch's cake
   6. watch a horror film
   7. 7 p.m.

3. (Answers will vary.)

4. 1 d 2 e 3 b 4 f 5 a 6 c 7 i 8 g 9 h

5. a 6 b 2 c 8 d 1 e 4 f 7 g 3 h 5

En plus: Mon chez moi
(Pupil Book pp. 80–81)

Learning objectives
- Talking about where you live

Framework objectives
2.2/Y8 Reading – (a) longer, more complex texts
2.4/Y8 Writing – (b) organising paragraphs
3.2/Y8 Culture – (b) customs/traditions
5.7 Strategies – planning and preparing
5.8 Strategies – evaluating and improving

FCSE links
Unit 10: Region and environment (Description and location of home; Opinions on different houses; Description and location of area; Facilities and activities within an area; Positive and negative aspects and opinions on a particular area)

Key language
Review of language from the module

PLTS
R Reflective learners

Resources
CD 2, track 28
ActiveTeach
p.081 Assignment 4
p.081 Assignment 4: prep

Starter
Aim
To develop listening skills

In groups of three, pupils do the prediction activity at the top of p. 80, in preparation for exercise 1.

1 Écoute. C'est vrai (✓) ou faux (✗)? (1–6) (AT 1.4)
Listening. Pupils listen to Nita talking about where she lives, then note whether the sentences in English about it are true (writing ✓) or false (writing ✗).

Ask pupils how the preparation they did in the Starter helped them tackle exercise 1. Explain that predicting in this way is an important and useful listening skill.

Audioscript CD 2 track 28

Salut! Je m'appelle Nita. J'habite dans un petit village en Guadeloupe.

J'habite au bord de la mer avec mon père, ma mère et ma sœur. On a une petite maison, c'est une sorte de bungalow. J'adore habiter ici.

Il y a la cuisine, le salon, deux chambres et une salle de bains. Il y a aussi une douche dans le jardin, mais il n'y a pas de télé parce qu'on aime regarder la mer!

Dans ma famille, le soir, on mange à sept heures. On mange beaucoup de poisson et quelquefois, on mange un colombo. C'est un curry de poulet.

Answers
1 ✗   2 ✓   3 ✓   4 ✗   5 ✗   6 ✓

2 Lis les textes et réponds aux questions. Écris le bon prénom. (AT 3.6)
Reading. Pupils read the two texts. They then answer the questions, identifying who is being described in each one. Some vocabulary is glossed for support.

Answers
1 Blaise   2 Stella   3 Stella   4 Blaise   5 Stella
6 Blaise   7 Stella   8 Blaise   9 Blaise   10 Stella

3 Choisis un pays. Prépare un exposé. Imagine que tu habites en Nouvelle-Calédonie, sur l'Île Saint-Pierre ou en Tunisie. (AT 2.4)
Speaking. Pupils choose one of the places described, Nouméa in Nouvelle-Calédonie, the island of Saint-Pierre or Djerba in Tunisia. They imagine they live there and prepare and give a presentation on where they live. Key language is supplied. *agneau* is glossed for support.

Encourage pupils to write out their presentation in full, then create note cards to use when speaking.

4 Trouve la fin de chaque phrase. Écris des phrases complètes. (AT 3.5)
Reading. Pupils match the sentence openings and endings, then write out the complete sentences.

En plus: Mon chez moi **Chez moi, chez toi** 4

Answers
1 c Je m'appelle Albert. J'habite dans un appartement à Yaoundé au Cameroun.
2 e J'adore habiter ici, mais un jour je voudrais habiter au bord de la mer.
3 a Chez nous, il y a trois chambres, deux douches, deux balcons, la cuisine et le salon.
4 d Normalement, le soir, on mange à sept heures. On mange du poisson avec des bananes plantains.
5 b Une fête importante au Cameroun, c'est la fête nationale. Il y a un défilé, on danse, on chante et on mange.

5 Écris un paragraphe sur le pays que tu as choisi pour l'exercice 3. Utilise les phrases de l'exercice 4 comme modèle. (AT 4.4)

Writing. Pupils write a paragraph on the place they chose in exercise 3, using the sentences in exercise 4 as a model. Draw pupils' attention to the tip box on checking their work using a checklist.

PLTS R

Encourage them to create and use a checklist like this to refer to whenever they do a piece of extended writing. Not only will it help them improve their second draft, it will also help them identify areas in which they need to improve.

Plenary
Agree on a UK celebration and ask pupils how they would describe it to a French visitor, using the structures supplied in exercise 5.

Worksheet 4.7 Une petite pièce

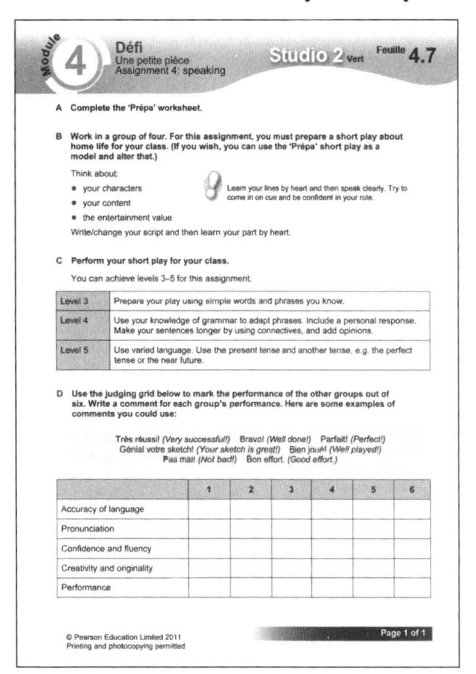

Answers
Assessed by teacher.

Worksheet 4.8 Une petite pièce. Prépa

Answers
A 1 Nita habite dans un petit village.
 2 Nita habite avec sa mère, son père et sa sœur.
 3 La famille habite dans une petite maison.
 4 On n'a pas de télé parce qu'on aime regarder l'océan.
 5 Au dîner, la sœur de Nita boit du jus de fruit.
 6 Au carnaval, on va danser.
B Assessed by teacher.

Studio Grammaire (Pupil Book pp. 82–83)

The *Studio Grammaire* section provides a more detailed summary of the key grammar covered in the module, along with further exercises to practise these points. The activities on ActiveTeach pages 82 and 83 are repeated from elsewhere in the module.

Grammar topics
- *je mange* or *je voudrais manger*?
- the partitive article
- *prendre* (singular, including *on*)
- *il faut* + infinitive
- the near future tense

je mange or *je voudrais manger*?

1 Match up the sentences and the pictures. Then translate the sentences into English.

Pupils match the sentences and pictures, then translate the sentences into English.

Answers
1 c I'm eating crisps, but I would like to eat pizza.
2 a I live in a little house, but I would like to live in a big castle.
3 b I'm listening to the teacher, but I would like to listen to music.

2 Fill in the gaps using the verbs below. Choose the present tense or *je voudrais* + infinitive.

Pupils complete the sentences using the verbs supplied.

Answers
1 **J'habite** dans une grande ville, mais **je voudrais habiter** au bord de la mer.
2 **Je joue** de la guitare, mais **je voudrais jouer** du piano.
3 **Je fais** mes devoirs, mais **je voudrais faire** du skate.
4 **Je vais** au collège, mais **je voudrais aller** au cinéma.
5 **J'achète** un scooter, mais **je voudrais acheter** une Ferrari.

The partitive article

3 Choose *du*, *de la* or *des* each time.

Pupils complete the text, choosing the correct form of the partitive article from the three supplied each time.

Answers
1 du 2 de la 3 des 4 des 5 du 6 des
7 de la 8 du 9 de la

prendre

4 Choose the correct answer each time. How do you say ... ?

Pupils choose the correct answer to each question from the two options given each time.

Answers
1 b 2 b 3 a 4 b

il faut + infinitive

5 Choose the infinitive form of the verb to complete each sentence. Match the French sentences with the English sentences.

Pupils complete the sentences, choosing the infinitive from the three verb forms supplied each time. They then match the sentences with their English translation.

Answers
1 Il faut **apporter** de l'argent. – b
2 Il faut **acheter** du fromage. – c
3 Il faut **aller** en ville. – a
4 Il ne faut pas **oublier** le chocolat. – e
5 Il faut **prendre** le bus numéro 2. – d

The near future tense

6 Fill in the gaps with the correct phrases from the list.

Pupils complete the gap-fill text using the phrases supplied.

Answers
1 vais porter 2 vais faire 3 vais aller
4 va regarder 5 va manger 6 va boire

Studio Grammaire   Chez moi, chez toi   4

7 Copy the table and write the sentences in the right column.

Pupils copy and complete the table, writing the sentences in the 'present' or 'future' column, as appropriate.

Answers

present	future
Je mange des crêpes au chocolat.	On va faire des crêpes.
On prend le petit déjeuner à huit heures.	Je vais manger au restaurant.
	Je vais manger une crêpe aux pommes.
	Tu vas regarder le défilé?

chez moi, chez toi 4 À toi (Pupil Book pp. 120–121)

Self-access reading and writing

A Reinforcement

1 Copie les phrases. Écris correctement les mots en désordre. (AT 3.2)

Reading. Pupils write out the sentences, unscrambling the words given as anagrams.

Answers
1 J'habite dans une petite **maison**.
2 Je voudrais habiter dans un vieux **château**.
3 Il habite à la **montagne**.
4 Elle habite au **bord de la mer**.
5 On habite dans un grand **appartement**.
6 Je voudrais habiter dans une vieille **chaumière**.

2 Lis le texte. C'est vrai (✓) ou faux (✗)? (AT 3.4)

Reading. Pupils read the text, then note whether the sentences about it are true (writing ✓) or false (writing ✗).

Answers
1 ✓ 2 ✗ 3 ✗ 4 ✓ 5 ✗ 6 ✗

3 Lis les listes. Qu'est-ce qu'il manque dans chaque panier? (AT 3.2)

Reading. Pupils read the lists and look at the pictures to work out what's missing from each basket.

Answers
A 300 grammes de fromage
B 250 grammes de fraises

4 Écris une liste de provisions pour ta fête. Utilise un dictionnaire, si nécessaire. (AT 4.2)

Writing. Pupils write a shopping list for a party, using a dictionary if necessary. A sample opening is given.

B Extension

1 Lis le texte. Copie et complète les phrases en anglais. (AT 4.4)

Reading. Pupils read the text. They then copy and complete the gap-fill sentences summarising it in English.

Answers
1 For breakfast, Manon usually has **bread** with **(strawberry) jam** and **(a big bowl of) hot chocolate**.
2 She and her family have their evening meal at **8 o'clock**.
3 First of all, they have **soup**.
4 Then they have **fish** or **pasta** with **salad**.
5 Manon's favourite dessert is **chocolate ice-cream**.
6 On Saturday evenings, she and her family have **a takeaway**.

2 Lis l'invitation. Puis choisis la bonne image dans chaque phrase. (AT 3.4)

Reading. Pupils read the invitation, then complete the sentences about it by choosing the correct picture from the two options given each time. Some vocabulary is glossed for support.

Answers
1 b 2 a 3 a 4 b 5 a

3 Écris une invitation à ta fête d'anniversaire. (AT 4.4)

Writing. Pupils write an invitation to their own birthday party, using the text in exercise 2 as a model. A list of features to change is supplied, along with a framework.

Module 5: Quel talent?! (Pupil Book pp. 86–105)

Unit & Learning objectives	PoS* & Framework objectives	Key language	Grammar and other language features
1 La France a du talent! (pp. 88–89) Talking about talent and ambition Using the infinitive	**2.1a** identify patterns **2.1c** knowledge of language **3.2/Y8** Culture – (a) young people: aspirations **4.5/Y8** Language – (b) range of modal verbs	*Mon talent, c'est …* *chanter* *jouer du piano* etc. *Un jour, je veux être …* *chanteur/euse* *professionnel(le)* *professeur (de musique)* etc. *Je veux jouer …* *dans un groupe de rock* *dans un grand orchestre*	**G** uses of the infinitive **G** *vouloir* + infinitive – developing writing skills
2 Je dois gagner! (pp. 90–91) Saying what you must and can do Using *devoir* and *pouvoir* + infinitive	**2.1a** identify patterns **2.2d** use correct pronunciation **2.2e** ask and answer questions **2.2f** initiate and sustain conversations **3b** sounds and writing **1.3/Y8** Listening – (a) understanding language for specific functions **1.3/Y8** Speaking – (b) using language for specific functions **4.5/Y8** Language – (b) range of modal verbs **5.1** Strategies – patterns	*Tu dois …* *aller à l'audition* *avoir confiance en toi* etc. *Je ne peux pas parce que …* *je dois faire mes devoirs* *je dois faire du babysitting* *Tu peux …* *faire tes devoirs demain* *répéter chez moi*	**G** *devoir* + infinitive **G** *pouvoir* + infinitive – pronunciation: –*oi* (*moi, toi, dois*)
3 Ne fais pas ça! (pp. 92–93) Telling someone what to do Using the imperative	**2.1a** identify patterns **2.1e** use reference materials **2.2i** reuse language **3.2/Y8** Culture – (a) young people: aspirations **5.5** Strategies – reference materials	*Change ton attitude!* *Chante plus fort!* *Enlève ton blouson!* *Éteins ton portable!* *N'oublie pas ta casquette!* etc.	**G** the imperative (*tu* form)
4 Les juges sont comment? (pp. 94–95) Describing people's personalities Using more adjectives	**2.2f** initiate and sustain conversations **1.4/Y8** Speaking – (b) unscripted conversations **1.5/Y8** Speaking – (b) using simple idioms **2.3/Y8** Reading – text features: emotive **4.2/Y8** Language – increasing vocabulary	*Il/Elle est …* *très/trop/assez/un peu* *arrogant(e)* *beau/belle* *cruel(le)* *gentil(le)* *vaniteux/vaniteuse* *sympa* etc.	**G** using *avoir* and *être* **G** adjective agreement

5 Quel talent?!

Unit & Learning objectives	PoS* & Framework objectives	Key language	Grammar and other language features
5 Et le gagnant est ... (pp. 96–97) Showing how much you can do with the French language Using a variety of structures	**2.1a** identify patterns **2.1b** memorising **2.2g** write clearly and coherently **1.5/Y8** Speaking – (a) unscripted talks **4.5/Y8** Language – (b) range of modal verbs	*j'aime gagner* *je dois gagner* *je peux gagner* *je voudrais gagner* *je vais gagner* *je veux gagner*	**G** verb + infinitive structures
Bilan et Révisions (pp. 98–99) Pupils' checklist and practice exercises			
En plus: Les vedettes de la musique (pp. 100–101) Writing a profile of a music star	**2.1d** previous knowledge **2.2b** skim and scan **2.1/Y8** Reading – authentic materials **2.5/Y8** Writing – using researched language **3.2/Y8** Culture – (a) young people: aspirations **4.2/Y8** Language – increasing vocabulary **5.4** Strategies – working out meaning **5.7** Strategies – planning and preparing	Review of language from the module *une vedette* *il est né/elle est née* *il/elle a gagné* *il est parti/elle est partie*	**G** the perfect tense – developing reading skills – developing writing skills
Studio Grammaire (pp. 102–103) Detailed grammar summary and practice exercises			**G** infinitives **G** modal verbs: *vouloir, devoir* and *pouvoir* **G** adjectives **G** using a variety of structures
À toi (pp. 122–123) Self-access reading and writing at two levels			

* In addition, the following Programmes of Study are covered throughout the module: 1.1–1.4, 2.2a, 2.2c, 2.2d, 3a, 3c, 3d, 3e, 3f, 4a, 4b, 4d, 4e, 4f, 4g. PoS 4c is covered in all Units 4 & 5 and *En plus* sections. See pp. 7–9 for details.

5 1 La France a du talent!

Quel talent?!
(Pupil Book pp. 88–89)

Learning objectives
- Talking about talent and ambition
- Using the infinitive

Framework objectives
3.2/Y8 Culture – (a) young people: aspirations
4.5/Y8 Language – (b) range of modal verbs

FCSE links
Unit 1: Meeting people (Personal information; Sports and hobbies)
Unit 6: Leisure (Sports/hobbies)

Grammar
- uses of the infinitive
- *vouloir* + infinitive

Key language
*Mon talent, c'est …
chanter
danser
faire de la magie
jouer du piano
jouer du violon
jouer de la guitare (électrique)
Un jour, je veux être …
chanteur professionnel/
chanteuse professionnelle
danseur professionnel/
danseuse professionnelle
magicien professionnel/
magicienne professionnelle
professeur (de musique)
Je veux jouer …
dans un groupe de rock
dans un grand orchestre*

PLTS
E Effective participators

Resources
CD 3, tracks 2–3
Cahier d'exercices Vert, page 43
ActiveTeach
p.088 Flashcards
p.088 Grammar
p.089 Thinking skills

Starter 1
Aim
To introduce the topic

Using the content of the module opener (Pupil Book pp. 86–87) as a starting point, ask pupils if they perform or have any ambitions to perform in the future, eliciting details of their talents and plans.

1 Écoute et mets les images dans le bon ordre. (AT 1.2)
Listening. Pupils listen to six people talking about their talents and note the letters of the pictures in the order they are mentioned (from **a–f**).

Audioscript CD 3 track 2
1 *Mon talent, c'est chanter.*
2 *Mon talent, c'est danser.*
3 *Mon talent, c'est faire de la magie.*
4 *Mon talent, c'est jouer du piano.*
5 *Mon talent, c'est jouer du violon.*
6 *Mon talent, c'est jouer de la guitare électrique.*

Answers
1 d **2** b **3** f **4** a **5** e **6** c

2 En tandem. Mime un talent. Ton/Ta camarade devine. (AT 2.3)
Speaking. In pairs: pupils take it in turn to mime a talent and to guess what it is. A sample exchange is given.

> **Studio Grammaire: uses of the infinitive**
> Use the *Studio Grammaire* box to cover some uses of the infinitive. There is more information and further practice on Pupil Book p. 102.

3 Lis la publicité. Complète les phrases en anglais. (AT 3.3)
Reading. Pupils read the advert, then read and complete the sentences in English summarising it. Some vocabulary is glossed for support.

Answers
1 talent contest/competition **2** dancing, magic **3** 18 **4** 24th July **5** 500, lessons **6** the website

135

5 Quel talent?! 1 La France a du talent!

Starter 2

Aim
To review talents vocabulary; To use grammar knowledge

Write up the following in two columns, jumbling the order of the sentence endings. Give pupils three minutes working in pairs to match the sentence openings and endings.

1 Mon talent, c'est
2 Je veux faire
3 Je joue du
4 Je
5 Je veux

danser.
de la magie.
piano.
veux être guitariste.
être danseur professionnel.

Check answers, asking pupils how they worked each one out.

Alternative Starter 2:
Use ActiveTeach p.088 Flashcards to practise talents vocabulary.

4 Associe les phrases suivantes aux phrases de l'exercice 1. (AT 3.2)

Reading. Pupils match the French sentences (**1–6**) to the images and phrases in exercise 1 (from **a–f**).

Answers
1 f 2 c 3 e 4 d 5 a 6 b

Studio Grammaire: *vouloir* (present tense singular) + infinitive

Use the *Studio Grammaire* box to cover *vouloir* (present tense singular, including *on*) + infinitive. There is more information and further practice on Pupil Book p. 102.

R Pupils choose four of the talents in exercise 1 on p. 88 and write a sentence using *Je veux* with each of them. They then translate the sentences into English.

5 Écoute. Copie et remplis la fiche pour chaque personne. (1–7) (AT 1.4)

Listening. Pupils copy out the form seven times. They then listen to the recording and complete a card for each of the seven speakers.

Pupils listen again to note in English any additional details given by the speakers about themselves.

Audioscript CD 3 track 3

1 *Je m'appelle Olivia. J'ai seize ans. Mon talent, c'est chanter. Mon style, c'est le R'n'B. Un jour, je veux être chanteuse professionnelle, comme mon idole, Beyoncé. Elle est hypercool!*

2 *Salut! Moi, c'est Nathan. J'ai quatorze ans. Mon talent, c'est jouer de la guitare électrique. Mon style, c'est le thrash métal. Un jour, je veux jouer de la guitare dans un groupe de rock, comme Megadeth ou Metallica!*

3 *Euh … Bonjour. Je m'appelle Félix. J'ai treize ans. Bon, euh … Mon talent, c'est faire de la magie. Un jour, je veux être magicien professionnel à la télé.*

4 *Je m'appelle Coralie. J'ai quatorze ans. Mon talent, c'est jouer du piano. Je joue de la musique classique avec mon ami Ryan. Un jour, je veux jouer dans un orchestre professionnel.*

5 *Salut! Je m'appelle Ryan. J'ai quinze ans. Mon talent, c'est jouer du violon. Je joue avec ma copine Coralie. Mais je ne veux pas être musicien professionnel. Un jour, je veux être professeur de musique dans un collège.*

6 *Salut. Je suis Lucas. J'ai quinze ans. Mon talent, c'est danser. Un jour, je veux être danseur professionnel. Mon style, c'est le hip-hop, le street-dance, la tecktonik. Je danse dans un groupe avec mes copains Malik et Charles. Le groupe s'appelle LMC. C'est L pour Lucas, M pour Malik et C pour Charles. Mais c'est aussi Les Mecs Cools!*

7 *Bonjour. Je m'appelle Laurine. J'ai douze ans. Mon talent? Je suis pompom-girl! Mon groupe s'appelle les Pompomstars. Un jour, je veux être professeur de danse.*

1 La France a du talent! Quel talent?! 5

Answers
1 Name: *Olivia*
  Age: *16*
  Talent: *singing*
  Ambition: *professional singer*
2 Name: *Nathan*
  Age: *14*
  Talent: *playing the electric guitar*
  Ambition: *play in a rock band*
3 Name: *Félix*
  Age: *13*
  Talent: *doing magic*
  Ambition: *professional magician on TV*
4 Name: *Coralie*
  Age: *14*
  Talent: *playing piano*
  Ambition: *play in a professional orchestra*
5 Name: *Ryan*
  Age: *15*
  Talent: *playing violin*
  Ambition: *music teacher*
6 Name: *Lucas*
  Age: *15*
  Talent: *dancing*
  Ambition: *professional dancer*
7 Name: *Laurine*
  Age: *12*
  Talent: *cheerleader*
  Ambition: *dance teacher*

6 Imagine que tu veux participer au concours de jeunes talents. Choisis A, B, C ou D et présente-toi. (Si possible, enregistre ta vidéo.) (AT 2.4)

Speaking. Pupils imagine that they want to take part in the talent contest. They choose an identity (A, B, C or D) and use the information supplied to introduce themselves. (If possible, make a video recording of their presentations.)

Answers
A *Je m'appelle Manu. J'ai douze ans. Mon talent, c'est chanter. Un jour, je veux être chanteur professionnel.*
B *Je m'appelle Clarisse. J'ai treize ans. Mon talent, c'est jouer de la guitare (électrique). Un jour, je veux jouer dans un groupe de rock.*
C *Je m'appelle Ludo. J'ai quatorze ans. Mon talent, c'est faire de la magie. Un jour, je veux être magicien professionnel.*
D *Je m'appelle Amélie. J'ai quinze ans. Mon talent, c'est danser. Un jour, je veux être professeur de danse.*

7 Choisis une autre personne de l'exercice 7. Écris un paragraphe. (AT 4.4)

Writing. Pupils choose another identity from those supplied in exercise 7 and write a paragraph about themselves. A sample opening is supplied. Draw their attention to the tip box, which offers language they can include to add interest and detail to their writing.

Plenary

If you are able to record the presentations in exercise 6, do so and then play them back to the class. If you are unable to record the presentations, ask a few pupils to give their presentations to the class.

PLTS E

Encourage the class to give constructive feedback on each one and to award one, two or three stars in each of the following categories: pronunciation, confidence and fluency, including a range of tenses. Encourage them to use in their feedback phrases like *Bravo! Super! Bon/Excellent effort! Intéressant! Très/Assez bien. Pas mal.*

Ask pupils how they could improve their next presentation, in response to the feedback they have all heard.

5 Quel talent?! 1 La France a du talent!

Workbook, page 43

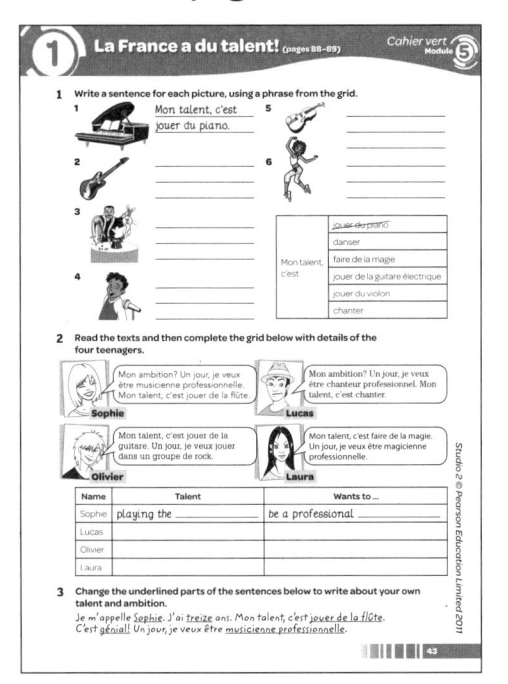

Answers

1 1 *Mon talent, c'est jouer du piano.*
2 Mon talent, c'est jouer de la guitare électrique.
3 Mon talent, c'est faire de la magie.
4 Mon talent, c'est chanter.
5 Mon talent, c'est jouer du violon.
6 Mon talent, c'est danser.

2

Name	Talent	Wants to ...
Sophie	*playing the* flute	*be a professional* musician
Lucas	singing	be a professional singer
Olivier	playing the guitar	play in a rock group
Laura	doing magic	be a professional magician

3 (Answers will vary.)

Worksheet 5.1 Understanding precise meanings

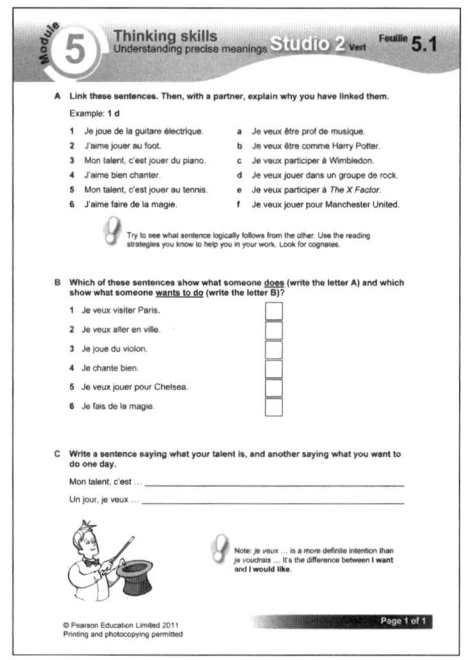

Answers

A 1 d
 2 f
 3 a
 4 e
 5 c
 6 b

B 1 B
 2 B
 3 A
 4 A
 5 B
 6 A

C (Answers will vary.)

5 | 2 Je dois gagner! (Pupil Book pp. 90–91)

Quel talent?!

Learning objectives
- Saying what you must and can do
- Using *devoir* and *pouvoir* + infinitive

Framework objectives
1.3/Y8 Listening – (a) understanding language for specific functions
1.3/Y8 Speaking – (b) using language for specific functions
4.5/Y8 Language – (b) range of modal verbs
5.1 Strategies – patterns

FCSE links
Unit 6: Leisure (Invitations – accepting and refusing)

Grammar
- *devoir* + infinitive
- *pouvoir* + infinitive

Key language
Tu dois …
aller à l'audition
avoir confiance en toi
faire un clip vidéo
participer au concours
répéter tous les jours
Je ne peux pas parce que …
je dois faire mes devoirs
je dois faire du babysitting
Je ne peux pas répéter chez moi.
Tu peux …
faire tes devoirs demain
répéter chez moi

PLTS
R Reflective learners

Resources
CD 3, tracks 4–5
Cahier d'exercices Vert, page 44
ActiveTeach
p.090 Flashcards
p.090 Grammar
p.091 Grammar
p.091 Grammar practice
p.091 Grammar practice
p.091 Grammar skills

Starter 1
Aim
To review infinitives

Write up the following. Give pupils three minutes working in pairs to write out the infinitive of the main verb form shown each time.

j'ai chanté   tu tchattes   il regarde   elle danse
je fais   elle est   je peux   on veut
je vais   tu as

Check answers (*chanter, tchatter, regarder, danser, faire, être, pouvoir, vouloir, aller, avoir*). Ask the class for examples of when the infinitive is used (e.g. after verbs of liking/disliking such as *aimer, détester*, etc.; in the near future tense; after *il faut*). Say that this unit focuses on another two uses of the infinitive.

Alternative Starter 1:
Use ActiveTeach p.090 Flashcards to introduce *devoir* + infinitive.

1 Écoute et mets les phrases dans le bon ordre. (1–5) (AT 1.3)
Listening. Pupils listen to five conversations and put the sentences listed (**a–e**) in the order they are mentioned.

Audioscript CD 3 track 4

1 – *Félix, tu dois participer au concours.*
– *Ah, non, Karim! Je ne peux pas.*
– *Mais, si, tu peux! Tu dois participer au concours!*

2 – *Alors, qu'est-ce que je dois faire?*
– *D'abord, tu dois faire un clip vidéo.*
– *Un clip vidéo!*
– *Oui, tu dois faire un clip vidéo.*

3 – *D'accord. Et ensuite?*
– *Ensuite, tu dois aller à l'audition.*
– *Ah, non! Je ne peux pas!*
– *Mais, si, tu peux! Tu dois aller à l'audition.*

4 – *C'est tout?*
– *Non. Après, tu dois répéter tous les jours!*
– *Tous les jours!*
– *Oui, tu dois répéter tous les jours.*

5 – *Et finalement, tu dois avoir confiance en toi!*
– *Mais, Karim, je n'ai pas de talent.*
– *Mais si, Félix! Tu as beaucoup de talent. Tu dois avoir confiance en toi. D'accord?*
– *D'accord. Je dois avoir confiance en moi.*

Answers
1 d **2** e **3** b **4** a **5** c

5 Quel talent?! 2 Je dois gagner!

2 En tandem. Choisis la séquence d'images A ou B et fais un dialogue. Utilise les phrases de l'exercice 1. (AT 2.3)

Speaking. In pairs: pupils choose a sequence of pictures, represented by A or B, and make up a dialogue, using the sentences from exercise 1. A framework is supplied.

Answers
A ● **Tu dois participer au concours!**
  ■ Qu'est-ce que je dois faire?
  ● D'abord, **tu dois avoir confiance en toi.** Ensuite, **tu dois faire un clip vidéo.**
  ■ D'accord. Et après?
  ● Après, **tu dois répéter tous les jours.** Et finalement, **tu dois aller à l'audition.**
B ● **Tu dois participer au concours!**
  ■ Qu'est-ce que je dois faire?
  ● D'abord, **tu dois faire un clip vidéo.** Ensuite, **tu dois aller à l'audition.**
  ■ D'accord. Et après?
  ● Après, **tu dois avoir confiance en toi.** Et finalement, **tu dois répéter tous les jours.**

Use the pronunciation box to review and practise the sound *oi*.

Studio Grammaire: *devoir* (present tense singular) + infinitive

Use the *Studio Grammaire* box to cover *devoir* (present tense singular, including *on*) + infinitive. There is more information and further practice on Pupil Book p. 102.

---

3 Écris un dialogue. Utilise la séquence d'images A ou B de l'exercice 2. (AT 4.3–4)

Writing. Pupils write a dialogue, using a sequence of pictures from exercise 2.

Starter 2
Aim
To review language for instructions/advice

Write up the following, jumbling the order of the words in each sentence. Give pupils three minutes working in pairs to write out the sentences correctly. Write out the first one correctly as a model and include capitals on starting words and full stops after the last word for support, if necessary.

1 *tu dois participer au concours*
2 *tu dois répéter tous les jours*
3 *tu dois aller à l'audition*
4 *tu dois avoir confiance en toi*
5 *tu dois faire un clip vidéo*

Check answers. Ask the class how *devoir* is used (with the infinitive). Ask which verb in the previous unit was also followed by the infinitive (*vouloir*).

Alternative Starter 2:
Use ActiveTeach p.090 Flashcards to practise the vocabulary for giving instructions/advice.

---

4 Lis les e-mails et réponds aux questions. C'est Olivia ou Nathan? (AT 3.4)

Reading. Pupils read the four emails and answer the questions in English by identifying who is being described each time: Olivia or Nathan.

Answers
1 Nathan 2 Nathan 3 Olivia 4 Nathan
5 Olivia 6 Nathan

Studio Grammaire: *pouvoir* (present tense singular) + infinitive

Use the *Studio Grammaire* box to cover *pouvoir* (present tense singular, including *on*) + infinitive. There is more information and further practice on Pupil Book p. 102.

---

5 Écoute et note les excuses et les solutions en anglais. (1–4) (AT 1.4)

Listening. Pupils listen to four conversations and for each note the excuse given and the solution proposed.

2 Je dois gagner! Quel talent?! 5

Audioscript CD 3 track 5

1. – Je ne peux pas aller à l'audition.
   – Pourquoi?
   – Parce que je dois faire du babysitting.
   – Je peux faire du babysitting pour toi.
2. – Je ne peux pas aller à l'audition.
   – Pourquoi?
   – Parce que je dois faire mes devoirs.
   – Tu peux faire tes devoirs samedi.
3. – Je ne peux pas participer au concours.
   – Pourquoi?
   – Parce que je ne peux pas répéter chez moi. Mes parents n'aiment pas le R'n'B.
   – Tu peux répéter chez moi. Mes parents adorent le R'n'B!
4. – Je ne peux pas participer au concours.
   – Pourquoi?
   – Parce que je dois faire un clip vidéo et je n'ai pas de caméra.
   – Tu peux faire un clip vidéo avec mon portable.

Answers

	excuse	solution
1	has to do babysitting	friend will do the babysitting for her
2	has to do homework	can do homework on Saturday
3	can't rehearse at home	can rehearse at friend's place
4	hasn't got camcorder to make video	can make video on friend's mobile

6 En tandem. Fais des conversations. (AT 2.4)

Speaking. In pairs: pupils make up four dialogues, using the framework + picture prompts supplied. Draw attention to the tip box on distinguishing *mes* and *tes*.

Answers
A ● Je ne peux pas aller à l'audition.
  ■ Pourquoi?
  ● Parce que je dois **faire du babysitting**.
  ■ Je peux faire du babysitting pour toi.
B ● Je ne peux pas participer au concours.
  ■ Pourquoi?
  ● Parce que mes parents n'aiment pas le **R'n'B/le thrash métal/le rock**.
  ■ Tu peux répéter chez moi. Il y a **un garage**.

7 Complète l'e-mail. Donne au moins trois excuses. (AT 4.3–4)

Writing. Pupils complete the email, giving at least three excuses why they can't take part in the talent contest. A sample opening is given.

PLTS R

When they have finished, pupils swap texts with a partner and check each other's work. They underline but don't correct the errors. They then write out a corrected second draft of their own work. Ask them to identify two areas in which they think they can improve.

Plenary

Play a game of Verb Tag to practise *devoir* and *pouvoir*. Put the class into teams and tell them to choose one of the verbs and study it for a minute. Put a sheet of paper for each team at the front of the class. On each paper write the verb chosen and the subject pronouns (singular, including *on*) in order. Tell pupils to close their books.

Team members take it in turn to come to the front of the class and fill in one of the verb forms. They then take the pen back and pass it to the next member of their team. The first team to complete the verb correctly is the winner.

Alternative Plenary:
Use the ActiveTeach p.091 Grammar practice activities to practise modal verbs.

5 Quel talent?! 2 Je dois gagner!

Workbook, page 44

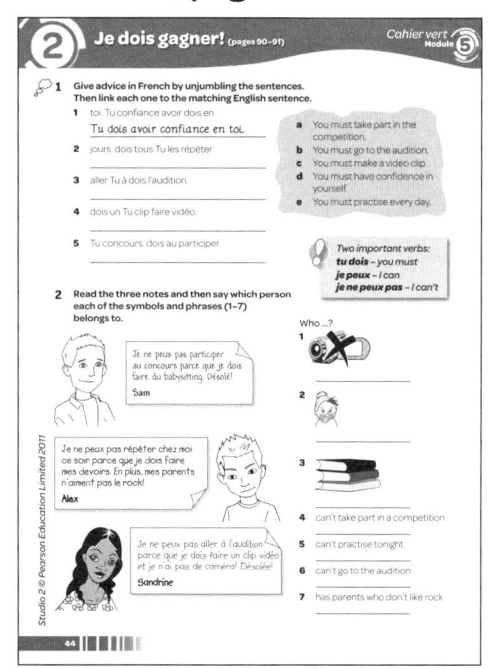

Answers
1 1 *Tu dois avoir confiance en toi.* **d**
   2 Tu dois répéter tous les jours. **e**
   3 Tu dois aller à l'audition. **b**
   4 Tu dois faire un clip vidéo. **c**
   5 Tu dois participer au concours. **a**
2 1 Sandrine 2 Sam 3 Alex 4 Sam 5 Alex
   6 Sandrine 7 Alex

Worksheet 5.2 Modal verbs

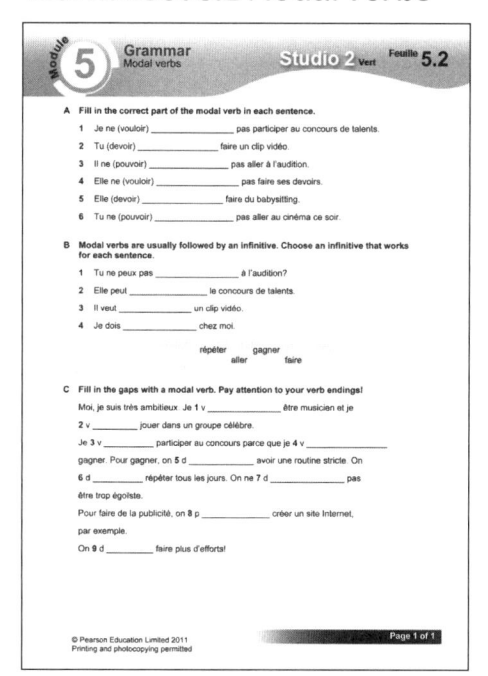

Answers
A 1 Je ne veux pas participer au concours de talents.
  2 Tu dois faire un clip vidéo.
  3 Il ne peut pas aller à l'audition.
  4 Elle ne veut pas faire ses devoirs.
  5 Elle doit faire du babysitting.
  6 Tu ne peux pas aller au cinéma ce soir.
B 1 Tu ne peux pas aller à l'audition?
  2 Elle peut gagner le concours de talents.
  3 Il veut faire un clip vidéo.
  4 Je dois répéter chez moi.
C Moi, je suis très ambitieux. Je **1 veux** être musicien et je **2 veux** jouer dans un groupe célèbre.
Je **3 veux** participer au concours parce que je **4 veux** gagner. Pour gagner, on **5 doit** avoir une routine stricte. On **6 doit** répéter tous les jours. On ne **7 doit** pas être trop égoïste.
Pour faire de la publicité, on **8 peut** créer un site Internet, par exemple.
On **9 doit** faire plus d'efforts!

5 Quel talent?! — 3 Ne fais pas ça! (Pupil Book pp. 92–93)

Learning objectives
- Telling someone what to do
- Using the imperative

Framework objectives
3.2/Y8 Culture – (a) young people: aspirations
5.5 Strategies – reference materials

Grammar
- the imperative (*tu* form)

Key language
Change ton attitude!
Chante plus fort!
Enlève ton blouson!
Éteins ton portable!
Fais plus d'efforts!
Jette ton chewing-gum!
Regarde la caméra!
N'oublie pas ta casquette!

PLTS
I Independent learners

Cross-curricular
ICT: internet research

Resources
CD 3, tracks 6–8
Cahier d'exercices Vert, page 45
ActiveTeach
p.092 Flashcards
p.093 Learning skills

Starter 1

Aim
To review *tu* forms, in preparation for learning the imperative

Write up the following, jumbling the order of the letters to make anagrams. (You can underline the starting letter each time for support, if necessary.) Tell pupils that they are all verb forms, all with the same subject pronoun. Give them three minutes working in pairs to unscramble and write out the verbs with the subject prounoun each time.

regardes   fais   aimes   habites   vas   dois   penses   veux

Check answers (as above: the subject pronoun is *tu*). Explain that the *tu* form is used to create the imperative, the verb form used for giving informal advice and instructions, and that the imperative will be introduced in this unit.

1 Un groupe de danse répète pour le concours. Que dit le prof de danse? Trouve la bonne phrase pour chaque personne. (AT 3.2)

Reading. A dance group is rehearsing for the talent competition. Pupils read and match the correct comment from the dance teacher for each person pictured.

Answers
See answers for exercise 2: pupils listen to the exercise 2 recording to check their answers.

2 Écoute et vérifie. (AT 1.3)

Listening. Pupils listen to check their answers to exercise 1.

Audioscript — CD 3 track 6

1. – OK, ce n'était pas mal, mais … Medhi.
   – Ouais.
   – Fais plus d'efforts!
   – Pardon?
   – Fais plus d'efforts!
   – D'accord.
2. – Flavie. Éteins ton portable.
   – Oh! Euh, oui?
   – Éteins ton portable.
   – Oh, pardon.
3. – Romain …
   – Jette ton chewing-gum.
   – Mais c'est bon pour la concentration.
   – Jette ton chewing-gum.
   – Oui, chef.
4. – Jade.
   – Oui?
   – Enlève ton blouson.
   – Mais j'ai froid!
   – Enlève ton blouson.
   – Ce n'est pas juste.
5. – Yanis.
   – Oui?
   – N'oublie pas ta casquette!
   – N'oublie pas quoi?
   – Ta casquette! N'oublie pas ta casquette!
6. – Alex …
   – Oui?
   – Regarde la caméra!
   – Regarde la caméra?
   – Oui.
   – Allez! On recommence! Musique, s'il vous plaît!

Answers
Medhi 3   **Flavie** 2   **Romain** 1   **Jade** 5   **Yanis** 6   **Alex** 4

5 Quel talent?! 3 Ne fais pas ça!

> **Studio Grammaire: the imperative (*tu* form)**
> Use the *Studio Grammaire* box to cover the *tu* form of the imperative.

R Write up: *regarder, enlever, faire, jeter, oublier*. Pupils working in pairs take it in turn to say the *tu* form of the imperative for each verb. Then ask them to identify in the phrases in exercise 1 the *tu* imperative form of *éteindre* (*éteins*) and the one verb that is given as a negative imperative (*oublier – n'oublie pas*).

3 À deux. Tu es le/la prof. Ton/Ta camarade est Hugo ou Marielle. (AT 2.3–4)

Speaking. In pairs: pupils take it in turn to play the part of the teacher and of Hugo or Marielle. As the teacher, they work out and give appropriate instructions, using the picture prompts. As the pupil, they respond appropriately.

Answers *(sample)*
● Hugo!
■ Oui?
● Jette ton coca.
■ Oh, pardon.
● Éteins ton iPod.
■ Oui, madame.
● Et fais plus d'efforts/regarde la caméra.
■ D'accord.

● Marielle!
■ Oui?
● Éteins ton portable.
■ Oh, pardon.
● Jette tes chips.
■ Oui, madame.
● Et n'oublie pas/enlève ta casquette.
■ D'accord.

4 Écris tes instructions pour Hugo et Marielle. (AT 4.3–4)

Writing. Pupils write out the instructions for Hugo and Marielle.

Answers *(sample)*
Hugo, jette ton coca. Éteins ton iPod. Fais plus d'efforts./Regarde la caméra.
Marielle, éteins ton portable. Jette tes chips. N'oublie pas/Enlève ta casquette.

Starter 2
Aim
To review the imperative (*tu* form)

Write up the following, omitting the text in brackets. Give pupils three minutes working in pairs to rewrite the sentences, each time changing the verb so that the sentence is logical.

1 *Regarde ta casquette!* [N'oublie pas]
2 *Fais ton blouson!* [Enlève]
3 *Enlève ton portable!* [Éteins]
4 *N'oublie pas plus d'efforts!* [Fais]
5 *Éteins ton chewing-gum!* [Jette]
6 *Jette la caméra!* [Regarde]

Check answers. Ask the class to summarise how the imperative is formed.

Alternative Starter 2:
Use ActiveTeach p.092 Flashcards to practise imperatives.

5 Lis le texte et réponds aux questions en anglais. (AT 3.4)

Reading. Pupils read the text, then answer the questions on it in English. *elle dit que* is glossed for support.

Answers
1 Sing in a talent contest.
2 *Any one of*: She has to do her homework./She has to help at home.
3 Ophélie's mother.
4 *Any two of*: Change your attitude./Listen to your mother./Make more effort at school./Do your homework./Help at home (e.g. make your bed and cook the dinner).
5 After two or three weeks.
6 *Pupils' own responses (with reason)*.

6 Écoute et choisis les bons conseils. (1–6) (AT 1.4)

Listening. Pupils listen to six conversations and choose the correct advice from the two options given each time. Some vocabulary is glossed for support.

3 Ne fais pas ça! Quel talent?! 5

Audioscript — CD 3 track 7

1
– Ouf! C'est difficile!
– Change ton attitude, Malik!
– Ce n'est pas juste! C'est difficile, la danse!
– Ce n'est pas difficile! Change ton attitude!

2
– Allô, oui? ... Salut, ça va?
– Coralie!
– Attends un moment. Oui?
– On répète! Éteins ton portable.
– Mais...
– Éteins ton portable!

3
– Bravo, Nathan!
– C'était bien?
– Oui, tu joues bien, mais jette ton bonbon.
– Pardon?
– Jette ton bonbon. Ce n'est pas professionnel.
– D'accord.

4
– Bravo, Félix, tu es un excellent magicien!
– Merci. Et mon costume, ça va?
– Ça va, mais je n'aime pas le chapeau. Enlève le chapeau.
– Le chapeau?
– Oui, enlève le chapeau.

5
– Olivia! Arrête!
– Qu'est-ce qu'il y a?
– Tu chantes trop doucement. Chante plus fort.
– Plus fort?
– Oui, chante plus fort.
– D'accord.

6
– Laurine! Regarde la caméra!
– Pardon?
– Regarde la caméra!
– D'accord!

Answers
1 ton attitude 2 portable 3 bonbon 4 chapeau
5 Chante plus fort 6 caméra

7 Écoute et lis la chanson. (AT 1.4)

PLTS

Listening. Read the *En France* box together. Ask pupils to look up the words of the original song on the internet for the next lesson.

Pupils listen to the song, following the text in the book. Some vocabulary is glossed for support.

Audioscript — CD 3 track 8

– Oh, c'est dur de devenir vedette!
  Oh, c'est dur de chanter et de danser!
– Toi, tu chantes trop doucement!
  Tu danses comme un éléphant!
  Chante plus fort! Chante plus fort!
  Fais plus d'efforts! Fais plus d'efforts!
– O-o-o-h!
  Oh, c'est dur de devenir vedette!
  Oh, c'est dur de chanter et de danser!

– Oh, c'est dur de devenir vedette!
  Oh, c'est dur de chanter et de danser!
– Toi, tu chantes un peu trop faux!
  Tu ne portes pas ton chapeau!
  La prochaine fois, la prochaine fois,
  N'oublie pas! N'oublie pas!
– O-o-o-h!
  Oh, c'est dur de devenir vedette!
  Oh, c'est dur de chanter et de danser!

– Oh, c'est dur de devenir vedette!
  Oh, c'est dur de chanter et de danser!
– Je n'aime pas faire de la danse,
– Je veux aller en vacances!
– De la danse! De la danse!
– En vacances! En vacances!
  O-o-o-h!
  Oh, c'est dur de devenir vedette!
  Oh, c'est dur de chanter et de danser!

8 Trouve dans la chanson l'équivalent des expressions en anglais. Utilise le Mini-dictionnaire, si nécessaire. (AT 3.4)

Reading. Pupils find in the song in exercise 7 the French for the English phrases given, using the Mini-dictionnaire if necessary.

Answers
1 (Toi,) tu chantes trop doucement.
2 Tu danses comme un éléphant.
3 (Toi,) tu chantes un peu faux.
4 Tu ne portes pas ton chapeau.
5 Je veux aller en vacances.

9 Chante la chanson! (AT 2.4)

Speaking. Pupils listen to the song in exercise 7 again and sing along.

Plenary

Ask pupils to summarise how the imperative is formed and give you examples, both from the unit and using other verbs they know.

Play the song in exercise 7 again for the class to sing along. This time fade out the recording and see if they can keep going on their own.

5 Quel talent?! 3 Ne fais pas ça!

Workbook, page 45

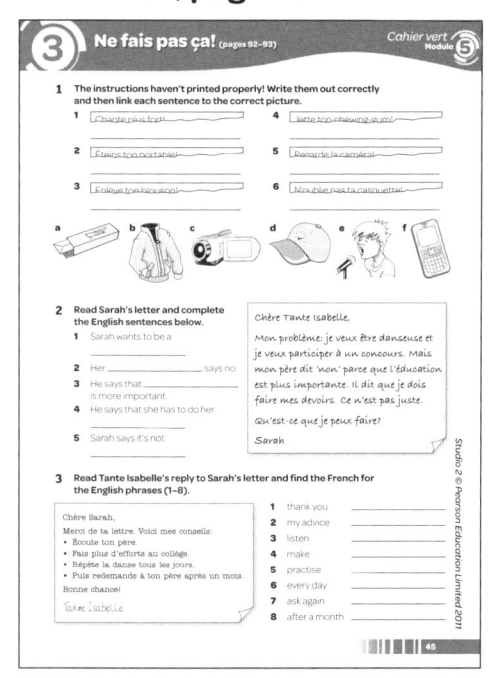

Worksheet 5.3 Working things out

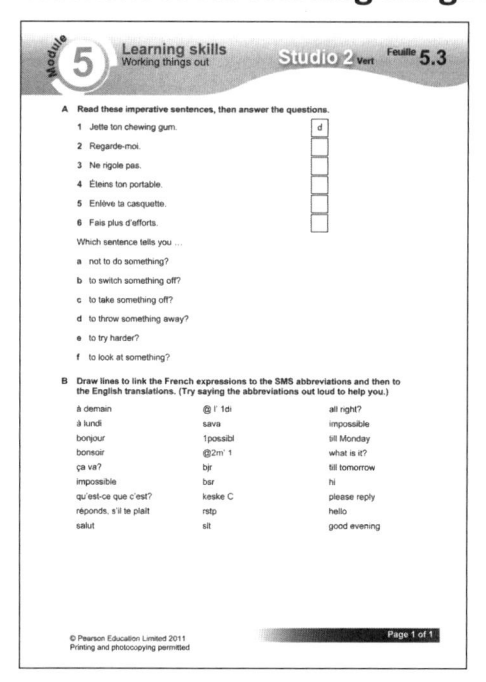

Answers

1
1. Chante plus fort! **e**
2. Éteins ton portable! **f**
3. Enlève ton blouson! **b**
4. Jette ton chewing-gum! **a**
5. Regarde la caméra! **c**
6. N'oublie pas ta casquette! **d**

2
1. Sarah wants to be a **dancer**.
2. Her **father** says no.
3. He says that **education** is more important.
4. He says that she has to do her **homework**.
5. Sarah says it's not **fair**.

3
1. merci
2. mes conseils
3. écoute
4. fais
5. répète
6. tous les jours
7. redemande
8. après un mois

Answers

A 1 d
  2 f
  3 a
  4 b
  5 c
  6 e

B à demain – @2m' 1 – till tomorrow
  à lundi – @ l' 1di – till Monday
  bonjour – bjr – hello
  bonsoir – bsr – good evening
  ça va? – sava – all right?
  impossible – 1possibl – impossible
  qu'est-ce que c'est? – keske C – what is it?
  réponds, s'il te plaît – rstp – please reply
  salut – slt – hi

4 Les juges sont comment?
(Pupil Book pp. 94–95)

Learning objectives
- Describing people's personalities
- Using more adjectives

Framework objectives
1.4/Y8 Speaking – (b) unscripted conversations
1.5/Y8 Speaking – (b) using simple idioms
2.3/Y8 Reading – text features: emotive
4.2/Y8 Language – increasing vocabulary

FCSE links
Unit 1: Meeting people (Physical/character descriptions)

Grammar
- using *avoir* and *être*
- adjective agreement

Key language
Il/Elle est …
très/trop/assez/un peu
arrogant(e)
beau/belle
cruel(le)
gentil(le)
impatient(e)
impoli(e)
intelligent(e)
marrant(e)
vaniteux/vaniteuse
sévère
sincère
stupide
sympa

PLTS
T Team workers

Cross-curricular
ICT: emailing

Resources
CD 3, tracks 9–10
Cahier d'exercices Vert, page 46
ActiveTeach
p.095 Grammar practice
p.095 Class activity
p.095 Video 9
p.095 Video worksheet 9
p.095 Learning skills

Starter 1
Aim
To review higher numbers

Write up the following. Give pupils three minutes to write the words in list A as numbers, then to write the numbers in list B as words, using A as a model.

A	B
quarante-quatre =	29 =
soixante-et-un =	34 =
trente-neuf =	48 =
cinquante-huit =	51 =
vingt-sept =	67 =

Check answers. Count round the class in tens from *dix*, then from *vingt* to *trente*, etc.

(Answers: 44, 61, 39, 58, 27; *vingt-neuf, trente-quatre, quarante-huit, cinquante-et-un, soixante-sept*)

1 Écoute et lis. On parle de quel juge? (1–5) (AT 1.3, AT 3.3)
Listening. Pupils read the summaries of the five judges. They then listen to the descriptions and identify which judge is being described each time (from **A–E**).

Audioscript — CD 3 track 9

1 *Elle a vingt-cinq ans. Elle est chanteuse et danseuse. Elle est intelligente et sympa.*
2 *Il a trente-et-un ans. Il est rock star. Il est égoïste et vaniteux.*
3 *Il a soixante-quatre ans. Il est présentateur de télévision. Il est gentil et sincère.*
4 *Elle a cinquante-deux ans. Elle est journaliste. Elle est sévère et impatiente.*
5 *Il a quarante-trois ans. Il est producteur de musique. Il est impoli et arrogant.*

Answers
1 B **2** E **3** C **4** D **5** A

2 Copie et complète les phrases. (AT 4.1, AT 3.3)
Writing. Pupils copy and complete the sentences describing the judges in exercise 1.

Answers
1 52, journaliste
2 Aimable, gentil
3 Michel, impoli, arrogant
4 Leïla Labelle, chanteuse
5 rock star, égoïste

3 En tandem. Jeu de mémoire! Ton/Ta camarade ferme le livre et tu poses des questions. (AT 2.3)
Speaking. In pairs: pupils play a memory game. They take it in turn to close their book and to ask questions about the judges in exercise 1.

5 Quel talent?! 4 Les juges sont comment?

> **Studio Grammaire: using *avoir* and *être***
> Use the *Studio Grammaire* box to cover using *avoir* and *être* correctly.

Starter 2
Aim
To review adjective agreement

Write up the following, jumbling the order of the adjectives (under correct column here for reference). Give pupils two minutes to copy out and complete the grid, writing the adjectives in the correct columns.

masculine	feminine	either
gentil	impatiente	sincère
beau	marrante	stupide
arrogant	intelligente	sévère
vaniteux	belle	sympa
impoli	cruelle	

Hear answers. Ask the class to summarise the rules of adjective agreement.

Alternative Starter 2:
Use ActiveTeach p.095 Grammar practice to practise using adjectives.

4 Écoute le commentaire des juges. (1–5) (AT 1.3)

a) Le commentaire est positif 😊 ou négatif 😞?
b) Tu es d'accord (✓) ou pas d'accord (✗) avec le/la juge?

Listening. Pupils listen to the five judges giving their comments and **(a)** identify whether the comment is positive (drawing a smiley face) or negative (drawing a sad face) and **(b)** say whether they agree with the comment or not, writing ✓ or ✗ as appropriate.

Audioscript CD 3 track 10

1 – Alors, quelle est votre opinion? Michel Méchant.
 – C'était ennuyeux. Très, très ennuyeux.
2 – À vous, Antoine Aimable. Quelle est votre opinion?
 – Bravo! C'était super! Génial!
3 – Eh, bien. Leïla Labelle. À votre avis, c'était comment?
 – C'était fantastique! Elle a beaucoup de talent!
4 – Quelle est votre opinion? Monique Maline.
 – À mon avis, c'était nul! Complètement nul!
5 – À vous, Damien Duroq. C'était comment?
 – Ouah! C'était bizarre. C'était bien? C'était nul? Alors, moi, je ne sais pas. Voilà.

Answers
a 1 😞 2 😊 3 😊 4 😞 5 😊/😞
b *Pupils' own opinions.*

> **Studio Grammaire: adjective agreement**
> Use the *Studio Grammaire* box to cover adjective agreement, including pronunciation. There is more information and further practice on Pupil Book p. 103.

5 Écris ton opinion sur trois célébrités ou personnages. (AT 4.3–4)
Writing. Pupils choose three celebrities or characters (from a book, TV or a film) and write their opinion of them. A framework is supplied for support.

➕ Pupils include other details about the people they are describing, such as their age, job, likes, dislikes, etc.

6 En tandem. Discute de ton opinion avec ton/ta camarade. (AT 2.4)
Speaking. In pairs: pupils exchange opinions on the people they wrote about in exercise 5. A sample exchange is given.

PLTS T 🖱

➕ Pupils exchange information via email on UK talent shows with pupils at your partner school in France, if you have one.

Plenary
Challenge the class (with books closed) to remember all the adjectives covered in the unit.

Review adjective agreement. Prompt with the masculine form of the adjectives in the unit for pupils to respond with the feminine form. Then prompt with the feminine form to test the masculine form.

4 Les juges sont comment? Quel talent?! 5

Workbook, page 46

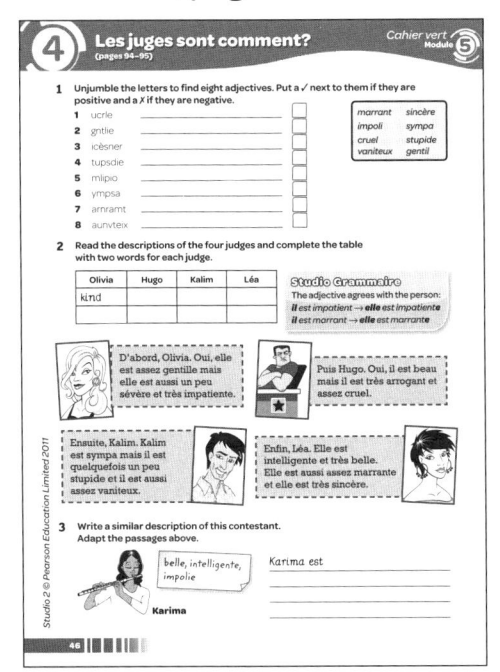

Worksheet 5.4 Quality of language

Answers
1 1 cruel ✗ 2 gentil ✓ 3 sincère ✓
  4 stupide ✗ 5 impoli ✗ 6 sympa ✓
  7 marrant ✓ 8 vaniteux ✗

2 (Any two words for each judge:)

Olivia	Hugo	Kalim	Léa
kind	good-looking	nice	intelligent
strict/harsh	arrogant	stupid	beautiful
impatient	cruel/nasty	vain	funny
			sincere

3 (Possible answer:)
Karima est belle et intelligente mais elle est aussi un peu impolie.

Answers
A a 3 and 6
  b 4
  c 2
  d 5
  e 1
  f 2 and 3

B Text **2** is better.
  Reasons:
  1 It uses a time marker (le weekend prochain).
  2 It uses connectives (mais, parce que).
  3 It expresses an opinion (À mon avis).
  4 It gives an explanation (parce que normalement, je ne chante pas devant mes copains).

C 1 À mon avis, Simon Cowell est **arrogant**.
  2 Je trouve que Lady Gaga est très **vaniteuse**.
  3 À mon avis, Wayne Rooney est un peu **impatient**.
  4 Mon père est très **gentil**.
  5 Kylie Minogue est **belle**.

5) Quel talent?!   4 Les juges sont comment?

Video

Episode 9: Un nouveau présentateur
The team interview a range of applicants for the new presenter's job at StudioFR. Video worksheet 9 can be used in conjunction with this episode.

> **Answers to video worksheet (ActiveTeach)**
> 1 **A** (Answers will vary.)
>   **B** Samira wants a new presenter for the team.
>   **C** Words used include: *ambitieux* (ambitious), *fort* (strong), *travailleur* (hard-working), *arrogant* (arrogant).
>   **D** (Answers will vary. They point up people's reactions.)
> 2 **A** It's a talent contest.
>   **B** He can't understand why Samira would want to hold a talent contest.
>   **C** He thinks Samira plans to replace Marielle.
>   **D** She is shocked at the idea she might be replaced.
>   **E** It's suspicious that she stammers and hesitates as she denies she is planning to replace Marielle.
>   **F** She looks as if she doesn't believe Samira.
> 3 **A** Because he's a rock singer, not a presenter.
>   **B** 'Suivant!'
>   **C** They can dance and sing.
>   **D** He says they are pretty (*jolies*). He also claims they have talent.
>   **E** 'You are wrong!'
>   **F** They don't seem very talented and they certainly aren't suitable for the job.
> 4 **A** Yes, they were interviewed on the street about fashion.
>   **B** They are hip-hop dancers.
>   **C** It seems terrible.
>   **D** Because they are boys and cool.
>   **E** Too ambitious, and anyway, they don't need three presenters.
>   **F** Pure jealousy. It would threaten her position.
>   **G** She's right to be worried!
> 5 **A** He has all the right qualifications.
>   **B** 'Félicitations!'
>   **C** (Answers will vary. Pupils may conclude that Lucie would probably have been the best choice.)
>   **D** Mehdi is male and doesn't pose a threat to her position.

5 Et le gagnant est ... (Pupil Book pp. 96–97)

Learning objectives
- Showing how much you can do with the French language
- Using a variety of structures

Framework objectives
1.5/Y8 Speaking – (a) unscripted talks
4.5/Y8 Language – (b) range of modal verbs

FCSE links
Unit 1: Meeting people (Sports and hobbies)
Unit 6: Leisure (Sports/hobbies)
Unit 12: Work choices (Future plans – career/studies/lifestyle choices)

Grammar
- verb + infinitive structures

Key language
j'aime gagner
je dois gagner
je peux gagner
je voudrais gagner
je vais gagner
je veux gagner

PLTS
S Self-managers

Resources
CD 3, tracks 11–12
Cahier d'exercices Vert, page 47
ActiveTeach
p.096 Grammar
p.096 Grammar practice
p.096 Grammar practice
p.097 Class activity
p.097 Video 10
p.097 Video worksheet 10
p.097 Grammar skills

Starter 1
Aim
To review structures using the infinitive

Write up the following, mixing both columns together (the second column here = the answers). Give pupils three minutes working in pairs to copy out all the expressions which can be followed by the infinitive, and to add an appropriate infinitive each time.

j'ai	je vais
je regarde	je peux
je m'appelle	j'aime
j'ai gagné	je veux
	je dois
	je voudrais

Check answers. Ask pupils if they remember any other expressions followed by the infinitive (*il faut*).

1 Écoute. Trouve la bonne phrase pour chaque personne. (1–6) (AT 1.3)
Listening. Pupils listen to six conversations with the contestants in the talent competition and identify the phrase each one mentions (from **a–f**).

Audioscript CD 3 track 11

1 – Je dois gagner, je dois gagner, je dois gagner...
  – Olivia, ça va?
  – Oui, mais je dois gagner!

2 – Coralie? Coralie!
  – Oui, Ryan?
  – Je veux gagner.
  – Oh, mais ...
  – Écoute! Je veux gagner!
  – D'accord, d'accord.

3 – Félix, répète après moi: Je peux gagner!
  – Euh ...
  – Répète! Je peux gagner, je peux ...
  – OK. OK. Je peux gagner. Je peux gagner!
  – C'est bien.

4 – Charles, Malik ...
  – Oui, Lucas?
  – Je n'aime pas perdre. J'aime gagner.
  – Oui, moi aussi, j'aime gagner.
  – Et moi, j'aime gagner.
  – Alors, tous ensemble!
  – J'aime gagner! J'aime gagner!

5 – Laurine, tu voudrais gagner?
  – Ah, oui! Je voudrais gagner.
  – Mais ...
  – Il y a beaucoup de talents, ici?
  – Oui, il y a beaucoup de talents.
  – Mais je voudrais gagner. Je voudrais gagner.

6 – Nathan. À mon avis, tu vas gagner.
  – Ah bon? Je vais gagner?
  – Oui, parce que tu as beaucoup de talent!
  – Merci. Mais ... je vais gagner?
  – Oui, tu vas gagner.

Answers
1 b **2** f **3** c **4** a **5** d **6** e

5 Quel talent?!   5 Et le gagnant est ...

2 Trouve l'équivalent des phrases en anglais. (AT 3.2)
Reading. Pupils find in exercise 1 the French for the English phrases given.

Answers
1 Je veux gagner!
2 Je vais gagner?
3 Je dois gagner!
4 J'aime gagner.
5 Je peux gagner!
6 Je voudrais gagner.

Studio Grammaire: verbs + infinitive
Use the *Studio Grammaire* box to cover a range of verb + infinitive structures. There is more information and further practice on Pupil Book p. 103.

3 Prépare cinq phrases. Utilise les infinitifs. (AT 2.1)
Speaking. Pupils make up and say five sentences using the verbs and the range of infinitives supplied.

Starter 2
Aim
To review verb + infinitive structures

Write up the following. Give pupils three minutes to complete each sentence.

1 Je d_ _ _ gagner.
2 Je v _ _ _ _ _ _ _ gagner.
3 J'_ _ _ _ gagner.
4 Je ve _ _ gagner.
5 Je va _ _ gagner
6 Je p _ _ _ gagner.

Check answers, asking pupils to translate each completed sentence. (Answers: *dois, voudrais, aime, veux, vais, peux*)

Alternative Starter 2:
Use the ActiveTeach p.096 Grammar practice activities to practise a variety of verb structures.

4 Qui gagne le concours? Écoute. Copie et remplis le tableau. (AT 1.5)
Listening. Pupils copy out the grid. They listen to the competition results and complete the grid with the details of who has won.

Audioscript CD 3 track 12

– *Votre attention, s'il vous plaît.*
– *Voici les résultats du concours de jeunes talents ...*
– *En troisième place: c'est le jeune magicien, Félix!*
– *Bravo, Félix!*
– *C'est génial! Merci, monsieur.*
– *En deuxième place: c'est une chanteuse avec beaucoup de talent: Olivia!*
– *Quoi! Deuxième place?! C'est nul!*
– *Bravo, Olivia.*
– *Mouais ... Merci quand même.*
– *Et finalement, les gagnants du concours ... !*
– *C'est un groupe de danseurs ...*
– *Ils sont fantastiques ...*
– *C'est: LMC!*
– *C'est pas vrai! On a gagné!!*
– *Oui! On a gagné! On a gagné!*
– *C'est hypergénial!*

Answers

	nom	réaction
Troisième place:	Félix	:)
Deuxième place:	Olivia	:(
Première place:	LMC	:)

5 Lis le texte et réponds aux questions en anglais. (AT 3.5)
Reading. Pupils read the text and answer the questions in English by identifying who is being described each time.

Answers
1 Olivia 2 Nathan 3 Lucas 4 Nathan
5 Olivia 6 Lucas

6 Imagine que tu es Ryan ou Coralie. Prépare un mini-exposé oral. (AT 2.5)
PLTS S

Speaking. Pupils imagine they are Ryan or Coralie, and prepare and give a short presentation on what they like and their future plans and hopes. A framework is supplied for support.

5 Et le gagnant est ...   Quel talent?!

Remind pupils how to approach a presentation: they write out what they want to say, then create notes to work from.

If you can, record the conversations, so pupils can listen and comment on how they might improve. Suggest that pupils record themselves speaking French at home, as this will help them develop fluency, accuracy and confidence.

Answers (sample)
Ryan
J'adore **jouer du violon**.
Un jour, **je voudrais jouer dans un grand orchestre**.
Mais d'abord, **je dois continuer mes études au collège**.
Après, **je veux aller à l'Académie des Jeunes Talents**.

Coralie
J'aime **jouer du piano**.
Un jour, **je veux être professeur de musique**.
La semaine prochaine, **je vais jouer du piano à la télé**.
Après, **je voudrais partir en vacances en Italie**.

7 Écris un paragraphe pour Ryan ou Coralie. (AT 4.5)

Writing. Pupils write a paragraph as though they were Ryan or Coralie, describing what they like and their future plans and hopes. Remind them to use the framework supplied in exercise 6.

➕ Read together through *Stratégie 5* on Pupil Book p. 105, covering more ways to learn vocabulary. Ask pupils to choose two new techniques (either from those listed or ones that they've thought up themselves) and use them to learn two different sets of vocabulary from the units from Module 5. Ask them in a subsequent lesson which method they found better and why.

Plenary
Ask the class to identify the sentence structures used by the contestants to express their feelings as they waited for the result (verb + infinitive).

Put the class into teams to write down all the verb + infinitive structures used in the unit. The team which finishes first wins – but warn them that each error earns a 10-second penalty on their total time.

Workbook, page 47

Answers
1.
   1. *Je dois continuer mes études.*
   2. *Je veux travailler en Afrique.*
   3. *Je vais chanter à la télé.*
   4. *Je voudrais être riche.*
   5. *J'aime jouer de la guitare.*
   6. *Je peux être chanteur professionnel.*
2. Moi, j'**adore** jouer du piano. Un jour, je **voudrais** être musicienne professionnelle. Mais d'abord, je dois continuer mes études au **collège** parce que l'éducation est **importante**. Après, je vais **étudier** la musique dans une école à **Paris**.

5 Quel talent?! 5 Et le gagnant est …

Worksheet 5.5 Using more than one tense

Answers

A 1 P – I must win.
2 F – I will try harder.
3 P – She's very determined.
4 F – I will practise.
5 F – I will become a musician.
6 F – She will be famous.
7 P – He has lots of success.
8 F – I will take part in the competition.

B 1 Je participe au concours.
2 J'ai participé au concours.
3 J'adore jouer de la guitare.
4 J'ai très bien joué au concours.
5 J'ai gagné le concours.
6 Je veux être prof de musique un jour.

C 1 would like to
2 going to
3 going to
4 would like to
5 would like to

Video

Episode 10: Le parcours de santé

Marielle, Hugo and new arrival Mehdi compete against each other on a fitness trail, while Alex and Samira record them. Video worksheet 10 can be used in conjunction with this episode.

Answers to video worksheet (ActiveTeach)

1 **A** He is not as fit and strong as he claimed to be.
  B Take off your jacket!
  Switch off your mobile!
  Throw away your chewing gum!
  Make more of an effort!
  Run faster!
  Stop talking!
  C Something like a 'fitness trail'.
2 **A** He says 'C'est facile.' – 'It's easy.' 'I'm going to win because I am the strongest and I have no fear.'
  B She's going to win actually! She says she's the strongest.
  C 'I'm the boss.'
  D You might think *chef* means 'chef' – but it means 'boss'.
  E Take off his jacket and join in.
  F Switch off her mobile.
  G Throw away his chewing gum.
  H Very strict and bossy.
  I A five-kilometre run with tasks every kilometre.
  J (Answers will vary.)
3 **A** 'On your marks!'
  B Ten press-ups.
  C Mehdi is finding it hard while Marielle isn't.
  D Twenty sit-ups.
  E Look at the camera and smile!
  F Yes, although Mehdi is actually the weakest.
  G Because he is tall.
  H He says 'Stop talking!' He is definitely picking on Mehdi because Marielle is in fact cheating.
  I 'fastest and most agile'. 'rapide' and 'agile' are both words that look similar in English and French but which are pronounced very differently. ['la plus rapide et la plus agile' are also examples of the superlative.]
  J He gets a Studio T-shirt and is welcomed into the gang.

5 Quel talent?! Bilan et Révisions (Pupil Book pp. 98–99)

Bilan
Pupils use this checklist to review language covered in the module, working on it in pairs in class or on their own at home. Encourage them to follow up any areas of weakness they identify. There are Target Setting Sheets included in the Assessment Pack, and an opportunity for pupils to record their own levels and targets on the *J'avance* page in the Workbook, p. 52. You can also use the *Bilan* checklist as an end-of-module plenary option.

Révisions
These revision exercises can be used for assessment purposes or for pupils to practise before tackling the assessment tasks in the Assessment Pack.

Resources
CD 3, track 13
Cahier d'exercices Vert, pages 48 & 49

1 Écoute les opinions sur les profs et coche (✓) les bons adjectifs. (1–6) (AT 1.3)
Listening. Pupils copy out the grid. They listen to six opinions on teachers and tick the adjective used for each of them.

Audioscript CD 3 track 13
1 Je n'aime pas Madame Lenoir. Elle est trop sévère.
2 J'adore Monsieur Levert. Il est très gentil.
3 J'aime bien Madame Lerouge. Elle est assez marrante.
4 Je n'aime pas Monsieur Legris. Il est un peu impatient.
5 J'aime beaucoup Madame Leblanc. Elle est très intelligente.
6 Je déteste Monsieur Lejaune. Il est très vaniteux.

Answers

	funny	impatient	vain	intelligent	strict	kind
1					✓	
2						✓
3	✓					
4		✓				
5				✓		
6			✓			

2 En tandem. Fais un dialogue. Utilise les images. (AT 2.4)
Speaking. In pairs: pupils make up a dialogue, using the framework + picture prompts supplied.

Answers
● Tu dois participer au concours de talents!
■ Je ne peux pas. Je dois **faire mes devoirs**.
● Tu peux faire tes devoirs demain soir.
■ Je ne peux pas. Demain soir, je dois **faire du babysitting**.
● Je peux faire du babysitting pour toi.
■ Je dois faire un clip vidéo, mais je n'ai pas de **caméra**.
● Tu peux faire un clip vidéo **avec mon portable**.
■ D'accord, merci.

3 Lis le blog et complète les phrases en anglais. (AT 3.5)
Reading. Pupils read the blog and complete the sentences summarising it in English.

Answers
1 One day, Samira wants to be **a professional singer**.
2 She would like to sing **on TV (with Rihanna)**.
3 But first she must **continue studying (at school)**.
4 Next week, she is going to **take part in a talent contest (in her town)**.
5 She is going to **rehearse** every day because she wants **to win**.

4 Tu es le/la prof. Écris quatre conseils pour cet élève. (AT 4.3–4)
Writing. Pupils imagine they are the teacher and write four pieces of advice for the pupil pictured.

Answers
Any four of: Jette ton chewing-gum! Éteins ton portable! Enlève ton blouson! *Enlève ta casquette!* Fais plus d'efforts!

5 Quel talent?! Bilan et Révisions

Workbook, pages 48 and 49

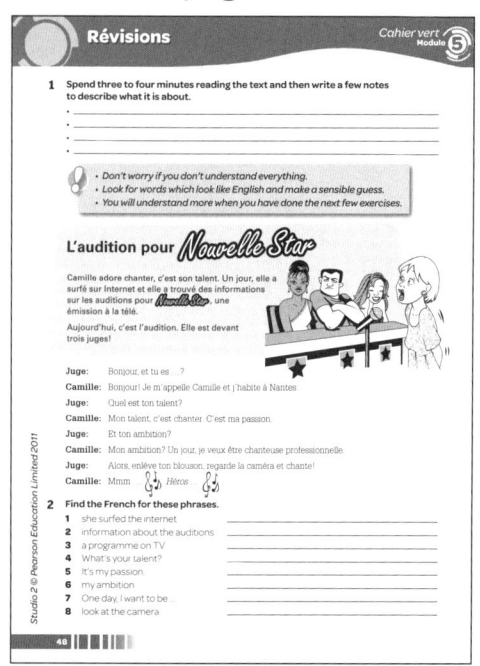

Answers

1 (Answers will vary.)
2
   1 elle a surfé sur Internet
   2 informations sur les auditions
   3 une émission à la télé
   4 Quel est ton talent?
   5 C'est ma passion.
   6 mon ambition
   7 Un jour, je veux être …
   8 regarde la caméra
3
   1 *Well done!*   2 natural talent
   3 you sing very well   4 let's vote
   5 you're going to return/come back   6 the final audition
   7 it's fabulous   8 every day
4 1 ✗   2 ✓   3 ✓   4 ✗   5 ✗   6 ✓   7 ✗
5 (Answers will vary.)

5 En plus: Les vedettes de la musique
Quel talent?! (Pupil Book pp. 100–101)

Learning objectives
- Writing a profile of a music star

Framework objectives
2.1/Y8 Reading – authentic materials
2.5/Y8 Writing – using researched language
3.2/Y8 Culture – (a) young people: aspirations
4.2/Y8 Language – increasing vocabulary
5.4 Strategies – working out meaning
5.7 Strategies – planning and preparing

FCSE links
Unit 1: Meeting people (Physical/character descriptions; Sports and hobbies)
Unit 6: Leisure (Sports/hobbies)

Grammar
- the perfect tense

Key language
Review of language from the module

une vedette
il est né/elle est née
il/elle a gagné
il est parti/elle est partie

PLTS
C Creative thinkers

Cross-curricular
English: reading for gist
ICT: internet research

Resources
CD 3, tracks 14–15
ActiveTeach
p.101 Assignment 5
p.101 Assignment 5: prep

Starter
Aim
To review the present and perfect tenses; To identify and apply grammatical patterns

Write up the following, omitting the words in italics. Give pupils three minutes to copy and complete the grid.

present	English	perfect	English
je gagne	*I win*	j'ai gagné	*I won*
je mange	*I eat*	j'ai mangé	*I ate*
je regarde	*I watch*	j'ai regardé	*I watched*
je pars	*I leave*	je suis parti	*I left*
je vais	*I go*	je suis allé	*I went*

Check answers. Ask pupils when the perfect tense is used.

1 Écoute et lis. Il s'agit de quoi? Choisis la bonne réponse. (AT 1.5, AT 3.5)
Listening. Pupils listen to the description of Christophe Willem, following the text at the same time. They answer the two questions, which focus on developing gist reading skills. Draw their attention to the tip box on reading for gist before they start. Point out that these are useful techniques to use when reading in English too.

Audioscript CD 3 track 14
Christophe Willem est né le 3 août 1983, à Enghien-les-Bains, en France. Son vrai nom est Christophe Durier. En 2006, il a gagné un concours de talents à la télévision qui s'appelle Nouvelle Star. Il a enregistré deux albums: Inventaire (2007) et Caféine (2009). Son premier album a été numéro un au hit-parade. En 2008, il est parti en tournée: il a donné des concerts en France, en Belgique et en Suisse. En général, Christophe a bon caractère: il est calme, généreux et très travailleur.

Answers
1 c
2 (*sample*) clues from words such as *albums, hit-parade, concerts*; knowing that *Nouvelle Star* is a singing contest

2 Qu'est-ce que c'est en anglais? Devine, puis vérifie dans le Mini-dictionnaire ou dans un dictionnaire. (AT 3.5)
Reading. Pupils translate the French expressions from the text in exercise 1, using the context and other reading strategies. They then check their answers in the Mini-dictionnaire or a dictionary.

Answers
1 his real name **2** his first album **3** tour
4 in Belgium **5** in Switzerland **6** calm **7** generous

5 Quel talent?! En plus: Les vedettes de la musique

> **Studio Grammaire: the perfect tense (*avoir* and *être* verbs)**
> Use the *Studio Grammaire* box to cover the perfect tense.

3 Lis et complète la traduction sans utiliser de dictionnaire. (AT 3.5)
Reading. Pupils read and complete the translations of the sentences without using a dictionary. Draw their attention to the tip box on using reading strategies to work out new words.

Answers
1 was born 2 won 3 recorded
4 number one, charts 5 on tour 6 gave

4 Écoute la description de Jenifer Bartoli et choisis la bonne réponse. (AT 1.5)
Listening. Pupils listen to the description of Jenifer Bartoli and complete the sentences by choosing the correct word/phrase from the two options given each time.

Audioscript CD 3 track 15

Jenifer Bartoli est née le 15 novembre 1982 à Nice, en France. Elle est chanteuse. En 1997, elle a gagné un concours de talents à la télévision qui s'appelle Star Academy. *Elle a enregistré trois albums:* Jenifer *(2002),* Le Passage *(2004) et* Lunatique *(2007). Son deuxième album a gagné un MTV Europe Music Award. Jenifer est sympa, enthousiaste et ambitieuse.*

Answers
1 le 15 novembre 1982 2 *Star Academy* 3 trois
4 deuxième 5 ambitieuse

5 Copie les phrases et corrige les erreurs. (AT 4.5)
Writing. Pupils copy out the sentences, correcting the errors: adding accents in 1–3, correcting spellings in 4–5 and inserting missing words in 6–8. Draw pupils' attention to the tip box on checking work for accuracy by checking features like these in any piece of written work in French that they produce.

Answers
1 Christophe est <u>né</u> le 3 <u>août</u> 1983.
2 Jenifer est <u>née à</u> Nice.
3 Christophe a bon <u>caractère</u>: il est <u>généreux</u>.
4 Christophe est aussi très <u>travailleur</u>.
5 Jenifer est <u>chanteuse</u>.
6 Elle <u>a</u> gagné un concours de talents.
7 En 2008, Christophe <u>est</u> parti en tournée.
8 Il a donné <u>des</u> concerts en France.

6 Fais des recherches sur Internet. Écris un paragraphe sur une star de la musique. Utilise le texte de l'exercice 1 comme modèle. (AT 4.5)

Writing. Pupils research a music star on the internet and write a paragraph about him/her, using the text in exercise 1 (p. 100) as a model. A list of details to include is supplied.

7 En tandem. Lis, vérifie et commente le paragraphe de ton/ta camarade. (AT 2.3–4)
Speaking. In pairs: pupils read, check and comment on the paragraph their partner wrote in exercise 6. A list of expressions to use in giving feedback is supplied.

> **Plenary**
> Ask some pupils to read out their descriptions from exercise 6: they omit the name of the person and pause after each piece of information to allow guesses. The rest of the class compete to see who can be the first to identify the music star correctly.

En plus: Les vedettes de la musique   Quel talent?! 5

Worksheet 5.6 Ta classe a du talent?

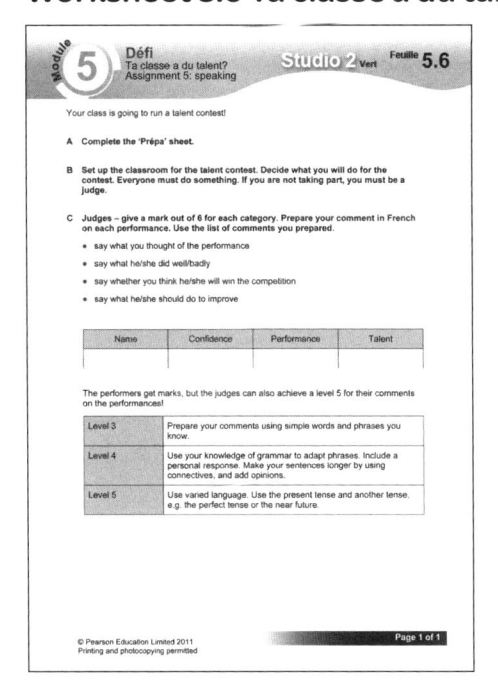

Answers
Assessed by teacher.

Worksheet 5.7 Ta classe a du talent? Prépa

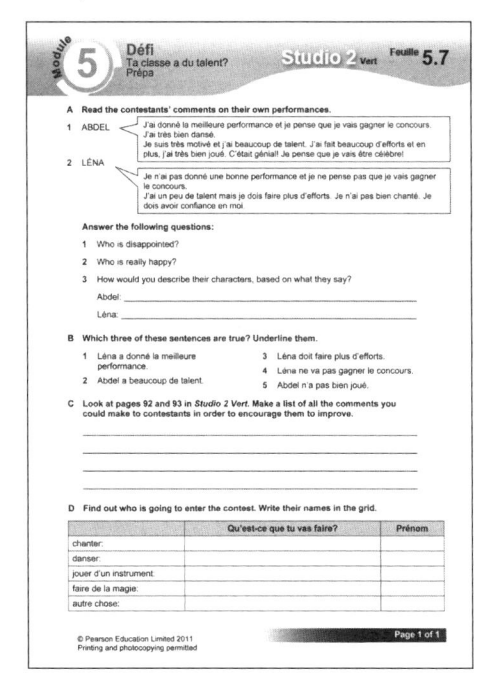

Answers
A 1 Léna
  2 Abdel
  3 Abdel: very confident, almost arrogant
     Léna: lacking in confidence
B 2 Abdel a beaucoup de talent.
  3 Léna doit faire plus d'efforts.
  4 Léna ne va pas gagner le concours.
C and **D** (Answers will vary.)

Studio Grammaire (Pupil Book pp. 102–103)

Quel talent?! **5**

The *Studio Grammaire* section provides a more detailed summary of the key grammar covered in the module, along with further exercises to practise these points. The activities on ActiveTeach pages 102 and 103 are repeated from elsewhere in the module.

Grammar topics
- infinitives
- modal verbs: *vouloir*, *devoir* and *pouvoir*
- adjectives
- using a variety of structures

Resources
Cahier d'exercices Vert, page 53

Infinitives

1 Complete each sentence with the correct infinitive.
Pupils copy and complete the sentences using the infinitives supplied.

Answers
1 faire 2 être 3 jouer 4 écouter 5 chanter
6 danser

vouloir

2 Translate these sentences into French. Use the infinitives and other words from exercise 1 to help you.
Pupils translate the sentences into French using the completed French sentences from exercise 1 as models.

Answers
1 Je veux danser.
2 Tu veux jouer.
3 Il veut chanter.
4 On veut écouter.
5 Je veux faire de la magie.
6 Elle veut être professeur.

devoir and *pouvoir*

3 Write out these sentences correctly. Then underline the modal verb in each sentence in red and the infinitive in blue.
Pupils write out the merged sentences, then in each one underline the modal verb (in red) and the infinitive (in blue).

Answers
(Modal verbs shown using underline; infinitives using italics.)
1 Je dois *faire* mes devoirs.
2 Je peux *faire* du babysitting.
3 Tu dois *avoir* confiance en toi.
4 Tu peux *répéter* chez moi.
5 On doit *faire* un clip vidéo.
6 Elle doit *aller* à l'audition.

Adjectives

4 Copy and complete the grid.
Pupils copy and complete the grid, supplying the correct form of the adjectives (masculine or feminine).

Answers
1 gentille 2 impatient 3 intelligente 4 marrant
5 vaniteuse 6 sévère 7 stupide 8 sympa

5 Write six sentences about different celebrities, using adjectives from the grid in exercise 4.
Pupils choose six celebrities and write a sentence for each one, describing him/her using the adjectives in exercise 4. Encourage them to choose a mixture of male and female celebrities.

Studio Grammaire Quel talent?! 5

Using a variety of structures

6 Write these sentences correctly, using the English translation to help you.
Pupils rewrite each scrambled sentence, using the English version to help them put the words in the correct order.

Answers
1 J'adore jouer de la guitare.
2 Je veux participer au concours.
3 Je dois faire un clip vidéo.
4 Je peux répéter dans le garage.
5 Je voudrais être guitariste professionnel.
6 Je vais gagner le concours.

7 Translate these sentences into French, using the infinitives below.
Pupils translate the sentences into French using the infinitives supplied.

Answers
1 Je peux gagner.
2 Je veux danser.
3 J'adore chanter.
4 Je vais jouer.
5 Je voudrais aller à Paris.
6 Je dois écouter.

8 Write six sentences about yourself, using a different structure at the start of each one (e.g. *je voudrais, je dois, je peux, j'aime, ...*). Use a dictionary if you need to.
Pupils write six sentences about themselves, using a different verb + infinitive structure for each one. They can use a dictionary for support if required.

Workbook, page 53

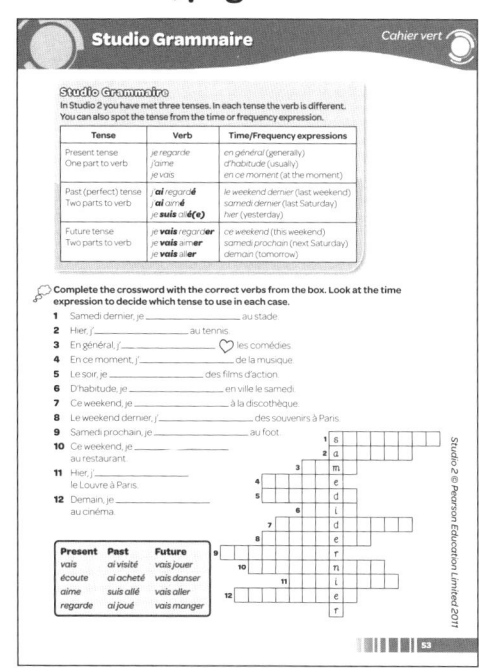

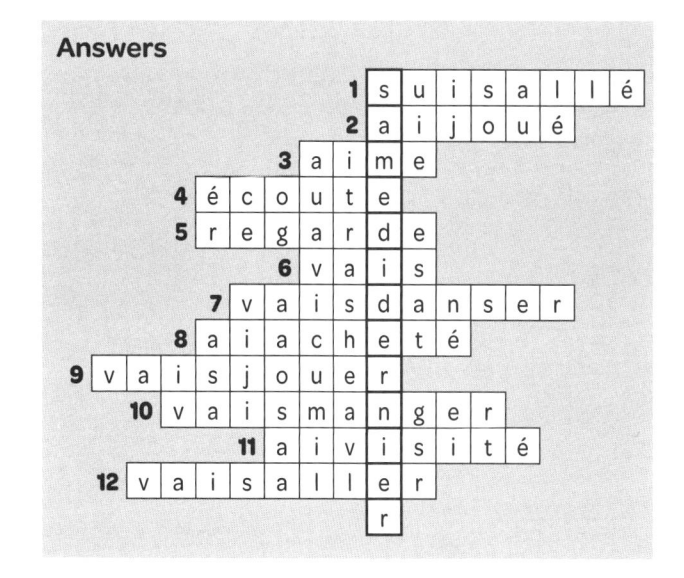

Answers

1	s	u	i	s	a	l	l	é	
2	a	i	j	o	u	é			
3	a	i	m	e					
4	é	c	o	u	t	e			
5	r	e	g	a	r	d	e		
6	v	a	i	s					
7	v	a	i	s	d	a	n	s	e	r
8	a	i	a	c	h	e	t	é	
9	v	a	i	s	j	o	u	e	r
10	v	a	i	s	m	a	n	g	e	r
11	a	i	v	i	s	i	t	é	
12	v	a	i	s	a	l	l	e	r

5 À toi (Pupil Book pp. 122–123)

Self-access reading and writing

A Reinforcement

1 Décode les conseils et trouve la bonne image. N'oublie pas les accents! (AT 4.2)

Writing. Pupils decode the pieces of advice, using the code supplied, and match each to the correct picture. They need to think about which accents to include, as these are not indicated in the code.

Answers
1 *Fais plus d'efforts!* – f
2 *Regarde la caméra!* – c
3 *Enlève ton blouson!* – d
4 *Jette ton chewing-gum!* – a
5 *Éteins ton portable!* – b
6 *N'oublie pas ta casquette!* – e

2 Lis et traduis les excuses bizarres en anglais. (AT 3.2)

Reading. Pupils read and translate the weird excuses into English.

Answers
1 I must babysit with my elephant.
2 I must go to the supermarket with Johnny Depp.
3 I must dance with Shrek in the swimming pool.
4 I must play the piano in the bathroom.
5 I must take part in the cheese sandwich contest.

3 Invente des excuses bizarres. Complète les phrases. Utilise un dictionnaire, si nécessaire. (AT 4.3–4)

Writing. Pupils make up their own weird excuses. The sentence openings are supplied for support. They can use a dictionary if necessary.

B Extension

1 Lis le texte. Copie et remplis les fiches d'inscription en anglais. (AT 3.4)

Reading. Pupils copy out the three cards. They read the text and complete the cards with the details in English.

Answers
Name: *Louise*
Age: *14*
Talent(s): *singing*, dancing, playing saxophone
Ambition: professional singer

Name: Yann
Age: 16
Talent(s): playing guitar (in a rock band)
Ambition: maths teacher

Name: Léo
Age: 9
Talent(s): doing magic
Ambition: magician on TV

2 Écris un paragraphe sur tes copains Charlotte et Fred. (AT 4.4)

Writing. Pupils use the information supplied on the identity cards to write two paragraphs: one about Charlotte and the other about Fred. A writing framework is also supplied.

Answers *(sample)*
Ma copine Charlotte a treize ans. Elle joue du piano et du violon. Un jour, elle veut être professeur de musique.

Mon copain Fred a quinze ans. Il chante et il danse. Un jour, il veut être danseur professionnel.

3 Copie et complète l'interview de Félix. (AT 3.5)

Reading. Pupils copy and complete the interview with Felix, using the words supplied.

Answers *(sample)*
1 adore 2 dois 3 être 4 continuer 5 peux
6 répéter

Module 6: Studio découverte
(Pupil Book pp. 106–113)

Unit & Learning objectives	PoS* & Framework objectives	Key language	Grammar and other language features
1 Le monde et les pays francophones (pp. 108–109) World geography and French-speaking countries	**2.1d** previous knowledge **2.2k** deal with unfamiliar language **2.2/Y8** Reading – (a) longer, more complex texts **2.5/Y8** Writing – using researched language **5.3** Strategies – English/other languages **5.4** Strategies – working out meaning	les pays francophones j'ai choisi j'ai étudié on parle français se trouve en … il y a En été/hiver, il fait …	– developing reading strategies – preparing an effective presentation
2 Les sciences (pp. 110–111) How to plant a garden	**2.2j** adapt previously learned language **2.2k** deal with unfamiliar language **1.4/Y8** Speaking – (a) classroom exchanges **4.2/Y8** Language – increasing vocabulary **5.7** Strategies – planning and preparing	Il faut … arroser les plantes préparer le sol choisir les plantes etc.	**G** il faut + infinitive – developing reading strategies
3 La Révolution française (pp. 112–113) The French Revolution	**2.2b** skim and scan **2.2/Y8** Reading – (b) personal response to text **2.4/Y8** Writing – (b) organising paragraphs **3.1/Y8** Culture – changes in everyday life **5.7** Strategies – planning and preparing	la Révolution française la fête nationale le quatorze juillet C'est le jour où … etc.	**G** using two tenses (present and near future) – preparing for an extended writing task

* In addition, the following Programmes of Study are covered throughout the module: 1.1–1.4, 2.2a, 2.2c, 2.2d, 3a, 3c, 3d, 3e, 3f, 4a, 4b, 4d, 4e, 4f, 4g. PoS 4c is covered in all Units 4 & 5 and *En plus* sections. See pp. 7–9 for details.

1 Le monde et les pays francophones

(Pupil Book pp. 108–109)

Studio découverte 6

Learning objectives
- World geography and French-speaking countries

Framework objectives
2.2/Y8 Reading – (a) longer, more complex texts
2.5/Y8 Writing – using researched language
5.3 Strategies – English/other languages
5.4 Strategies – working out meaning

FCSE levels
Unit 10: Region and environment (Description and location of area; Facilities and activities within an area)

Key language
les pays francophones
j'ai choisi
j'ai étudié
on parle français
se trouve en …
on trouve
il y a
En été/hiver, il fait …
Si vous allez visiter …
il faut emporter (vêtements légers)

PLTS
I Independent enquirers

Cross-curricular
Geography: world geography; Francophone countries
ICT: internet research

Resources
CD 3, tracks 16–17
Cahier d'exercices Vert, pages 54–55
ActiveTeach
p.109 Learning skills

Starter 1
Aim
To encourage a broader cultural discussion on France

Using the content of the module opener (Pupil Book pp. 106–107) as a starting point, ask pupils to share what they know about French culture and what new things they have learned about France in the course of the year.

1 Regarde la carte. Écoute et lis le texte. (AT 1.4)
Listening. Pupils look at the map of the world. Ask what the green shading on the map represents (Francophone countries). Pupils then listen to the recording, following the text at the same time. Some vocabulary is glossed for support.

Audioscript CD 3 track 16

La géographie est l'étude des continents et des océans qui existent sur notre planète.

Les six continents sont l'Afrique, l'Europe, l'Océanie, l'Amérique, l'Asie et l'Antarctique. On parle français sur tous les continents à l'exception de l'Antarctique.

Les océans recouvrent soixante-et-onze pour cent de la surface de la Terre. Il y a cinq océans: l'océan Pacifique, l'océan Atlantique, l'océan Indien, l'océan glacial Arctique et l'océan glacial Antarctique.

Il y a beaucoup de climats différents dans le monde:
– le climat tropical (avec une saison sèche et une saison humide, et souvent avec des moussons)
– le climat désertique (qui est sec et chaud)
– le climat tempéré (avec des étés frais et des hivers doux)
– le climat polaire (qui est très froid).

Notre Terre est très belle. On trouve beaucoup de paysages différents du nord au sud, de l'ouest à l'est: des forêts, des déserts, de grandes plaines, des volcans, des montagnes, des lagunes, de jolies plages, des rivières, des lacs …

2 À trois. Fais une liste des mots apparentés dans le texte de l'exercice 1. (AT 3.4)
Reading. In threes: pupils make a list of all the cognates in the text in exercise 1. They then discuss in their groups how the different reading strategies listed can help them work out the other new words in the text. Point out that using strategies like these will help them tackle texts which initially look too challenging. Draw their attention to the tip box on using their knowledge of geography to help them.

1 Le monde et les pays francophones — Studio découverte 6

Answers
la géographie – geography
continents – continents
océans – oceans
existent – exist
planète – planet
six – six
Afrique – Africa
Europe – Europe
Océanie – Oceania
Amérique – America
Asie – Asia
Antarctique – Antarctica
exception – exception
surface – surface
Pacifique – Pacific
Atlantique – Atlantic
Indien – Indian
Arctique – Arctic
différents – different
climat – climate
tropical – tropical
saison – season
humide – humid
tempéré – temperate
polaire – polar
forêts – forests
déserts – deserts
plaines – plains
volcans – volcanoes
montagnes – mountains
lagunes – lagoons
rivières – rivers
lacs – lakes

3 En tandem. Lis le texte à voix haute et joue au 'BIP'! (AT 2.2)
Speaking. In pairs: pupils play 'Bip.' One pupil reads out the text in exercise 1, stopping at random and saying *Bip!* The other says the next word. They take it in turn to read and answer. A sample exchange is given.

4 Relis le texte et choisis la bonne réponse. (AT 3.4)
Reading. Pupils read the text in exercise 1 again and complete the sentences summarising it by choosing the correct word from the two options given each time.

Answers
1 Il y a **six** continents et **cinq** océans.
2 On ne parle pas français en **Antarctique**.
3 Les **océans** recouvrent 71% de la surface de la Terre.
4 Le climat polaire est très **froid**.
5 Les paysages sont **différents** du nord au sud.

➕ Pupils make up true/false sentences about the text and, working in pairs, take turns to identify their partner's sentences as true or false.

Starter 2
To review vocabulary for geographical features

Put the class into teams. Give them three minutes to write down in French as many geographical features as they can.

The teams swap and check each other's answers, awarding a point for each correct item. Reward the team with the most points.

5 Écoute. Copie et complète le texte. (AT 1.5)
Listening. Pupils copy out the text, leaving spaces for the missing words. They listen and fill the gaps to complete the text. Some vocabulary is glossed for support.

Audioscript — CD 3 track 17

En Martinique, on parle français.

La Martinique se trouve en Amérique. C'est une petite île dans la mer des Caraïbes.

J'ai étudié la géographie du pays.

On trouve toutes sortes de paysages en Martinique.

Il y a des montagnes et une forêt tropicale.

En été, il fait chaud. C'est la saison sèche avec un climat tropical, humide.

En hiver, il pleut beaucoup.

Si vous allez visiter la Martinique, il faut emporter un maillot de bain et un chapeau.

Answers
1 français 2 Amérique 3 Caraïbes 4 paysages
5 forêt 6 climat 7 hiver 8 chapeau

6 Studio découverte   1 Le monde et les pays francophones

6 Trouve la fin de chaque phrase. Écris des phrases complètes. (AT 3.5)

Reading. Pupils match the sentence openings and endings, then write out the complete sentences.

Answers
1 d Le Canada se trouve en Amérique du Nord.
2 g On trouve toutes sortes de paysages au Canada.
3 a Il y a de grandes plaines, des forêts et dans le nord, la toundra.
4 e En été, il fait beau, il y a du soleil et il fait assez chaud.
5 b En hiver, il fait très froid et il neige beaucoup.
6 f Si vous allez visiter le Canada en été, il faut emporter un tee-shirt et un pull.
7 c Si vous allez visiter le Canada en hiver, il faut emporter des skis!

7 Regarde la carte d'identité. Prépare un exposé. (AT 2.5)

Speaking. Pupils look at the identity card for Lebanon, then prepare and give a presentation on it. A framework is supplied for support. Draw pupils' attention to the tip box on which resources to use for further support.

Answers
Comme pays francophone, j'ai choisi le Liban.
Au Liban, on parle français.
Le Liban se trouve en Asie, entre la Syrie et Israël.
J'ai étudié la géographie du pays.
On trouve toutes sortes de paysages au Liban.
Il y a des montagnes, des fleuves, des cascades, des plaines fertiles et des plages.
En été, il fait beau. Il y a du soleil et il fait chaud.
En hiver, il fait un peu froid et il neige dans les montagnes.
Si vous allez visiter le Liban en été, il faut emporter des vêtements légers.
Si vous allez visiter le Liban en hiver, il faut emporter un manteau.

8 Choisis un pays francophone. Fais des recherches et écris la carte d'identité de ton pays. (AT 4.5)

PLTS

Writing. Pupils copy out a blank identity card. They choose a Francophone country and research it (either on the internet or using books, travel brochures, etc.), then complete the card with the details.

Plenary

Ask pupils how they would describe their own country, using the headings in the identity card in exercise 7 as prompts.

Workbook, pages 54 and 55

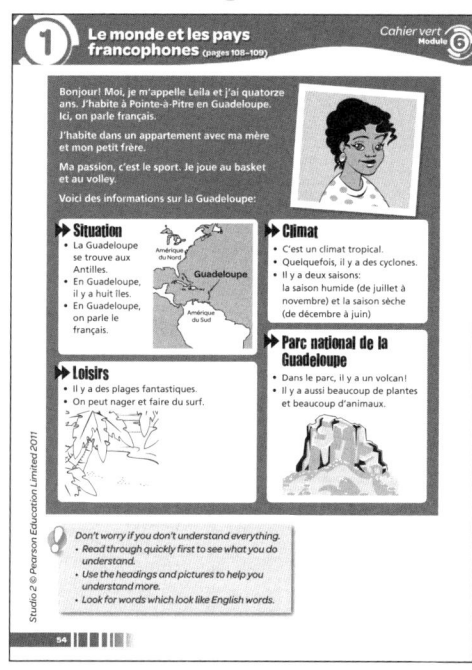

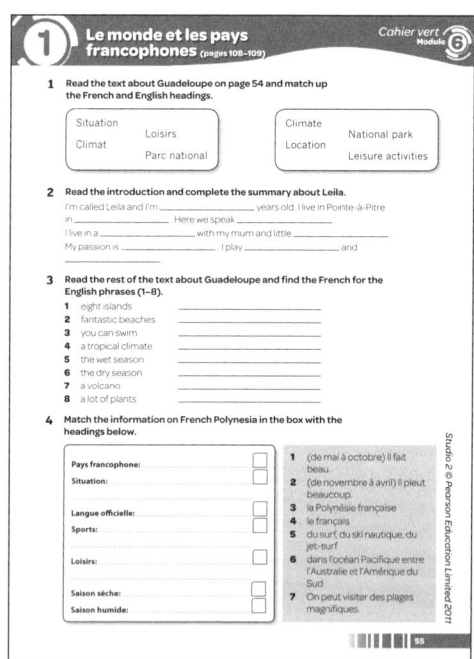

1 Le monde et les pays francophones   Studio découverte 6

Answers

1. Situation – Location
   Loisirs – Leisure activities
   Climat – Climate
   Parc national – National park
2. I'm called Leila and I'm **fourteen** years old. I live in Pointe-à-Pitre in **Guadeloupe**. Here we speak **French**.
   I live in a **flat** with my mum and little **brother**.
   My passion is **sport**. I play **basketball** and **volleyball**.
3. 1 huit îles
   2 plages fantastiques
   3 on peut nager
   4 un climat tropical
   5 la saison humide
   6 la saison sèche
   7 un volcan
   8 beaucoup de plantes
4. Pays francophone: **3**
   Situation: **6**
   Langue officielle: **4**
   Sports: **5**
   Loisirs: **7**
   Saison sèche: **1**
   Saison humide: **2**

Worksheet 6.1 Predicting language

Answers

A (Answers will vary.)
B (Answers will vary.)
C Notre planète tourne tout le temps. Il y a six continents sur la Terre. Dans l'espace, il y a beaucoup de satellites en orbite autour de la Terre. Ces satellites donnent des informations sur la météo et des images de la surface de la planète. On peut observer les dépressions et les anticyclones, les orages et les tempêtes. Un satellite a aussi d'autres fonctions: il prend des photos de la Terre pour Google Earth, par exemple. Les satellites facilitent aussi les communications comme la télévision et la téléphonie et bien sûr, ils sont utilisés pour la recherche.
D 1 T
  2 F
  3 T
  4 F
  5 NM
  6 F

2 Les sciences (Pupil Book pp. 110–111)

Studio découverte 6

Learning objectives
- How to plant a garden

Framework objectives
1.4/Y8 Speaking – (a) classroom exchanges
4.2/Y8 Language – increasing vocabulary
5.7 Strategies – planning and preparing

Grammar
- *il faut* + infinitive

Key language
Qu'est-ce qu'il faut faire pour créer un jardin?
Il faut …
arroser les plantes
préparer le sol
choisir les plantes
bien surveiller les jeunes pousses
planter les graines
manger les légumes
D'abord, il faut …
Ensuite,/Puis …
Finalement, …
Et voilà!

PLTS
T Team workers

Cross-curricular
Science: plants

Resources
CD 3, tracks 18–19
Cahier d'exercices Vert, pages 56–57
ActiveTeach
p.111 Thinking skills

Starter 1
Aim
To review the infinitive

Give pupils three minutes to look at sentences 1–6 in exercise 1 (Pupil Book p. 110) and identify all the infinitives used, then come up with three more infinitives.

Check answers (**1** *arroser* **2** *préparer* **3** *choisir* **4** *surveiller* **5** *planter* **6** *manger*).

Ask pupils how they were able to identify an infinitive even when they didn't know what the word meant (*–er/–ir* ending and used after *il faut*).

1 Trouve la bonne phrase pour chaque image. (AT 3.3)
Reading. Pupils find the correct caption (from **1–6**) for each picture (**a–f**). Draw pupils' attention to the tip box on reading strategies.

Answers
a 2 **b** 4 **c** 3 **d** 1 **e** 6 **f** 5

2 Écoute. Mets les étapes dans le bon ordre. (AT 1.3)
Listening. Pupils listen and write the number of the stages (**1–6** in exercise 1) in the order they are mentioned.

Audioscript — CD 3 track 18

– *Qu'est-ce qu'il faut faire pour créer un jardin potager?*
– *D'abord, il faut choisir les plantes.*
  Ensuite, il faut préparer le sol … et il faut planter les graines.
  Puis il faut bien surveiller les jeunes pousses.
  Tous les jours, il faut arroser les plantes.
  Finalement, il faut manger les légumes.

Answers
3, 2, 5, 4, 1, 6

3 Écoute à nouveau. Mets les expressions de temps dans le bon ordre. (AT 1.1)
Listening. Pupils listen to the exercise 2 recording again and note the time expressions (**a–f**) in the order they hear them.

Audioscript — CD 3 track 19
As for exercise 2.

Answers
b, c, e, d, f, a

4 Écris quatre phrases. Utilise tous les mots dans le pot. Traduis tes phrases en anglais. (AT 4.4)
Writing. Pupils write four sentences, using all the words supplied. They then translate the sentences into English.

2 Les sciences Studio découverte 6

Answers
D'abord, il faut préparer le sol. – First you need to prepare the soil.
Ensuite, il faut choisir les plantes. – Then you need to choose the plants.
Puis il faut planter les graines. – Then you have to plant the seeds.
Finalement, il faut bien surveiller les jeunes pousses. – Finally, you have to look after the young shoots well.

Starter 2
Aim
To review language from the unit

Write up the following incorrect sentences, omitting the text in brackets. Give pupils three minutes to copy and correct the sentences.

1 *Il arroser les plantes.* (*il* **faut** *arroser* …)
2 *Il faut prépare le sol.* (*il faut* **préparer** …)
3 *Il planter faut les graines.* (*il* **faut planter** …)
4 *Il faut les manger légumes.* (*il* **faut manger les** …)

5 Lis le texte. Corrige les erreurs dans les phrases en anglais. (AT 3.5)
Reading. Pupils read the text. They then read the sentences in English summarising it and rewrite them, correcting the errors. Some vocabulary is glossed for support.

Answers
1 You need **an egg cup** and an empty eggshell to make your egg man.
2 First you have to draw a **face** on the egg, **two eyes, a nose, a mouth, a beard, glasses …**
3 You have to put the egg into **the egg cup**.
4 You have to put cotton wool **inside the empty eggshell**.
5 You have to sow the **cress seeds**.

6 Associe les mots français aux mots anglais. (AT 3.1)
Reading. Pupils match the French words with the English translations. Draw their attention to the picture and remind them that using clues like this is an important reading strategy.

Answers
du papier – paper
des paillettes – sequins
dessiner – to draw
coller – to stick
de la colle – glue
des plumes – feathers
découper – to cut out

7 À quatre. Prépare un projet pour la classe. (AT 2.4)
PLTS T

Speaking. In groups of four: pupils prepare a project and explain to the class what you have to do to make the item they have designed. They can use the mask shown in exercise 6 or come up with an idea of their own. Encourage them to be as imaginative as possible, using a dictionary as necessary. A framework is supplied.

Plenary
Challenge the class to come up with the longest list they can of structures featuring *il faut* + a different infinitive. Get them to set a target number, then see if they can beat their target.

6 Studio découverte 2 Les sciences

Workbook, pages 56 and 57

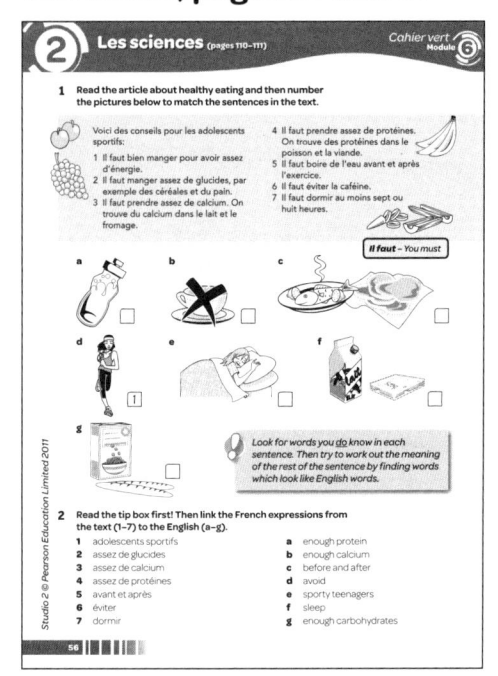

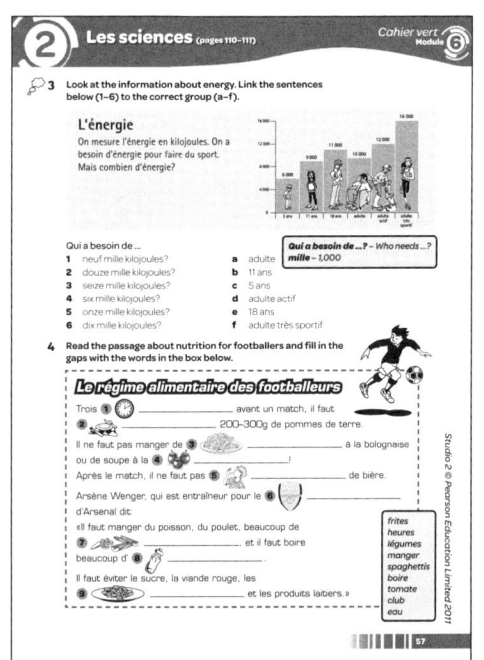

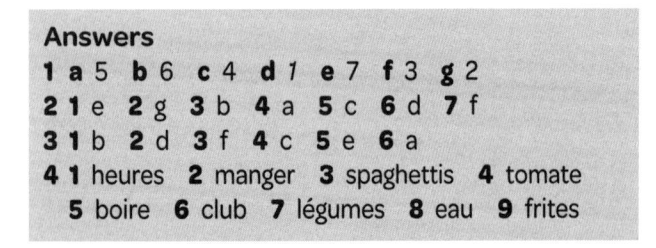

Worksheet 6.2 La vie d'un scientifique

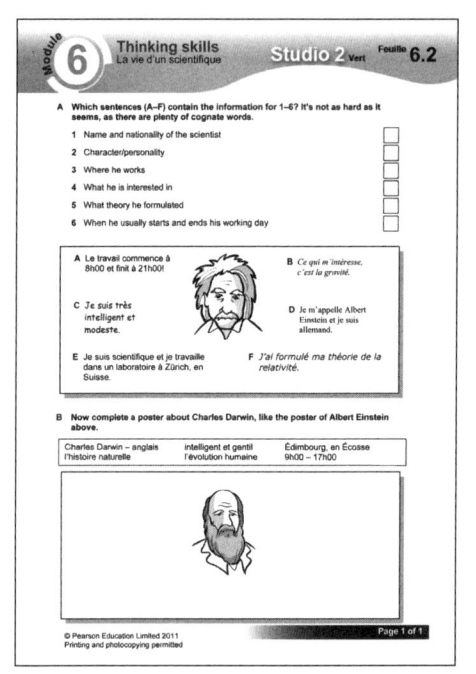

Answers

A
1 D
2 C
3 E
4 B
5 F
6 A

B Je m'appelle Charles Darwin et je suis anglais.
Je suis scientifique et je travaille dans un laboratoire à Édimbourg, en Écosse.
Le travail commence à 9h00 et finit à 17h00.
Je suis intelligent et gentil.
Ce qui m'intéresse, c'est l'histoire naturelle.
J'ai formulé la théorie de l'évolution humaine.

Answers

1 a 5 b 6 c 4 d 1 e 7 f 3 g 2
2 1 e 2 g 3 b 4 a 5 c 6 d 7 f
3 1 b 2 d 3 f 4 c 5 e 6 a
4 1 heures 2 manger 3 spaghettis 4 tomate
5 boire 6 club 7 légumes 8 eau 9 frites

3 La Révolution française
(Pupil Book pp. 112–113)

Studio découverte 6

Learning objectives
- The French Revolution

Framework objectives
2.2/Y8 Reading – (b) personal response to text
2.4/Y8 Writing – (b) organising paragraphs
3.1/Y8 Culture – changes in everyday life
5.7 Strategies – planning and preparing

FCSE levels
Unit 7: Celebrations (Celebrations/festivals in target language country)

Grammar
- using two tenses (present and near future)

Key language
la Révolution française
la fête nationale
le quatorze juillet
C'est le jour où …
en 1789
la Bastille
un jour férié
traditionnellement
un défilé militaire
partout
les feux d'artifice
Normalement/D'habitude, …
Demain, …

PLTS
R Reflective learners

Cross-curricular
History: the French Revolution
ICT: internet research

Resources
CD 3, tracks 20–21
Cahier d'exercices Vert, pages 58–59
ActiveTeach
p.113 Thinking skills

Starter 1
Aim
To introduce the topic (the French Revolution)

Ask pupils why the 14th of July is special in France: what happens then and what is being celebrated? (If they don't know, encourage them to speculate.) Ask if there is a similar celebration in the UK. Elicit their thoughts on why not and whether there should be some kind of national day.

1 Lis le texte. Mets les images dans l'ordre du texte. (AT 3.5)
Reading. Pupils read the text about Bastille Day and note the letters of the pictures in the order they are referred to.

Answers
d, a, b, c

2 Relis le texte et termine les phrases en anglais. (AT 3.5)
Reading. Pupils read the text in exercise 1 again and complete the sentences summarising it in English.

Read together through the *En France* text on the origins of the French Revolution. Ask the class for their thoughts on the information here.

Answers
1 14th of July 2 the Bastille 3 Revolution
4 parade 5 fireworks 6 dances or concerts

3 Écoute et choisis la bonne réponse. (AT 1.4)
Listening. Pupils listen to the description of a Canadian holiday and complete the sentences by choosing from the two options given each time.

Audioscript CD 3 track 20

Le premier juillet, c'est la fête du Canada.

C'est un jour férié.

Traditionnellement, il y a un spectacle et un concert et des feux d'artifice dans tout le pays.

On fait la fête, on chante et on danse.

Answers
1 juillet 2 C'est 3 un concert 4 fait la fête

4 Choisis une de ces dates. Fais des recherches: Quelle est l'importance de cette date en France? Prépare un exposé pour ta classe. (AT 2.4)

Speaking. Pupils choose one of the dates supplied and do some research (using books or the internet) to find out why the date is important in France. They then prepare and give a presentation on it to the class. A framework is supplied.

171

6 Studio découverte 3 La Révolution française

Starter 2

Aim

To review time expressions used with different tenses

Write up the following in jumbled order. Give pupils two minutes to copy and complete the grid using the time phrases supplied.

aujourd'hui, d'habitude, normalement

demain, la semaine prochaine, demain soir

present	future

Check answers (1st row = present, 2nd row = future), asking pupils to translate them into English. Remind the class that identifying time expressions like this will help them work out which tense is being used.

5 Écoute et lis. Une aristocrate parle de sa vie. Copie et remplis le tableau en anglais. (AT 1.5, AT 3.5)

Listening. Pupils copy out the table. They listen to a young French female aristocrat from before the French Revolution talking about her life and follow the text at the same time. They then complete the table with the details. Some vocabulary is glossed for support.

Audioscript CD 3 track 21

Normalement, je me lève vers onze heures du matin. Je prends mon petit déjeuner tout de suite. D'habitude, je mange de la brioche et je bois du thé.

Ensuite, je me prépare dans ma chambre. D'abord, je m'habille. Je porte une robe en soie avec des chaussures en daim. J'adore les chaussures. Les vêtements, c'est ma passion!

Quelquefois, je fais de l'équitation dans le parc ou je fais des promenades. Je joue du piano tous les jours parce que j'adore ça.

Souvent, je discute avec mes amies, on parle de musique et de vêtements. Le soir, quelquefois, je dîne au château de Versailles avec le Roi. Après le dîner, on va à l'opéra.

Demain, je vais aller à la chasse. Le soir, on va dîner et après, on va danser et écouter de la musique. J'aime beaucoup danser.

Answers

daily routine	breakfast	pastimes	plans for tomorrow
gets up at about 11 eats breakfast gets dressed evening: has dinner	brioche tea	horse-riding walking playing the piano chatting with friends	hunting dinner dancing listening to music

Give pupils a few minutes to read the text in exercise 5 again and, in pairs, to discuss in English what they found interesting about it. Ask some pairs to tell the class their opinions, encouraging them to refer directly to the text as much as possible.

If this activity works well with your class, you could bring in a range of short, simple texts from French magazines, books or internet sites on one of the topics already covered in the course and have pupils discuss these.

6 Imagine que tu es un paysan ou une paysanne. Décris ta vie avant la Révolution. (AT 4.5)

Writing. Pupils imagine that they are a peasant living before the French Revolution and describe their daily life. They can do some research (either on the internet or using books) or use any knowledge they have from studying the period in history. Draw their attention to the tip box on how to approach the task. Frameworks for spider diagrams are also supplied for support.

Ask pupils to summarise in English how things have changed since the time of the French Revolution, comparing the life of a French peasant to the life of an ordinary worker today.

Plenary

PLTS R

Ask pupils to look at the texts they wrote for exercise 6 and identify two areas in which they could improve (e.g. tense formation, spelling accuracy, range of vocabulary, adjective agreement, including connectives/intensifiers, using a wider variety of structures, etc.).

3 La Révolution française   Studio découverte 6

Workbook, pages 58 and 59

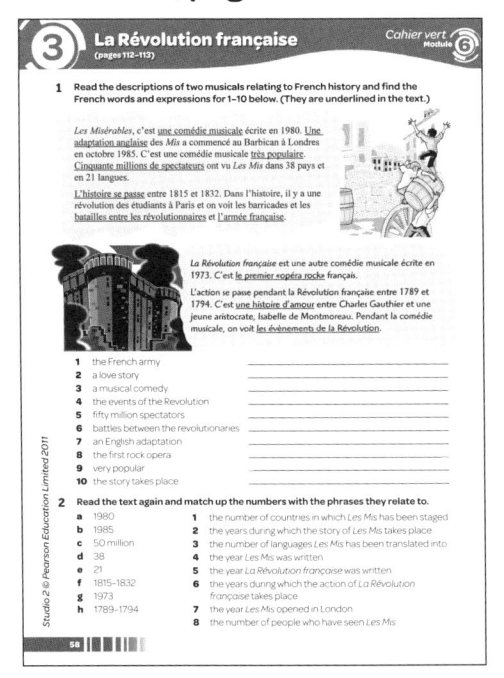

4 (Possible answer:)
Ma passion, c'est le théâtre musical.
J'adore chanter et danser. Un jour, je veux être chanteur professionnel/chanteuse professionnelle au théâtre.
J'adore aussi regarder des spectacles. Mon spectacle préféré, c'est **Le Roi lion**.
Le weekend dernier, je suis allé(e) à Paris avec **mon père** et j'ai vu **Le Roi lion** au théâtre. On a voyagé en **bus**.
Avant le spectacle, j'ai visité **le Louvre**, puis je suis arrivé(e) au théâtre **à deux heures de l'après-midi**.
J'ai adoré la musique!
Après le spectacle, je suis allé(e) **au café** et j'ai mangé **une crêpe**. C'était délicieux.
Ce weekend, je vais retourner à Paris et je vais voir **Mamma Mia!** Super!

Worksheet 6.3 Un cours d'histoire

Answers

1
1 l'armée française
2 une histoire d'amour
3 une comédie musicale
4 les évènements de la Révolution
5 cinquante millions de spectateurs
6 batailles entre les révolutionnaires
7 une adaptation anglaise
8 le premier «opéra rock»
9 très populaire
10 l'histoire se passe

2 a 4 b 7 c 8 d 1 e 3 f 2 g 5 h 6

3 1 ✗ 2 ✓ 3 ✗ 4 ✓ 5 ✓
  6 ✗ 7 ✓ 8 ✓ 9 ✗ 10 ✗

Answers

A 1 In 1066
   2 France

B 1 1940
   2 1789
   3 1998
   4 1804
   5 1889
   6 1999

C 1066 Battle of Hastings
   1789 French Revolution
   1804 Napoleon becomes Emperor
   1889 Eiffel Tower built
   1940 German occupation
   1998 France wins the Football World Cup
   1999 Introduction of the euro

173